SOWING CHAOS
Libya in the Wake of Humanitarian Intervention

BY
PAOLO SENSINI

TRANSLATED FROM THE ITALIAN BY
ALEXANDER M. SYNGE

Clarity Press, Inc

In-house editor: Diana G. Collier
Cover: R. Jordan P. Santos

Library of Congress Cataloging-in-Publication Data

Names: Sensini, Paolo, author.
Title: Sowing chaos : Libya in the wake of humanitarian intervention / by
  Paolo Sensini.
Description: Atlanta, GA : Clarity Press, 2016. | Includes bibliographical
  references and index.
Identifiers: LCCN 2016007061 (print) | LCCN 2016008805 (ebook) | ISBN
  9780986085314 (alk. paper) | ISBN 9780986085383 ()
Subjects: LCSH: Regime change--Libya. | Libya--History--Civil War, 2011- |
  Libya--History--20th century. | Libya--Politics and government--1969- |
  Libya--Foreign relations.
Classification: LCC DT236 .S46 2016 (print) | LCC DT236 (ebook) | DDC
  961.205--dc23
LC record available at http://lccn.loc.gov/2016007061

Clarity Press, Inc.
2625 Piedmont Rd. NE, Ste. 56
Atlanta, GA. 30324 , USA
http://www.claritypress.com

TABLE OF CONTENTS

PART II: JAMAHIRIYYA

PART III: RECIPE FOR DISASTER

FOREWORD

The 80-20 Rule

In an extremely important and revealing speech before Stanford University Business School graduate students, former World Bank director James Wolfensohn spoke to the 80–20 rule he grew up with. He said that all of his life, he had the 80–20 rule tucked neatly in his back pocket, so that no matter where he went in the world, he was able to enjoy the privileges of this rule. The rule, quite simply, was that 80% of the world's GDP was to be enjoyed by approximately 1 billion people while the rest of humanity had to get by on the remaining 20%. All of the world's institutions were created to reflect that fact. Therefore, whether it is the United Nations, the World Bank, the International Monetary Fund, or any other multilateral institution established by the United States in conjunction with the world's former colonizers, the 80-20 rule must be kept in mind.

The 80-20 rule merely extended and institutionalized into the post-colonial period the global economic imbalances caused by colonialism. Wolfensohn's 80–20 rule is a nice way of saying that the world is an apartheid world with the former colonizers, in league with the United States, in charge.

"Western European/US-style "White" supremacy is quite evident when one travels around the world as I do. Much of Russian history consists of trying to prove to its Western European cousins that it truly is "European," but the Russians could never be accepted into the club on Russian terms. Turks were ready to deny their very identity in order to gain admission to the exclusive club, only to be rejected when the time came to issue the membership cards.

Nearly everyone wants to be a member of this exclusive club, and some will do anything in order to get even a temporary membership card. This prolonged collaboration created a colonial mindset in the victims of colonialism, as exquisitely explained and revealed by Frantz Fanon. Because of the colonial practice of establishing rewards for collaboration in one's own oppression, the colonial mindset proved much harder to eliminate.

Universal apartheid then has resulted in a universal type of mind control that exists on every corner of the planet because, as Fanon correctly pointed out, the violence of colonialism works both ways: on the colonized as well as on the colonizer. And further, the damage is not just physical, but is much more deeply psychological—a psychopathology that reaches deep into one's very identity.

Universal Apartheid, Universal Mind Control

So, the former colonizers have a very useful tool. Steve Biko said that "the most useful tool in the hands of the oppressors is the mind of the oppressed." So, a kind of self-denial takes root in the pursuit of all things "White." That's why to marry "up" for a person of color is to marry White. We can witness this phenomenon all over the world. Thus, in Korea, eye surgery and rhinoplasty are extremely popular. "Fair" skin is aspired to by all and hence the ubiquitous skin bleaching cream from which Western corporations bank unmerited profit. In the shadow of one of humanity's greatest triumphs, The Pyramids, I found some skin whitening cream in a local store. Thus, the scramble to be light, almost White, or so compliant that the temporary membership card might be earned for just one night.

"I'm not an African."

I was left speechless recently when, in Tunisia, I was chatting with my taxi driver. A darker-skinned woman darted into the street, hand outstretched, begging for a dime. The taxi driver yelled her to get out of the way, and then he purposely hit her with his car, not enough to hurt her, but enough to tell her to get out of the way. I vigorously objected, saying she's your fellow Tunisian and you should care enough about her as a human being, at least enough not to hit her with your car. He responded that she's an African. I asked him, well, where are you from? He responded that he's Tunisian. I asked him if he was born in Tunisia and he said yes. And then with a straight face, he told me, I'm not an African. I asked the driver on what continent Tunisia was located and he dutifully responded "Africa. But I'm not African."

Even in Bangladesh, I have yet to see a child's doll that is actually the skin color of the majority of the population there. Just imagine the psychological damage done on a daily basis as a result of the adoration of all that is "White." Television shows in Latin America rarely depict darker-skinned Latin Americans in non-subservient roles. Even on the African continent, the women in the poorest of countries find a way to remove or hide their natural curls in exchange for wigs, creams, presses, hot combs, or anything that will transform their beautiful hair to "White" hair. And everywhere, status is attained by possessing Michael Kors, Chanel, Ferragamo, etc. instead of the beautiful, diverse, indigenous arts of Asia, Latin America, the Caribbean, and Africa. "Modernity" means abandoning cultural dress and looking more like the men and women of the colonizer—and sharing their values.

So real change means completely changing the power configuration, not just the faces that represent it.

Cui bono?

There is no such thing as a broken system. Any system reflects the choices of those who wield power within it. It is Spain, France, England, Holland, Belgium, Portugal, Germany, Italy, England, who, in the colonial era, went into other parts of the world and settled their people on the lands of others. Countries like Switzerland allow their corporations to enrich themselves and the Swiss people by shielding the hot money that flees all the dominated countries where corporations bribe governments, steal resources, and exploit the labor of the subject peoples. Of course, more recently, we have Israel as a settler colonial state on Palestinian land. And it is the United States, with its nearly 1000 overseas bases, and a military divided into nine globe-spanning Unified Combatant Commands of the United States Armed Forces, that backs it all up. It is these countries that reap the rewards of the current system and work to prolong its present power configuration.

So now, what does all this have to do with Libya?

Libya's Jamahiriyya As One Solution

Libya's Jamahiriyya, which means masses of the people, was the outgrowth of Muammar Gaddafi's thinking about the failures of "representative" democracy. As a U.S. citizen who understands the role of the U.S. economic hitman, I can confirm it's a lot easier to bribe the necessary number of parliamentarians to get what you want done than it is to bribe every citizen/voter in a direct democracy. Gaddafi's ideas were outlined in *The Green Book*, one of the first book burnings that took place in embassies around the world after the U.S. destroyed Africa's first post-colonial experiment in direct democracy. The very idea of direct democracy and self-government for the former colonialized peoples of color is an affront to the Western-inherited power systems and economies, and most importantly, an affront to the presumed superiority of the "Western" way of doing business.

The Jamahiriyya recognized that colonialism and its

vestiges had to be confronted on multiple levels. The Jamahiriyya recognized that the most precious asset of the state is its sovereignty and that direct democracy was the best way to assure that the state did not interfere with, and instead satisfied, the rights of the people.

When I was in Libya, the question that was being put before the entire people was how the oil revenues should be spent: as a subsidy of the price of gasoline or on education. The ultimate objective of the Jamahiriyya was self-government for the Libyan people and liberation of the African Continent. The Jamahiriyya looked south and focused its energies on Africans (not just Libyans) in the Diaspora, and the entire African Continent. With its huge oil wealth, it had the means, motive, and opportunity to carry its revolution throughout the Continent.

Of course, such a plan would be challenged on every front by the power wielders in the current power configuration. And it was. It was this effort to free itself and the rest of Africa from what Nkrumah called the last stage of imperialism, neo-colonialism, that doomed the Libyan experiment—not a fundamental unsoundness of direct democracy, but the colonial mindset of some Libyans (who also happened to live inside the U.S and/or serve on paid projects of the U.S.) who demanded the U.S.-led bombing of their own country. Joining in that level of perfidy were South Africa's Jacob Zuma, who was helped into power by Libya and then used the South African seat on the Security Council to vote yes with the U.S. against Libya; the Europeans who cooperated in the allied bombing campaign; and the Arabs, Africans, and African Americans who said nothing to defend Libya's right not to be wiped off the map. For such Libyans, Arabs, Africans, and African Americans, I can only muse at the level of psychopathology and identity crisis that leads to such behavior. It is this same phenomenon that exists in Syria where some Syrians actually want their country to be bombed and become another Libya.

And in yet another extraordinary display of such psychopathology, African Americans are giving their votes to Hillary Clinton, the "We came, we saw, he died" Secretary of State.

Not satisfied with bombing and destroying one African country, President Obama is also bombing Somalia. Therefore, the U.S.'s first President of African descent is responsible for the destruction of African countries and the recolonization of the African Continent for "Western" (anti-African sovereignty) interests. And against this backdrop, these same "Western" countries have the nerve to be complaining about African and Asian migration to Europe, though likely this migration is being facilitated not to help, but to further hurt the countries of origin of these migrating Asians and Africans, with agents provocateurs among them.

Conclusion

I have to conclude that these Western Europeans and the U.S. (and Israel) have much to atone for because of the multi-layered mass-scale global human tragedy that they have continuously ignited for the past five hundred years. Recognition without behavioral change is just words on a paper that's then torn up. Even as I write, Western powers are voicing the need to invade Libya once again. One wonders at the pretext. This time, to root out the very chaos that they have sown?

Surely the "West" deserves to lose its world leadership role. All that is delaying this process of de-Westernizing of the world are those who still don't realize that a new age of dignity for them is just around the bend.

If not, what has been sown, will also be reaped. Or, as Paolo says, "What goes around, comes around."

I thank Paolo for writing this powerful exposé of "Western" treachery, corruption, criminality, and holocaust creation in Libya.

Cynthia McKinney
former US Congresswoman
fomer Green Party Candidate for President
author of *The Illegal War on Libya*
May 1, 2016.

PART I

FALL OF THE OTTOMANS, WARS AND MONARCHY

"Italy repudiates war as an instrument offending the liberty of the peoples and as a means for settling international disputes"

Constitution of the Italian Republic,
Fundamental Principles, Article 11

"Time is running out for regimes that hide the truth [...]. Time is running out for cosmetic, limited reforms"

Giorgio Napolitano
President of the Republic of Italy
General Assembly of the United Nations
New York, 28 March 2011

"The contribution of the missions of the UNO, NATO and the European Union has highlighted the truly marked sensitivity of our military forces, the quality of their actions and their spirit of sacrifice, which I once more pay homage to. This contribution has also brought with it further credit to Italy within the international community, and it should therefore be valorised and sustained."

Giorgio Napolitano
Associazione Nazionale Mutilati e Invalidi di Guerra
(national association of disabled servicemen)
Rome, 26 April 2011

"War is Peace, Freedom is Slavery. Ignorance is Strength"

"These contradictions are not accidental, nor do they result from ordinary hypocrisy; they are deliberate exercises in DOUBLETHINK. For it is only by reconciling contradictions that power can be retained indefinitely."

George Orwell
The Theory and Practice of Oligarchical Collectivism, in
Nineteen Eighty-Four (Part II, Ch. IX)

2011: CENTENARY OF ITALY'S ATTACK ON LIBYA

For Italy, 2011 was a centenary year. The events of one hundred years ago remain. They have left an indelible mark on Italy's history. Italy's first war against Libya commenced in October 1911. The centenary 'commemorations' coincided with the 'decision' in Rome to embark on a second colonial war against Libya.

The first invasion of Libya was the fruit of nearly three decades of diplomatic and intelligence groundwork.[1] Accompanying the aggression was a popular song, a melodic chart topper of the period, *Tripoli, bel suol d'amore* (Tripoli, beauteous land of love). Francesco Saverio Nitti charmingly described the invasion as the taking of a "sandbox".[2]

It was the fourth government of Giovanni Giolitti. Other celebrations were under way (1911 marked the fiftieth year of Italian unity). Notably, Giolitti's administration pursued many leftist policies. At the time, France held Algeria, Morocco and Tunisia. Britain controlled Egypt, a key nation of the Mediterranean (though still formally a part of the Ottoman Empire). To gain for itself the status of a major European power, Italy, too, required its own "place in the sun".

At the turn of the century, the Banco di Roma had already embarked upon a policy of 'peaceful penetration' of Tripolitania and Cyrenaica, and was gradually increasing its control over local light industry, agriculture, and shipping and trading concerns. It opened branches in Tripoli, Benghazi, Zliten, Al Khums (or Khoms) and Misrata. Indeed, alleged Ottoman interference in the commercial affairs of Italians served as one of the pretexts for Italian military intervention in 1911.

As the tensions rose, Italy's major newspapers campaigned in favor of the seizure of Libya—described by the renowned poet, Gabriele D'Annunzio, as Italy's *Quarta sponda*, or fourth shore.[3] Each newspaper had its own approach. Behind Frassati's *La Stampa* and Olindo Malagodi's *La Tribuna*, both supportive of Giolitti, we find the FIAT motor vehicles company and the Banca Commerciale. *Il Giornale d'Italia* and *Il Resto del Carlino* represented the interests of the bourgeoisie and landed classes of Emilia and Romagna. *Il Messaggero* and the Catholic press had ties with the Banco di Roma, as did *Il Corriere d'Italia*, *l'Avvenire d'Italia*, *Il Corriere di Sicilia* and *Rassegna Nazionale*. Two major Milanese papers, *Il Corriere della Sera* and *Il Secolo*, stood by and watched. However, on 14 September, just twenty days before the troops finally disembarked, *Il Corriere della Sera*, under Luigi Albertini, joined the pro-war camp.[4]

In order to bring Italian public opinion around to the Libya project, most of the papers dwelt on the "extraordinary opportunities" that the territory represented, and its "wealth". Concern over the scale of Italian emigration also played a part. A further concern was the security of Italy's coastline. In its own way, Libya became a sort of 'Promised Land', which had to be "occupied at the earliest opportunity", since France and Germany had for some years already set their sights on this territory. Proponents were eager to point out how easy the campaign would be, relatively speaking.

The Sultans of Constantinople returned to the regions now known as Libya in 1835. The Ottoman forces were poorly armed. It was rumored that the Libyan Arabs eagerly awaited outside intervention to "liberate" them from the "appalling Ottoman yoke". In the meantime, subject to various centrifugal forces, the Ottoman Empire itself was slowly but surely disintegrating.

Fifteen years after the tremendous defeat in the battle of Adwa at the hands of the Ethiopian Empire, naval squads under the admirals Faravelli and Borea Ricci were already shelling Tripoli.[5] On 3 October 1911, Giolitti turned down a proposal for compromise submitted by the Ottoman Empire. This proposal might have averted a war whose duration no one could be sure about, nor could one estimate its repercussions for Italy and Europe as a whole.[6] The war—over what Gaetano Salvemini was to call an "enormous bottomless pit of sand"[7]—was to continue practically without interruption until 1932.

'LIBERAL ITALY'
GIRDS FOR WAR

From the very start, this new phase of Italian colonialism set off a series of violent shocks that rocked Italy's political system to the core. The Socialist Party (PSI) was divided. Not two but three currents emerged during the run up to the Libyan war. Filippo Turati (the PSI's longstanding leader) openly opposed wars of conquest. However, neither he nor the socialist newspaper, *Avanti!*, knew how to oppose this particular adventure. Then we have the left wing within the youth federation, which included Benito Mussolini—a leading militant fresh from the barricades.[8] Mussolini, who radically opposed the war, extended the invitation to workers to "familiarize themselves [...] with the arm of sabotage, to fully understand the revolutionary import of the general strike".[9] The third current was made up of right wing reformers under Ivanoe Bonomi, Angelo Cabrini and Leonida Bissolati, who believed instead that the Libyan adventure was "not incompatible with the ideals of socialism". The reformers were thus able to establish a link with the revolutionary syndicalist headed by Angelo Oliviero Olivetti, Arturo Labriola and Paolo Orano, who considered colonial expansionism beneficial to Italian workers and conducive to a "social revolution".[10] A number of leading writers also expressed their support for intervention.

The Italian task force was originally made up of 34,000 men, 6,300 quadrupeds, 10,500 carriages, 48 field guns, 24 mountain guns, and 4 field communication stations.[11] The quantities soon multiplied. At the close of 1911, an imposing army of 103,000 men had been assembled under 24 generals. Leading the operations was the elderly general, Carlo Caneva, whose experiences during the 1896-97 Africa campaign were to cast a long and dark shadow over his actions in Libya.[12]

To resist Italy, the Ottomans had only one division. Indeed, not even a full division, since four battalions had been transferred to Yemen to put down a revolt there. In other words, the Ottomans had hardly more than 4,000 troops on the ground (3,000 in Tripolitania with its 523,176 inhabitants, and 1,200 in Cyrenaica, with a population of 198,345). The population of Fezzan was estimated at approximately 20,000. In addition, the Turks' arms were generally rather antiquated compared with those of the Italians.

Further Turkish forces consisted of 1,500 men from the gendarmerie and 3,000 native militia men.[13] However, the Ottomans reckoned on arming between 25,000 and 30,000 members of the Sanusi Muslim Brotherhood (a religious movement that would play a decisive part in later wartime developments, and, more importantly, in developments surrounding the political future of a unified Libya).[14] The following pages outline the key characteristics of this highly significant Sanusi movement, shedding light also on many very recent developments in Libya's history.

3

THE SANUSIS

The Sanusis make up a Sunni Islamic mystical, missionary and militant brotherhood (*tarikha*) belonging to the Maliki 'school'.[15] The brotherhood was founded in 1837 on Mount Abu Qubais (located in the Arabian Peninsula, in the vicinity of Mecca). Sayyid Muhammad ibn Ali as-Senussi (1787?-1859)—the founder, known in Libya as *Al-Sanusi al-Kabir* (the Grand Sanusi)—was a Berber of the Algerian Walad Sidi Abdallah tribe. His family believed itself to descend from the Prophet of Islam by the Prophet's daughter, Fatima. The doctrines and rituals of this Islamic purification movement consisted of tasks described as reminding the indifferent, teaching the ignorant, and guiding those who have lost their way.[16]

Unlike many others of the same ilk, this *tarikha* brotherhood does not quite simply seek (as do the Wahhabis,[17] for example, and, perhaps, the Zaydis[18]) the return of the faithful to the Qur'an and the Sunna, traditions based on the life and teachings of the Prophet Muhammad. This brotherhood proclaims and demands renouncement of mere *taqlid* (imitation) of the ways set forth by the major and traditional Islamic scholars or masters. It also proclaims and demands a systematic and precise reopening of the "gate of *ijtihad*" (the independent or original interpretation of problems not precisely covered by the Qur'an, Hadith [traditions concerning the Prophet's life and utterances], and *ijmā* [scholarly consensus]), which, according to most historians of the customs and practices of this religion, had been definitively closed in the fourth century of the *Hijra* (10th Century AD).[19]

After lengthy peregrinations, Muhammad ibn Ali as-Senussi, who had studied in Fes and Mecca, created the first *zawiya* (place for the teaching of the Qur'an, and a caravan and trading post), so that he might draw the local tribes to the cause of his *tarikha*. He then moved to Egypt. When the Ottomans occupied Ghadames in 1843, the Grand Sanusi had settled in Cyrenaica. In the same year, he founded the *al-zawiya al-bayda* ("white religious house or lodge") in the Gebel al Akhdar region.

Relying on its followers, called the *ikhwan* ("brethren"), in order to propagate the vision of the founder, the Sanusi movement rapidly created a number of lodges in Cyrenaica, the most important of which was located at the Al Jaghbub Oasis.

While not officially recognized as a kingdom or principality, the movement nevertheless rapidly developed a vast territorial State in Cyrenaica, whose capital was the settlement of Jaghbub, where the affairs of public and private life were conducted strictly in accordance with the precepts of Islam and the example of Muhammad.

With its focus on Islamic practices characterized by asceticism and purification, accompanied by promises of solidarity and support, we should not be surprised that the Sanusi doctrine reached into the heart of Cyrenaica and its tribal spirit.[20] Cyrenaica at the time was still an isolated land, traversed only by nomadic or semi-nomadic tribes of Arabic origin. By demanding taxes, and providing social services, peace and the awareness of an identity, Muhammad ibn Ali as-Senussi endowed the various tribes with a rudimentary structure of government. The Ottoman rulers, who were engaged in securing Tripolitania and Fezzan, were content to let the Sanusis manage their own affairs, and approved the movement's anti-French stance.

Right from the onset of its activities in Libya, the political and religious conduct of this sect was markedly dynastic and hierarchic. The descendants of the progenitor did not stray from this model.

After the founder's death, under his son, Sayyid Muhammad al-Mahdi (1844-1902), the brotherhood's influence spread to western Egypt and Sudan. It also reached out to Fezzan, Algeria, Tunisia, Morocco, Arabia, Northern Chad, Niger and even distant Senegal. We note, however, that the sect found few followers among the cosmopolitan inhabitants of Tripoli.

In 1894, in order to block the French advance, Sayyid al-Mahdi left Al Jaghbub for Kufra, and then proceeded southward to Dar Guran in Chad. On his death in 1902, command fell to Sayyid al-Mahdi's brother, Sayyid Ahmad al-Shariff (al-Mahdi's sons, including the future King of Libya, Idris, were still minors). Given the number of *zawiya* houses scattered across northern Africa, the influence of the brotherhood was not, in the strict sense, merely religious. Initially, the Italians were totally unaware of the extent of the brotherhood's political and economic outreach.

The Sanusi movement is headed by the *Shaikh al-kabir* (the great sheikh, the possessor of the Holy *Barakah*, the "wisdom" or "blessing" of Muhammad). This role always fell to the latest of the descendants of the family of the first founder. We then have the three most important dignitaries: the Great Caliph (taking on the functions of the Supreme Sheikh), the *Wakil* (administrator and treasurer) and the head officer responsible for all the *tolba* (Qur'anic students)[21] of the sect's *zawiya* houses.

Occupying a position only slightly inferior, we have the *Shuyukh al-zawiye*. These are the qualified officers responsible for the various regional religious centers of the brethren. Below these come the many minor or middling *Mokkaddem* (directors or superintendents), generally a lifelong post within the various regions and provinces of greatest interest to this congregation. Alternatively, the *Mokkaddem* carry out the functions of itinerant missionaries.

The dignitaries mentioned above must possess what is termed an *Ijaza* ("mystic diploma"). To obtain the diploma, they must study long and hard the religious curricula of the major madrassas (Qur'anic schools) of their congregation.

Lastly, occupying the lowest tier of this hierarchical organization are the affiliates. Among them, various distinctions apply. The affiliates are responsible for cells, militants or mere supporters.

From the picture that we have provided of this peculiar community of the faithful, what emerges is a very rigorously ordered, highly structured and disciplined organization of initiates (*ikhwan*). It is a sort of hierarchically ordered *corpus*. Its members are programmed for strict obeisance to the particular doctrine of Islam with which the *corpus* identifies. Furthermore, the movement must seek out all means to further the aims set by the *corpus* leaders.[22]

4

THE LANDING FORCES REACH THE COASTAL CITIES

The Italians under the command of Vice-admiral Luigi Faravelli shelled Tripoli during the afternoon of 3 October 1911. The attack began at 15:30 and went on until the early evening. It recommenced the next morning. Following the destruction of the Turkish fortifications, the first landing forces reached the city in the early afternoon of 5 October. The landing encountered no serious problems. From the start, it appeared that the people were happy to welcome the "*boni 'taliani*" (good Italians).[23] There were no incidents, and the Italian soldiers were not subject to any attacks during their first fortnight in Libya.[24]

Then, on 23 October, an incident banished all illusions of peace. It was a bitter foretaste of future events. The Turks and, above all, hordes of Arabs, bore down on the Italians stationed at the Sciara Sciat outpost, slaughtering many. Sciara Sciat is located on the outskirts of Tripoli, within the area of the oasis.[25] With this bloodbath the attackers—badly armed and worse provisioned—showed the Italian settlers and, above all, Italy's soldiers, what the immediate future held in store for them. Three days later, another raid took place between Bu Meliana, Sidi Messri and the higher ground of Henni. In this case, however, after strenuous efforts, the forces of the commander Nesciat Bey had to withdraw under shelling from land and sea.

The Italian central command bodies of Tripoli and Rome vetted the news for the Italian public, as is typical of wars of conquest. Until spring 1912, the Italian press was prevented from entering Cyrenaica. In this region, the war between Italians and Turks gradually became a war between Italians and Bedouins, led by the Sanusis.[26]

The new year started off fairly calmly, as the military command engaged in building bridges between Italians and Arabs. Work on large-scale public projects and other activities sought to advance such ties. The citizens of Tripoli received wages about five times higher than those offered by the Turks.

However, clashes were inevitable. As expected Turkish and Arab raids began again at the end of February. The most important raid was against the belt of defenses around Benghazi. Here, thanks to use of barrage fire from his artillery, General Giovanni Ameglio was able to follow the attackers to the oasis of Suani Abd el-Rani. Here, the attackers entrenched themselves. The (unprecedentedly brutal) struggle at the oasis came to be called the Battle of the Two Palms.

According to Italian estimates, 745 Turks and Arabs died, 38 Italians lost their lives and 144 were wounded. Despite the pincer movement and the use of artillery on a massive scale, many of the foe escaped the trap. Yet again, the Italians failed to achieve a decisive victory, sought since the start of the war, with the destruction of enemy forces.[27]

Months had gone by since the Italians had landed in Libya, and yet they had made very little progress. Despite the optimistic forecasts, the task force was still within its enclaves along the Mediterranean coast. The largest enclave, at Tripoli, was only ten miles deep.[28]

The Arab-Turkish forces in Tripolitania and Cyrenaica—under the Commanders in Chief Nesciat Bey and Enver Bey respectively—were not as well equipped as the Italians. They knew they could count on a degree of complacency on the part of the Egyptians, and some support. More to the point, however, was the fact that the two commanders were fine tacticians, and this was a great source of concern for the Italians, who were effectively barred from taking the initiative.[29]

A "diplomatic formula" was found, much to the relief of the Italian soldiers and their officers, exhausted by the stalemate. Much to the relief also of the Great Powers of Europe, which—one after the other, starting with Russia and followed by Austria, Germany, Great Britain and France, in that order—recognized Italian sovereignty over Libya.

A rough estimate can be made of the losses incurred during this North African campaign:

> According to the official figures, 3,431 died. 1,438 died in combat and 1,949 died of diseases. Of the 1,391 who died in the field 92 were officers [...]. There were 4,220 wounded in all. Only one figure is to be found in regard to Arab and Turkish losses: 14,800.[30]

Both the war and the peace process continued. Or so it seemed. As the Turks were being demobbed and readied for their return home, a number of Berber tribal chieftains announced that they did not recognize the terms of the Treaty of Ouchy, purporting to end the conflict.

Fighting broke out toward the end of March in the Asbi'ah basin. Libya was once more in the spotlight. The Italian commanders decided to take Fezzan, in Libya's southern desert. It was a complex task, given the considerable distance between the Fezzan region and the coastline. Furthermore, Fezzan hosted many tribes who were determined to block the Italian advance. The Italians called in the Lieutenant Colonel of the General Staff, Antonio Miani. After operations covering vast distances (Sirte, Bu Njem, Sawknah, Umm al-Abid, Sabha), despite the logistical and military problems, Miani finally marched triumphantly into Murzuk, the region's capital.[31]

Fezzan was conquered, but Miani's problems didn't end there. His main concern was supply routes through thousands of kilometers of hostile territory.

Following the start of the war on the continent in July 1914, Italy's already precarious position in Fezzan became untenable. Italy entered the Great War only in 1915. However, Turkey and the central Empires already considered Italy an enemy. They wanted chaos, and therefore encouraged the revolt in Libya by organizing landings in the coastline area of Sirte. In the meantime, the Sanusis mobilized against the Italians, deploying their Libya-wide network of assets, their more than two million affiliates in North Africa, and their 300 *zawija* houses.[32]

Abandoning an entrenched warfare approach, the Sanusis split their forces into small groups and adopted guerrilla warfare tactics. This decision was particularly appropriate in view of their own military tradition, and also in view of the type of arms available to them. With the Sanusi forces deployed in this manner, the Italian commanders were in turn obliged to review their own position and engage in anti-guerrilla activities.

Between February and July 1914, inflicting enormous losses on the Sanusis, General Ameglio managed to achieve practically all the goals he had set himself. During one of the battles, Ameglio—appointed the governor of Cyrenaica— was opposed for the first time by the guerrilla leader, 'Omar

Al-Mukhtar. Al-Mukhtar would guide the resistance in Cyrenaica during the 1920s and pose very real problems, later, for Field Marshal Graziani. By the end of May, as a result of Ameglio's successful campaigns, all the major field positions of the Sanusis in western and central Cyrenaica had been pulverized. But the war was anything but over.

Many Arab revolts erupted throughout Libya. By the close of 1914 the Italian position, while not catastrophic, was still highly unstable. The Fezzan and the Ghibla regions were entirely lost and the Sirtica area, with the exception of the small port of Sirte, was practically all lost. At the close of 1914, Italy had very little to show for itself. The prospects for 1915 were also quite discouraging. On 29 April 1914, during the battle of Gasr Bu Hadi, a column headed by Colonel Miani was totally destroyed by the mujahideen under Safi ed-Din.[33]

After a number of crushing defeats, the only territories fully under the control of the Italians lay within the coastal strip (i.e. more or less the areas held in 1912). The revolt even reached Tripoli, where the troops erected a line of defense only 32 kilometers long. We see here the picture of defeat, perhaps even more humiliating than Adwa.

Then, on 21 August 1915, Italy declared war on Turkey. Six days later, she also declared war on Germany. The Libyan resistance had just gained two major allies capable of providing it with arms, equipment and military training.

COMING TO TERMS WITH THE SANUSIS

The Ottomans persuaded Ahmad al-Shariff, in Cyrenaica, to attack the British forces in Egypt. As a result, Ahmad al-Shariff was obliged to hand over leadership of the Sanusis to his cousin, Sayyid Muhammad Idris Al-Sanusi, a grandson of the Grand Sanusi and the son of al-Mahdi al-Sanusi. But Idris was not up to the political duties arising out of his important position, which he disliked. He opposed the campaign against the British, with whom he had established ties (it was an alliance that would last for five decades).

As a result of this cleavage, Sayyid Idris and his Sanusi order became significant players on a diplomatic level. Idris was considered the spokesman for the Bedouins of Cyrenaica. In July 1916, with the intermediation of the British, he began negotiations with the Italians. This led to the Bur 'Akrama (or Acroma) agreement of April 1917, according to which the Sanusis were to autonomously administer all Cyrenaica except the coastal strip. Sayyid Muhammad Idris (now addressed as His Highness) was to be titled, al-Amir al-Sanusi. The rank would be hereditary. These agreements represented a great victory for Sayyid Muhammad Idris over his cousin, Ahmad al-Shariff.[34]

Ahmad al-Shariff opposed these agreements. He moved from Al Jaghbub to the military position of Ben

Gauad in Sirtica. His intention was to continue the war against Italy in Tripolitania itself. However, in August 1918 he abandoned Libya by submarine. From Pola he proceeded to Vienna and then to Constantinople. He had truly abdicated, and was never to return to Libya. Muhammad Idris now had no rivals, and proceeded to consolidate his power as Grand Sanusi, biding his time before reaching out for true independence.

The Sanusi State clung to its power until about 1923, when Italy annulled the previous agreements and, through the force of arms, restored direct sovereignty over all Cyrenaica.[35]

6

STALEMATE

The war had practically ended in Tripolitania, but the forces on both sides were now faced with a new enemy— famine. The Italians had to face the hardship imposed upon them by Germany's intense submarine warfare campaign. The rebels' hardship was imposed upon them solely by General Giovanni Ameglio, who had adopted a scorched earth policy in order to force capitulation upon the Arabs. While decisive battles were under way in Europe, in Tripolitania the action was limited to pillage and plunder by both sides.

At Khallet ez-Zeitu, worn down by the hostilities, the Italians and the Arab chiefs finally agreed upon a Statute according to which the

> inhabitants of Tripolitania are to be raised to the moral and political dignity of citizens accorded the same rights as those enjoyed by Italian citizens, and are called upon to take part in the governing of public affairs and in the administration of the territory in the broadest and most concrete senses, under terms of freedom and civil progress, as a pledge, for them, that shall ensure prospects of peace.

While the Statutory Charter of Tripolitania can hardly be considered an instrument of democracy, it was hoped it would foster the maturing of democratic conditions within Libya.

However, no moves were actually made in the direction of even rudimentary local government. Two years later, more or less, the Libyan Statute had already lost all meaningful purpose. The only real plan left was that of domination over the Arabs.[36]

Italy's real intentions became clear in July 1921 when Giuseppe Volpi—a banker and politician, and one of the peace negotiators at Ouchy—was appointed governor of Tripolitania. His first significant political move was to occupy Qasr Ahmad (otherwise known as the Misurata Marina). This was widely resented in Tripolitania.[37] However, Volpi's heavy-handed approach—coming after a period of relative calm—received the full backing of the government and of the new colonial minister, Giovanni Amendola.[38] The new approach to Libya was epitomized by the actions of General Rodolfo Graziani.

5

THE COLONIZATION POLICY IN LIBYA DURING THE ERA OF FASCISM

On seizing power, Mussolini did not have a specific policy regarding the colonies. However, already in 1922, it became quite clear that his approach would differ considerably from that of his predecessors.

The "new Italy" would not seek 'arrangements' with its foes. The country would forge on, carrying all before it.

The new minister for the colonies, Luigi Federzoni, was determined to put the new philosophy into effect. Federzoni and the Governor, Emilio De Bono—freshly appointed in 1925—perfectly embodied the spirit of the dawning fascist era. This break with the past meant tactical changes and changed approaches in the field, and of the task force itself. A new force was brought in, made up almost entirely of mercenaries (from Eritrea, Ethiopia, Sudan, Yemen and Libya itself). The war would drag on for a decade, but it was hardly noticed in Italy.

Thus, between 1923 and 1932, Italy, having learned the political and military lessons of engagement in a World War, reconquered first Tripolitania, then Fezzan and, lastly, Cyrenaica. This return to the division of the territory into zones (as was the case under the Ottomans) augmented Mussolini's prestige, both nationally and internationally.

There was just one problem to be solved before full victory could be declared. This hurdle was the aforementioned Sanusi *shaykh*, Sayyid 'Omar Al-Mukhtar. The sheikh had fought side by side with Ahmad al-Shariff before joining the exiled Sayyid Idris in Cairo (where he resided until 1923).[39] 'Omar Al-Mukhtar, for about eight years, was the leader of bands of Bedouin warriors engaged in a desperate and increasingly bitter struggle against fascist Italy. These small bands successfully engaged a much larger force of about 20,000 Italian troops. The Italians were not only better equipped; they also received support from one of the most advanced air forces of the times.

For a decade, 'Omar practically always waged a war of attack, as can be seen from the numbers of battles (53) and skirmishes (210).

> 'Omar struck and then disappeared, infuriatingly for 'Omar's adversaries who hoped for but failed to find a final pitched battle. His name soon became the symbol of the resistance in Cyrenaica. It was pronounced by the mujahideen with respect and devotion.[40]

And so the struggle dragged on until the early months of 1931. Italy's fortunes finally changed when the new commander of the Cyrenaica Jebel troops, Colonel Giuseppe Malta, reorganized his forces during the summer of 1931. Malta created cavalry units to be deployed for mass maneuvering. The mobile mixed groups were tasked to block the routes along which the enemy armed bands (*duar*) would retreat.[41]

The Sanusi guerrilla campaign was at last crushed on 11 September 1931. Following the last of many clashes,

Sheikh ʻOmar Al-Mukhtar was captured by Captain Bertè's men. His fate was certain. A hanging.[42]

8

THE ERA OF
ITALO BALBO

After the bloody defeat of Libya's anti-Italian resistance movement, Libya was to be transformed.[43] Once an "exploitation colony", henceforth it would be a "settler colony", much in the manner of the French, above all in Algeria and Tunisia. However, some time would pass before the State moved decisively in the direction of demographic colonization of its "Fourth Shore".[44]

This new phase was inaugurated by Governor Italo Balbo, whose name is linked to the *Litoranea Via Balbia* (Italy's first great highway in Africa, between Cyrenaica and Tripolitania). Balbo initiated other public works, too, during his mandate in Libya. He was noteworthy, above all, for his entirely new approach to colonization.[45]

The settlers in Libya were mainly northern Italian farmworkers from the Po valley districts of the regions of Venetia and Emilia. During the previous era of Liberal Italy, it was thought that Libya would be settled essentially by southern Italians, for their benefit.[46] Balbo believed colonization should, so to speak, be packaged in bright colors. He would create a grand spectacle of the whole process. The idea, of course, was to bring prestige to the regime. But, more importantly, to himself![47]

According to this overall vision of migration of masses, as Balbo put it, "Libya is not just a stretch of Mediterranean coastline: it is Empire. The entire system upon which the future overseas Italy depends hinges upon Libya".[48] Balbo evidently considered these settlers "rural troops", primarily farmers armed with hoes, ploughshares and rifles. He envisaged the "peasant-soldier" dedicated to tilling the land and "devoted to the prospects of his homeland".[49]

Between 1938 and 1939, more than 30,000 new settlers reached Libya's shores. These figures denote the peak of Italy's efforts to put the colony to best use.[50] During this period, Mussolini decreed that he should be ordained the *"Protettore dell'Islam"* (protector of Islam) in Tripoli. It was an initiative of some symbolic significance.

During the 1930s, archaeological excavation work continued at the ruins of Roman cities along the coastline, such as Leptis Magna, Sabratha, Cyrene and Apollonia. According to Libyan historian Angela Del Boca, Balbo "insisted that the work should proceed as an absolute priority because he believed in Libya's future tourism potentials." Del Boca adds that "rather than farming, development of tourism was uppermost in his mind".[51]

This 'expansion' came to a halt when Italy entered World War II. The war took its toll on Libya, lying between Tunisia and Egypt, respectively under French and British rule. A further key development was Balbo's accidental death on 28 June 1940 when flying over Tobruk (an Italian anti-aircraft unit in Tobruk mistook his plane for a British bomber).

Pietro Badoglio[52] proposed that General Rodolfo Graziani should take over as Governor General of Libya and as field commander of the North African forces. Graziani's approach would be quite different from that of his predecessor.

Following clashes with the British on Egyptian soil, Graziani's first great challenge—and defeat—came on 5 February 1941. The tenth Italian army was crushed by the British, leading, within a matter of days, to the total loss of Cyrenaica. Cyrenaica had sustained enormous damage both during the Italian-German offensives and the subsequent British counteroffensives and occupations.

Graziani had gained fame and fortune in Libya and Ethiopia as the commander of operations conducted against poorly armed partisan bands. These brave bands were tenacious, but, technically speaking, they were an inferior sort of enemy. Graziani was then faced with an army representing the greatest Empire that the world had ever seen, and the legend of his '*condottiero*' standing soon crumbled to dust.

Following tremendous losses of territory, Graziani (at his own request) was relieved of his duties. General Ettore Bastico succeeded to the post of Governor of Libya. However, the Axis Powers were losing on all fronts. The Italians and Germans commenced their retreat on 4 November 1942 before the advancing British Eighth Army under General Bernard Law Montgomery. After the second battle of El Alamein, all was lost. General Erwin Rommel—commanding the Germans and Italians—had resisted with all his might. In less than three months, Cyrenaica and much of Tripolitania had been lost. Without the means to defend itself against the constant attacks of the British, the Axis forces finally evacuated Tripoli on 20 January 1943.

It was the end of a brief imperial Era—three decades of occupation and violence with episodes of apparent pacification, followed by the call to 'abandon ship'.

9

BRITISH MILITARY ADMINISTRATION OF LIBYA AND CORONATION OF KING IDRIS

With the war over, the British Military Administration (BMA) overseeing Tripolitania and Cyrenaica[53] embarked upon the project of unifying Libya under the sovereignty of the emir, Sayyid Idris—the recognized leader of the Sanusis. This solution was feasible in Cyrenaica, where the Grand Sanusi was indeed the undisputed leader. However, it would be harder to establish Idris' sovereignty over Tripolitania and Fezzan.[54]

Following the institution of the General Assembly in 1946, UN Resolution no. 289 of December 1949 declared that the country was to be an independent and sovereign State. The High Commissioner assigned to the Libya 'desk' was a Dutchman, Adriaan Pelt. On 29 March 1951, the new Libya assumed its first federal government. The opinions of the citizenry were disregarded. The government came out of agreements between Great Britain and the designated King, Muhammad Idris.

The defeated Italians, too, suffered at the hands of the British occupier. Many settlers left the country. The modest urban artisans and manual workers of the cities were among those less eager to leave. In the early 1950s, about 45,000

Italians remained. By the mid-1960s the number had fallen to about 27,000 (24,000 in Tripoli alone).

On 7 October 1951, the Assembly definitively approved Libya's twelve-chapter federal Constitution. In it, Libya was declared an independent, sovereign State ruled over by a hereditary monarchy. It was to be a federal nation, subject to parliamentary government. Officially known as the United Kingdom of Libya, the country was made up of the three *wilayah* of Cyrenaica, Tripolitania and Fezzan. King Muhammad Idris al-Mahdi al-Sanusi became the Supreme Chief of State and commander of the armed forces of Libya. He was an 'untouchable' King, accountable to no one. He would act through his ministers, who would bear responsibility for the decisions they made.[55]

This was what had been agreed before the ceremony of the declaration of independence, taking place at midnight simultaneously in Benghazi, Tripoli and Sabha. Thus, the British and French finally handed over their powers to this new United Kingdom. A few hours later, at the al-Manar palace in Benghazi (the former residence of Rodolfo Graziani), King Idris proclaimed Libya's independence.

This independence, however, was strictly *pro forma*. British control was everywhere. The British had been here since 1942, and furthermore, King Idris immediately granted them military bases and portions of sovereignty.[56] It was quite clear who ruled over Libya. Britain would act both politically and militarily as Libya's overseer. One might concur with Dirk Vandewalle's view that the United Kingdom of Libya was an "accidental state", modelled according to the interests and desires of the Great Powers of the day, and with the assent of the provincials who feared the alternatives.[57]

Libya's neighbors achieved independence only after long struggles, and the sentiment of their national identity was forged by these struggles. In Libya's case, lying between the Maghreb and Mashreq, political independence came suddenly, at a moment's notice. It was unexpected. Ten years later, the country effortlessly achieved economic independence, with no effort on the part of the citizenry. This independence would bring about deeply significant, irreversible changes in the lives of Libyans.[58]

Following the war, with the permission of the British (September 1954), the Americans held the Wheelus Field air base in the vicinity of Tripoli. According to this agreement, the Americans

> would remain until 24 February 1970. They also received authorisation to considerably enlarge the military base. When the work was completed, it was one of the most important anti-Soviet strategic bases in the world and a facility for training air force personnel in the Mediterranean area.[59]

The British were based in El Adem, near Tobruk, not far from the frontier with Egypt. Territorially speaking, in the light of the emerging situation in the Mediterranean and Middle East during the Cold War, the sites of the two bases were of enormous strategic importance.[60]

The scope for 'collaboration' with the United States broadened. New agreements were reached regarding health care, education, agriculture and natural resources, involving the sum of $100 million dollars.[61] Libya moved toward client-state status, shielding itself from the winds of change that blew so forcefully after the Egyptian revolution of 23 July 1952 (during which the Free Officers under Gamal Abdul Nasser seized power).[62]

In Libya, the undercurrents of discontent gained in strength, inexorably. Young graduates from Egyptian universities, trade union militants and the members of disbanded Arab nationalist parties all felt the mounting pressure.[63] In the early 1960s, in an atmosphere of growing discontent, the Libyans found in their midst communists, Nasserians and many Ba'ath Party members (Ba'ath, an Arab-nationalist, lay-spirited and socialist party dedicated to an Arab resurrection, was founded in Damascus in 1940 by Michel 'Aflaq; the Libyan authorities soon also considered the Ba'ath Party a threat).

While their outreach was greatly conditioned by family, tribal and regional ties, these movements clung to the demands circulating between 1945 and 1951 (the founding of a republic, the formation of a unitary State, and federation with the other States of the Arab world).[64]

A huge oilfield was discovered in Cyrenaica in the late 1950s, at Bi'r Zaltan. However, the imbalances resulting from the flow of oil incomes destabilized Libyan society and constituted a key factor in the overturning of the political order and national institutions.[65] The Rockefellers were the sole short term beneficiaries of the birth of this 'new Texas'.[66] A company under their control, Esso Standard Libya, traded some 17,000 barrels per day.[67] The pace of prospecting activities accelerated, and enormous oilfields were found in the areas granted to major operators such as Royal Dutch Shell, Amerada and Continental (Oasis group), Gulf, Texas, and American Overseas Petroleum. Smaller companies— including the two Italian concerns, CORI (Compagnia Ricerca Idrocarburi), a company allied with AGIP mineraria (belonging to the AGIP, Azienda Generale Italiana Petroli, group), and AMI (Ausonia Mineraria), owned by Edison— soon joined the 'big boys'.[68]

Laden with Libya's 'black gold' for the markets of the West, the Esso-Canterbury set sail from a dedicated port served by a 160-kilometer pipeline, Marsa al-Burayqa

(Brega). Suddenly and unexpectedly, the State of Libya became rich. By the mid-1960s, the enriched Libya had become little more than a 'backyard' for the oil majors. As the largest oil producer in Africa, it boasted sales of 58.5 million tons. In 1968, the Libyan monarchy issued 137 concessions to 39 companies, major and independent. Total production rose to 2.6 million barrels per day.[69]

The social and political tensions within the country rose accordingly. The regime persecuted the youngsters and workers who organised demonstrations in the various cities, but the extremely harsh persecution did little to calm Libya's waters. It required just a spark for open revolt to erupt, as on 5-10 June, in the wake of the Israeli so-called "six day war". The Jews in Libya paid a heavy price. Seventeen Libyan Jews died, and the vast majority fled to Italy. Of the 5,000 Jews in Libya prior to the revolt, hardly more than a hundred remained in Tripoli (with only two remaining in Benghazi).[70]

Change was in the air, social and political. When "nationalism became the new mode of loyalty, especially among the new generations, the Sanusi movement began to decline".[71] The State, it must be remembered, had created a power structure based entirely on the equilibria established between tribes, and upon a system of military serfdom marking the kingdom's 'hallmark' quality (rejection of true statehood).[72]

This was a traditional society, indigent and illiterate, whose people had few interests outside their family circle, tribe or province. It suddenly saw prosperity coming its way. Strong ideological currents also emerged, and these currents brought with them a nagging sensation of uncertainty. While taking refuge in precedent, the Libyans would have to manage the brand new needs and discontinuities of an oil producing State.[73] King Idris' regime was in critical condition. The crisis might be delayed, but it could not be prevented.[74]

10

THE FREE OFFICERS SEIZE POWER AND EXPEL THE ITALIANS FROM TRIPOLI

A group of young men, the Free Unionist Officers (*al-Dubbat al-ahrar al-wahdawiyyun*), ousted King Idris. These officers had almost all risen from the poorer rural classes. Their leader was Mu'ammar ("he who builds") Gaddafi. This twenty-seven year old captain had been considering a revolt for years, and had planned it with great patience and attention to detail.[75]

Meetings were held to fine tune the operation in Tripoli and northern Italy, at Abano Terme. In Italy, during the last meeting of 24-27 August 1969, the final details of the plan were discussed, and the various tasks were allocated to the conspirators.

Asked about involvement of the Italian secret service in the Gaddafi coup d'état, a leading Italian magistrate, Rosario Priore, replied,

> The *coup d'état* was organised in a hotel in Abano Terme. I believe the Italians had a hand in it. As soon as Gaddafi assumed power, for the triumphal parade, we immediately sent him ships loaded with tanks, entire divisions,

even to the point of weakening the national defences of our own borders [...]. We knew about the oil [under that 'box of sand'] and we knew that the fields were immense. Libya was a tempting proposition. It constituted a strategic reserve, fuelling our economic development. And this is how it turned out [...]. The Libyans immediately closed the British and American bases and expelled the personnel [and] Italy immediately became Gaddafi's major economic partner.[76]

This certainly wasn't the first time secret services had intervened in order to modify the political conditions of a Middle Eastern nation, and it certainly won't be the last. On 6 October 1999, testifying to the parliamentary commission investigating acts of terrorism in Italy (*Commissione stragi*), Admiral Fulvio Martini—who, for seven years, had headed *SISMI* (Italy's Military Intelligence and Security Service) under the Craxi, Fanfani, Goria and Andreotti governments—outlined another extremely bold operation undertaken by Italy's intelligence community. "In 1985-87," he declared, "we organised a sort of *coup d'état* in Tunisia, to have President Ben 'Ali at the helm of the State, replacing Bourguiba who wanted to escape." Martini confessed quite openly, "Our country organized a coup [during the night of 6-7 November 1987] to oust a sick leader who posed a threat to the stability of the entire Maghreb area, and we installed a president favored by Italy".[77] A month after Ben 'Ali had taken up office, the chairman of *ENI*, Franco Reviglio, "rushed to Tunis to stipulate an agreement".[78]

Let us now return to Libya. At 2.30 a.m. on 1 September 1968, "Operation Jerusalem" commenced in all locations with a significant military presence (Benghazi,

Tripoli, Sabha, Derna and Bayda). The name, "Operation Jerusalem", was selected to honor the Palestinian liberation movement.

The surprise facilitated the taking of the various barracks, police command structures, radio stations and airports, which all fell into the hands of the Revolutionary Command Council (RCC) with no bloodshed whatsoever. Indeed, the Praetorian Guard units of the Cyrenaica Defense Force (CYDEF) and the Tripolitania Defense Force (TRIDEF) decided not to intervene.

The coup was over at 7.30 a.m. The monarchy's key functionaries had been taken into custody. The only resistance encountered was at Tobruk where about 600 members of the royal guard held out until 4 September. However, a platoon of the 5th regiment of the Libyan army, by now under the control of the young officers, forced the guards to surrender, again with no bloodshed.[79] Victory also depended on the tribal factor. The Warfalla and Magariha tribes in the west were allied with Gaddafi's own Qaddhafa tribe.[80]

At daybreak, after learning that the coup d'état had been successful in practically all locations, the young Gaddafi broadcast a proclamation via the radio in Benghazi, in which he declared that the old regime had come to an end. The Libyan Arab Republic was born. The *putsch* (the work of a hundred young men below the age of thirty) was a triumph.[81] King Idris learned of the coup while in Turkey, where he was undergoing treatment for rheumatism. He had no choice but to abdicate.

A devoted admirer of Nasser,[82] Gaddafi was now a colonel, and the commander in chief of the armed forces. During the first weeks of the new regime's rule, the RCC [83] had already begun to 'Libya-ize' and nationalize the banks of foreign countries operating locally (*Banco di Roma, Banco di Napoli* and 50% of Barclays Bank).[84] The royalties due from oil companies were raised, as were the wages of the Libyan oil sector's workforce.[85]

However, this was just the first step in the execution of a strategy that Gaddafi famously described as the use of oil as a "political weapon". Over the next four years, the RCC nationalized the assets and interests of the nine major American oil companies, transferring them to the National Oil Company (NOC), a concern controlled by the Libyan State.[86]

The British and American military personnel of El Adem and Wheelus Field were soon expelled. The revolutionaries would accept "no bases, no foreigner, no imperialist, and no intruders".[87] The Libyans threw down the gauntlet, and the Americans complied with the order. They packed their bags and left by 30 June 1970.[88]

What principles underpinned this revolution? Three key themes dominated the thinking of Gaddafi and the RCC: "freedom, socialism and unity", to which we can add the struggle against Western influences within the Arab world, and, in particular, the struggle against Israel (whose very existence was, Gaddafi stated, a confirmation of colonization and subjugation).[89]

Please note that the "socialism" part of the Free Officers' 'package' was not, strictly speaking, what Westerners generally understand by the term 'socialism'. It was not accompanied by the usual anti-religious sentiment. It was, rather, as Gaddafi saw it, an Islamic socialism that respects private property.[90] Here, Gaddafi's reference to Islam came as a presentation of his credentials, as one who opposes the old 'ulama once associated with Sanusi authority. These Sanusi elements would become the revolution's bitterest enemies. They fought the regime from within.[91] In brief, Libya under Gaddafi was to institute an "Islamic socialism" that deploys "national capital to aid the development of the country".[92]

The revolution represented primarily a determined effort to bring about Arab unity, around which all energies should converge. Over time, the seven Arab unity projects pursued by Gaddafi all failed (with Egypt and Sudan in 1969, Egypt, Sudan and Syria two years later, Tunisia in 1974, Morocco in 1984), but they, too, reflected Tripoli's own interest in this great dream.[93] Over the following two decades, the pan-Arab project was replaced by the ideal of a pan-African unity.[94]

The aim of the RCC's people's revolution (*thawra*)—one which, as Gaddafi insisted from the very start, sets the revolution apart from a merely military coup *d'état* (*inqilab*)—was to form a young ruling class rooted in its territories and drawn from the petty bourgeoisie and proletariat. This degree of integration within society and the level of education displayed would distinguish this class from Libya's traditional élites, and from the background and education of these strata. The embers that lay below monarchic Libya had been fanned to life. They embodied one of the "most original and most widely discussed" experiments of the Middle East.[95] This vision of a complete break with a colonial past underscores the importance of the experience of colonialism in forming Gaddafi's thought and his Revolution. Italy had concretely epitomized Western imperialism, against which the country had struggled.[96]

On 21 July 1970, the RCC accordingly issued three laws ordering confiscation of all the assets of the Italians and Jews and expulsion of all the members of both communities. This harsh measure led to the reluctant exodus of some 20,000 Italians.[97]

About 500 Italians remained. These had been acknowledged as 'good' by the authorities. In 1972, the remains of the 20,000 troops that had fallen in Libya were also sent back to Italy. We note, however, that the 500

Italians who did not leave Libya were soon to be joined by other incoming Italians (this 'post-colonial invasion' would bring the Italian population back up to more than 16,000 in 1978).[98]

Despite these dramatic twists and turns, the authorities of Tripoli and Rome remained on speaking terms. As pointed out above, it seemed likely that commercial and political relations between the two nations would remain (discreetly) solid.[99]

This picture finds confirmation in the fact that the Italian multinational oil company, ENI, was able to set up a joint venture with Libya, with both parties enjoying an equal standing (the American and British concerns had been nationalized). The SNAM Progetti company constructed Libya's first large refinery at Tripoli (capable of handling 2 million tons). Dozens of Italian companies operating in various other sectors thrived.[100] With the pace of business increasing over time, the former colony was fast becoming one of Italy's leading commercial partners.[101]

11

THE JAMAHIRIYYA
GREEN BOOK

The most important measure adopted to overcome the slowness of the desired reforms was the institution in 1973 of "power of the people" (*sult ash-sha'b*). While dealing with the affairs of his own country and deriving his actions from the domestic context, Gaddafi's thinking was never limited to Libya alone. His policies took the form of a world theory. He worked towards a human destiny that is universal in nature.

The programmatic ideas underpinning his fairly unique vision of the world had not yet found a unitary form. The revolutionary fervor of his *Green Book* (*al-Kitab al-akhdar*)—a rather brief work published in three separate sections between 1973 and 1979—brought the parts together.[102]

Change did not take the form of a smooth transition. On the one hand, the Libyan revolutionaries were implementing increasingly radical policies in the direction of entrusting the State with management of all economic activities. On the other, they were undermining the State as a fulcrum of political identity,[103] via the institutionalization of *Green Book* democratic theory based on the exercise by the people of direct democracy. How were these two tendencies to be reconciled?

Conflicts emerged during the first four years of the new regime (we note Gaddafi's impatience with the red tape and with the political practices that he believed prevented the people from directly participating in the country's revolution). Furthermore, we note his diffidence toward traditional sources of power. These factors assumed capital importance, in his thinking, for what he called the "Third Universal Theory".

The *Green Book* (with its three parts, dedicated to politics, economics and society) outlined the *Third Universal Theory*, which Gaddafi saw as an alternative to capitalism and Marxism.

The book—whose language reflects the author's Bedouin cultural background—wished to go beyond the socialist political experimentation of the past, replacing it with a radical reform of the country's political structures. These structures were to serve as a means of transforming Libya's citizens and turning them into active creators of a Stateless society. The theories of the French Revolution come to mind. The noted Italian journalist of the left, Valentino Parlato, observed that "Gaddafi is an attentive reader of Rousseau and the thinkers of the Enlightenment, and he loves Dickens".[104]

The book came out at a crucial time for the young nation, and it soon became the ideological focal point of domestic and international policy making.

Its directives—reflecting a deep-seated mistrust of political parties, representative government and bureaucratic institutions, as barriers to the participation of the people— provided the rationale for a series of increasingly bold economic, social and political initiatives. These directives culminated in the birth of the *Jamahiriyya*—a nation governed directly by its citizens without the intervention of intermediaries.

Put simply, Gaddafi aimed for a political community in which *consultation* as opposed to *representation* played the key role. Within this community, the resources of the nation were to be held by the citizenry, with the citizenry directly managing the administration and bureaucracy of the State through a system of Popular Conferences and Peoples' Committees (each handling a specific sector of administration). These organs were to have the power to enact decisions nationwide. The intended political system was seen as a 'bottom up' construct, and not 'top down'.[105]

One of the most famous principles of the revolution was *shuraka'la ujara'* ("partnership and not a wage system"). The *Green Book* established that neither private nor public concerns could employ "wage-earners"; such relations lead quite simply to the "exploitation of man by man". Workers must therefore abolish both the bureaucracy of the public sector and the dictatorship of the private sector by directly taking control of economic enterprises. These ideas clearly implied that the wealth of the nation must be shared out fairly, and that equality can only be established when no one depends economically upon others.

Gaddafi hoped that his work would serve as a practical manifesto. He wanted to intensify his previous attempts at mobilization. He had been impeded, he believed, by the country's political system, which was incapable of expressing the true voice of Libyans, because the people did not directly control their economic resources, and because of the antiquated nature of present social structures. His ideas were, we see, quite clear. Furthermore, combined with his insistence on egalitarianism and the absence of hierarchies, they tended to reflect a tribal *ethos*.

This new system of political government—with the deployment of nearly one thousand representatives nationwide—was finally set up in 1977. On 2 March at Sabha, on the day of inception, Gaddafi announced that the *"era of the masses"* had begun (from the Arabic root, *ja-m-ha-ra*, meaning "to gather together or convene a multitude"; he thus coined the term *Jamahiriyya*, which we might translate as "State of the masses").[106] He called Libya, *Al-Jamahiriyya al-'Arabiyya al-Libiyya ash-Sha'biyya al Ishtirakiyya* (the "Socialist People's Libyan Arab Jamahiriya"). The nation adopted the directives of the *Green Book* as the juridical guiding principles of Libyan society. The *Green Book* took the place of the first Constitution of December 1969, by means of which the Libyan Republic had been founded.

The reordering of the legal system was completed in 1988, with the announcement of *Al-Wathiqa al-khadra al-kubra lil-huquq al-insan fi 'asr al-jamahir* ("the great green charter in the era of the masses"), which, in twenty-seven articles, announced "to the popular masses the advent of a new Era from which corrupted regimes will be banished and all traces of tyranny and exploitation eradicated".[107]

Gaddafi then stepped down from his official posts. His title from then on would be, quite simply, *Qa'id* ("leader")—the permanent "guide" of the revolution.

As one observer noted:

> Gaddafi—the agitator and propagandist, the Utopian, the pragmatist—seems to be reviving a model that mirrors aspects of the 'democracy of the desert' such as the tribal assembly and the oral tradition of law.[108]

His was a charismatic, 'deinstitutionalized' role much in keeping with the ambit created by the *Jamahiriyya*.[109]

Further, as another observer remarked, Gaddafi's

ability to insinuate himself—and the Libyan

people simultaneously—into the troubled
history of his country by claiming that he
followed in the footsteps of Umar Al-Mukhtar
and all who had resisted the West forged a
sense of solidarity among Libyans.[110]

To substantiate Gaddafi's claim, we might briefly
consider the relations between the Libyan State and the
Christian churches (Christians representing the largest
among the minority religious communities). The Libyan
government's policy in favor of religious pluralism was
clearly intended as a means of bolstering the sentiment of
solidarity among all components of society, and was in
accordance with Islamic principles.

In the wake of the 1969 revolution and of the
expulsion of the Italians in 1970, the Catholic Church's new
identity had become more Afro-Asian.

The two milestone events of this period of dialogue
between Christians and Muslims were:

1) The Islamic-Christian conference in Tripoli
(February 1976). This event showed the world that closing
the churches at the time of the expulsion of the Italians was
not a move against the Catholic Church as such, but, instead,
against Italian colonialism (with which the Church was, in
one way or another, associated);

2) Establishment of diplomatic relations between the
Great Jamahiriya and the Holy See on 10 March 1997. This
development was much appreciated by the Libyan authorities
because it came during the embargo imposed by the United
States after the Lockerbie disaster. Through this agreement,
the Holy See showed the world that conflicts are resolvable
not by embargos but, rather, by dialogue.

Other significant events of this period concern the
dialogue seminars organized by *Al Daawa Al Islamiya*, the

visit paid by the Patriarch, Bartholomew of Constantinople, on the invitation of the Libyan government, and the prize awarded by the Gaddafi Prize Association for Peace and Promotion of Human Rights to the Coptic Orthodox Patriarch of Alexandria, Amba Shenouda.

On 29 December 2006, the various churches of the Christian community of Tripoli, headed by the Catholic Bishop of Tripoli, Monsignor Giovanni Martinelli OFM, were invited to meet the leader of the Great El Fatah Revolution, Mu'ammar Gaddafi, to exchange greetings on the occasion of the festivities of Eid Al-Adha, Christmas and New Year's Day, all occurring in the same week.

On 9 March 2007, the first Church in the Old City of Tripoli was reopened by the Libyan authorities, and use of it was granted to the local Anglican community (formerly the Church of Santa Maria degli Angeli).

On 24 October 2008, Theodore II, Patriarch of Alexandria and of All Africa, paid a visit to Libya's Greek Orthodox community. Also honoring the Catholic community with a visit, he met Monsignor Martinelli.

On 28-30 January 2009, the Archbishop of Canterbury, Dr. Rowan Douglas Williams, paid his first visit to Libya, and to the Anglican Church.

From the mid-seventies on, in the face of growing internal opposition, organized above all by fundamentalist groups, who accused him of "heresy", Gaddafi turned more and more to his own family and to the Qaddhafa tribe. This was vital if he was to have control of the security services and ensure his own personal safety.[111]

In the controversy over the rights and freedoms of women, for example, the 'ulama saw heresy at work. As he furthered his project for female emancipation, Gaddafi encountered bitter opposition not only from the most conservative exponents of the religious party but also from a number of his fellow revolutionists.[112]

Gaddafi's fundamental principle was that "Discrimination against woman by man is a flagrant act of oppression without justification".[113] Equality was required in the sphere of study and within the armed forces. A women's academy was founded in Tripoli in 1978. This principle was also applied to marriage, divorce and inheritance. The 'traditionalists', instead, proposed segregation and separation of the sexes, strict compliance with Qur'anic norms, and discrimination against women in many fields. Hence Gaddafi's famous description of Islamists as "reactionaries in the name of Islam".[114]

A small (but most determined) component of Libyan society detested Gaddafi. The Islamic clerics had lost economic prerogatives enjoyed for decades. This Islamic opposition was fomented by the Muslim Brotherhood, in particular. Harsh measures were taken to curb the influence of this latter organization. Significantly, in 1996, Libya was the first country to issue an international arrest warrant with Osama bin Laden's name on it.[115]

Islamic student groups emerged once more—mainly in Cyrenaica, and above all in Benghazi. The Islamists set up a number of very well organized, generously funded organizations. The revolt that received global attention in early 2011 spread outward precisely from these centers. This question shall be discussed in Part II.

Gaddafi's approach to these numerically small groups of Arab fundamentalists wavered between the rod and the carrot (the latter in the form of "national reconciliation").[116]

His conduct is of some interest, in the light of his ability to govern the country for so long without any formal powers conferred upon him. By focusing on the material needs of the people and widely distributing the proceeds of the oil industry (42% of the GDP), Gaddafi managed to prolong his rule and impede the formation of alliances among politicians eager to destabilize the existing governmental structure.

Admittedly, Libya's economy was client-, patronage- and favor-based. In terms of efficiency, the country's bloated bureaucracy and its 'social contract'—that was based on distribution of the proceeds of oil sales—undermined the system as a whole.[117]

Little progress was made regarding the *Green Book*'s intended "direct democracy". A process of "institutionalization of tribal power" came about, that suffocated all ideas of self-government of the people.[118] As Gaddafi himself wrote, "Theoretically, this is genuine democracy but, realistically, the strong always rules, i.e., the stronger party in the society is the one that rules".[119]

Here, we see the Jamahiriyya's 'learning curve'. Indeed, Gaddafi's Utopian vision—at least as originally formulated—failed to emerge as a credible systemic alternative.[120]

With equal objectivity and frankness, we note also that, in terms of living standards, Libya's economy had clearly developed into the most prosperous of the continent of Africa. Libya's living standards also placed the country ahead of the Arab Middle East.[121]

In any case, these factors of socio-economic stabilization, complemented by a potent blending of charismatic power and skilled use of the instruments of myth and rhetoric, provided the key to Gaddafi's position of leadership over a period of four decades.

Let us round off this chapter with a quick look at the foundations upon which this enormous social experiment rested. In a word, immense oil revenues (estimated at about 95 billion dollars). Thanks to these resources, the average incomes of Libyans rose from 2,216 dollars in 1969 to nearly 10,000 dollars in 1979. At the close of the 1970s, per capita spending on development in Libya was four times greater than that of all the other Arab States combined.[122] Unsurprisingly, the oil facilities were carefully cordoned off from all revolutionary fervor of the kind that might be found elsewhere in Libya.

12

COVERT OPS
AND TALES OF
'TERRORISM'...

The United States, France and Great Britain were not pleased with Gaddafi's deep commitment to the international political scene, and his frequent meddling in the affairs of the Middle East and Africa (e.g. the considerable economic and military support provided to the African National Congress (ANC)). They resented Libya's role in the South African anti-Apartheid struggle.[123] They decided he'd overstepped the mark, repeatedly. Something had to be done about him.

On 18 July 1980, the remains of a Libyan MIG-23, piloted by Captain Ezzedin Khalil, were discovered in the vicinity of the village of Castelsilano, in the Sila area of the province of Catanzaro, Italy. The MIG accident may have had something to do with the Ustica air disaster. On 27 June, a DC-9 ITAVIA airliner exploded in the skies of the island of Ustica, to the north of Sicily. All 81 passengers died. In the absence of concrete evidence, one can only speculate about possible connections between the two incidents.

Years and years have gone by. The investigators are still groping in the dark. Rosario Priore—the investigating magistrate mentioned above, who had been called in also to investigate the Ustica disaster—stated that elements and information [exist] that lead us toward the truth. But it's an 'unutterable' truth. A truth that could not be revealed at the time of the judicial investigation, as is the case for many other enquiries into mysterious episodes in Italy's recent past, be these massacres or international links with our terrorists. The truth of Ustica was buried under the absolution sentences passed, but even certain individuals occupying the highest offices of power have now pronounced that truth, albeit under their breath.[124]

So what is this "unutterable" truth? Priore openly describes a very real "war scenario [...] buried under an international conspiracy of silence (*omertà internazionale*)". On the basis of the judicial proceedings, Priore concludes that

the DC-9 was downed by one or more military aircraft, guided toward the target by a powerful, efficient radar fighter control system (*guida caccia*) capable of 'seeing' even over distances of hundreds of kilometers.[125]

The scene was described by two fighter pilots of the *Stormo di Grossetto* squad based at Grossetto, Italy—Mario Naldini and Ivo Nutarelli. That evening, aboard their TF 104, they were flying right behind the DC-9. When they returned to their base, they told their colleagues that "something terrible happened. A dogfight that could have led to all-out war".[126]

Tragically, the two pilots never made it to the courtroom. While awaiting the hearing, "they both died as a result of a strange accident at Ramstein"[127] in Germany. The German judicial authorities failed to reach a final verdict in regard to their deaths. Equally mysterious are the "episodes of false testimony, destruction of documents, disappearances of witnesses, tapes from which the portions of radar data for the minutes of greatest interest had been removed, records gone missing",[128] and the "strange deaths" of military personnel ("at least ten"), who had the very bad luck to be on duty that night in the radar room covering the skies above Ustica.

All truth has been sucked out of reality, and has disappeared into an *enormous black hole*. The evidence that might lead us to those responsible for the massacre has disappeared. Priore concludes, "There clearly was a plan to, at all costs, prevent us from finding out what took place in the sky over Ustica".[129]

The conclusion reached by the Roman magistrate was that the downing of the DC-9 "was an error. The objective was in all likelihood something else: the plane that at that time flew under the 'cover' of the DC-9, to protect it from radar interception. Perhaps it was the Libyan MIG that crashed onto the Sila".[130]

So, what was the real target? He adds, "as emerged during our enquiry, and [as became] clearer over time [....] the target was an aircraft carrying Gaddafi. The flight plans held by our air force mention a VIP flight that evening from Tripoli to Warsaw".[131]

Libyan aircraft were not allowed into European airspace: "if military aircraft from a non NATO country had been detected, the system would have immediately considered them enemy flights to be downed".[132] We must remember that the NADGE system (the radar network protecting the European countries belonging to the Atlantic alliance) "had 'gaps' along the Italy stretch", which could be breached by sufficiently well informed persons, thus enabling undisturbed journeys "to the very heart of Europe". This was possible "because the Libyans had privileged relations with Italy [...]. Basically, we're dealing with people who needed to travel safely and, in one way or another, we provided them with our protection".[133]

The Ustica affair sounds like the stuff of spy thrillers. The more you delve into it, the clearer the picture becomes.

> More recent hypotheses have it that those fighters were to join the Libyan leader over the Tyrrhenian Sea to escort him on a journey to eastern Europe. However, a warning of imminent danger was received while the plane was in the area of Malta. The plane suddenly changed its route and returned to Libya. It is quite clear that anyone who wanted to attack Gaddafi's plane would have to down the escort planes first.[134]

Who could have carried out such a daringly complex plan? Priore believes that "from a technical angle, at that time, and in the Mediterranean, only two countries were able to carry out a military operation of this kind—the United States and France".[135] Data emerging during the enquiry and the public declarations (placed on record) of the former President of the Italian Republic, Francesco Cossiga, fairly clearly indicate "the responsibility of France".[136]

Priore also concludes that

> the elimination of the Libyan leader over Ustica would have been just the first stage of a much greater, more complex plan that would have entailed intervention on the

ground in Libya. The fall of the Tripoli regime would have led to a revision of the entire order in North and Sub-Saharan Africa and a separation of areas of influence in these decidedly resource-rich areas, with Italy losing out on all fronts.[137]

If this is how the incident occurred, we can also suppose the plan to finally "remove" Gaddafi had never been abandoned. Indeed, incidents surrounding Gaddafi multiplied over the years.[138]

The Americans detested him. President Reagan called him a "mad dog", and engaged in repeated covert attempts at destabilizing Libya.[139] This destabilization consisted in direct intervention (a grave violation of norms) and a "reported disinformation program" (with the involvement of the major television and press networks, now eager to demonize Gaddafi).

The disinformation campaign was conducted on such a scale that it prompted top-ranking official Bernard Kalb to resign in protest in 1986. Kalb was Assistant Secretary of State for Public Affairs, and, at that time, the right hand man of Secretary of State George Schultz. He claimed that his conscience would not permit him to engage in the disinformation (psyops) actions desired by the American administrative apparatus.[140] The scandal was aired by the mass media.

Starting in January 1986, the USA imposed, first, an oil embargo and then a total block on all trade with the Jamahiriyya. This economic embargo was intensified by the UN on 31 March 1992 (Resolution 748), and intensified yet further on 11 November 1993 (Resolution 883). After a temporary suspension in April 1999, the embargo ended in 2003.[141]

As relations between the United States and Libya worsened in the 1980s, Vice-President George H. W. Bush went so far as to claim that the Libyan government's policies and actions represented an extraordinary threat to the national security and foreign policy of the United States. A mechanism—now familiar to us all—was being set up. These people wanted Gaddafi out of the way.[142]

Following the terrorist attack of 5 April 1986, the anti-Gaddafi campaign went on unabated. An explosion occurred at the "La Belle" discotheque in West Berlin (a nightspot favored by American servicemen).

As Libyan historian Angelo Del Boca points out, here (as on other similar occasions)

> there is no proof that the Libyans were involved. Actually, the most likely trail points to Syria [...]. Even without concrete evidence of Libyan involvement in the Berlin attack, as soon as he was informed of the incident Reagan decided to move. The episode had all the prerequisites for dealing a blow to a man who so justly deserved punishment, whom he had already called a 'mad dog'. Reagan approved adoption of a policy based on the force of might. He started with the invasion of Grenada.[143]

According to Noam Chomsky, the Reagan administration came to power with three basic programs in mind: transferring resources from the poor to the rich, supporting hi-tech industry through the military system, and expanding forceful intervention in the third world. While the public had to be mobilized via the constant threat of war, direct confrontation with the Empire of Evil was too dangerous. A safer target was required—Libya was the perfect candidate. Gaddafi had already been made eminently detestable in the public mind, and armed conflict with Libya was risk free. The war drums rolled. The scenario had already been prepared in 1981, with the trap set for Libya in the Gulf of Sirte. The idea was to augment consensus for the presence of the US Rapid Deployment Force in the region, and for other military measures.[144]

The American attack (code name: Operation Colorado Canyon) got underway in the early hours of 15 April 1986, with airstrikes against Tripoli and Benghazi using 272-kg and 952-kilo laser-guided bombs. The main target was Gaddafi himself, at his family's normal place of residence, the bunker complex of Bab al 'Aziziyah. Despite the devastation, the Colonel survived. One hundred civilians died, including Gaddafi's sixteen-month old adopted daughter, Hana'.

Just a few hours later, by way of reprisal, the Libyans launched two Scud-B missiles against a LORAN-C telecommunications station on the Italian island of Lampedusa. Coordination between the Sixth Fleet and USAF planes, which had flown in from Great Britain, was handled by the Beacon system located at the base on Lampedusa. The two Libyan missiles caused very little damage but the media resonance was enormous. As a precautionary measure, the Italians set up a naval plan for the Strait of Sicily, named *Operazione Girasole* (Operation Sunflower).[145]

The Americans failed in their attempt to get rid of Gaddafi, but failure was no deterrent. After the airstrikes, they deployed US-trained guerrillas whose mission was to destabilize the regime.[146] This was yet another fiasco.

However, the matter was not to end there. The Democratic President, Bill Clinton, would carry on 'the good work' of his predecessor. Washington did not intend to give up its role as "world cop", as we shall see in some detail in the second part of this book.

The crisis worsened relations between Italy and Libya, but the bridges were gradually rebuilt. In 1993, partnering with Italy's major oil company, AGIP-ENI, the National Oil Company (NOC) laid out a 5.5 billion dollar natural gas agreement for development in western Libya. The plan was to lay down an immense underwater gas pipeline between Libya and Italy. Over the years, for both partners, the project assumed the proportions of a major strategic move.[147]

However, the main obstacle to such agreements was the unpaid war reparations due to Libya as a result of Italy's colonial adventures. Again and again, the ghosts of the past returned, until a Libya-Italy Friendship, Partnership and Cooperation Treaty was drawn up and finally signed in Benghazi on 30 August 2008 by Italy's PM, Silvio Berlusconi, and the leader of the Great Socialist People's Libyan Arab Jamahiriya, Mu'ammar Gaddafi.[148]

After four decades of turbulence, the prospects for Gaddafi seemed at last to be improving. This was not to be. It was just the calm before the storm.

In February, the Gaddafi dossier was back on the table: *Gaddafi the bloodthirsty dictator! Gaddafi the madman!*

While the scenario is familiar, the quantities of disinformation flooding the media were unprecedented. Like a full blown symphony the campaign had its very own overture—a spectacular movement, called "Arab Spring".

PART II

JAMAHIRIYYA

*"Serpens, sitis, ardour harenae dulcia uirtuti; gaudet
Patientia duris; laetius est, quotiens mango sibi
constat, honestum. Sola potest Libye turba praestare
malorum, ut deceat fugisse uiros"*[149]
(Lucan, *Pharsalia*, Book 9, 402-407)

1

"ARAB SPRING"

On 14 January 2011, Tunisia's Zayn al-Abidin Bin 'Ali was forced out of office following widespread unrest. He had been the President of Tunisia since 1987.

Weeks later, on 11 February, Hosni Mubarak fell from power after thirty years on the throne as Egypt's unchallenged *dominus*. Those three decades had earned Mubarak the (not altogether affectionate) nickname, "Pharaoh". The sensationalist Western press transformed these events into a spectacle. Buzzwords like "jasmine revolution" and "lotus revolution" abounded.

What of the governments of Tunisia and Egypt today? With the insurrections over, and after the thousand or so deaths in the two countries, the old men are back. The same 'wolves' in a new 'sheep's clothing'.[150] Pareto's thesis of the circulation of élites appears to hold as true in North Africa as anywhere else...

No genuine process of democratization has come about. The regimes were to be aided in their efforts toward economic integration with the United States and EU. Economic reforms (rather vaguely defined) would be accompanied by new foreign investments.[151]

The wave of protest moved on. It came to Jordan, Yemen, Algeria and Syria. Unexpectedly, the wave also broke against the shores of Oman and Bahrain. Here, the regimes brutally crushed the protests. On 14 March, Saudi Arabia mobilized its special forces to assist the Bahraini government. No condemnations were forthcoming from the governments of the West.[152]

The Saudis greatly feared the spread of protests from Bahrain into Saudi Arabia, across the stretch of sea traversed by the twenty-six-kilometer raised superhighway bridge, the King Fahd Causeway. Over and above the Shiite question, and the considerable discrimination against them both in Bahrain and in Saudi Arabia, the living standards of the people in Saudi Arabia are very low indeed. While the kingdom is one of the greatest oil producers in the world, 40% of the population (made up mainly of young people) live below the poverty line. These people have, in effect, little access to education or jobs. Most of the skilled and unskilled jobs go to foreigners.

In a timely move, the King of Morocco broke away from the pack. On 10 March, he announced constitutional reform.

2

UN RESOLUTIONS 1970 AND 1973 AND THE 'NEW INTERNATIONAL LAW'

The Tunisian and Egyptian 'spring' events were conveniently side lined[153] so that the media could focus on the "gross and systematic violation of human rights" (Resolution 1970, passed by the UN Security Council on 26 February 2011), on the "crimes against humanity" (Resolution 1973, passed by the UN Security Council on 17 March 2011), and a long list of other crimes reportedly committed by Gaddafi against his own people.[154]

Resolution 1973, with its very many discrepancies, was totally lacking in juridical value. It represented a very clear breach of the UN Charter based upon the sovereignty of states. With the imposition of a no-fly zone and the resolve to "take all necessary measures" (except military occupation) to protect Libyan civilians, a number of functions of the Security Council were transferred to certain member States. The measures included a naval blockade to prevent arms supplies from reaching Libya.[155]

The measures were quite simply illegal. Over and above the question of concrete implementation itself, we note that only in cases of conflicts between States can the UN intervene as per Chapter I, article 2(4), and Chapter VII of the United Nations Charter. The UN cannot intervene in cases of domestic conflict (i.e. conflicts within States), these being the internal affairs of the countries affected (i.e. domestic jurisdiction). The Security Council members must therefore abide by Article 25 of the Charter. Exceptions to the prohibition on the use of force appear in article 51 and Chapter VII. Various provisions (article 42) allow the Security Council to take actions "necessary for the purpose of maintaining international peace and security".

Resolutions 1970 and 1973 included the specification that they were in accordance with the letter and spirit of Chapter VII of the UN Charter. A closer look tells us that both resolutions clash with Article 42. Article 42 can apply only when measures "not involving the use of armed force" have failed.

From the very onset, the media cast its veil of obscurity over events on the ground. At the very least, any decision made should have been based on an enquiry conducted in Libya itself. No investigating committees under the orders of the UN Human Rights Council or Security Council actually went to Libya.

While international law permits States to have recourse to force in extremely limited circumstances, the rules applying to non-State actors in regard to the use of arms are even stricter. One instance in which arms use on the part of non-State actors is recognized bases itself on the right to self-determination against an oppressive occupying foreign power. This circumstance may legitimize the use of force by Iraqis or Afghans, for example, against an occupying army. However, it does not authorize Libyan 'rebels' to rise up in arms against their own government. The double standards underpinning these criteria fuel the arguments of critics, who claim that the two resolutions—like other similar resolutions in the past—undermine the very foundations of international law. In the Kellogg-Briand Pact, or World Peace Act, of 1928 and in the UN Charter of 1945, the signatories agreed to renounce the use of force against each other for the purposes of furthering their foreign policy agendas. Over the last two decades, various Western powers have repeatedly violated this principle. Many have noted the eagerness with which these powers attack prevalently Muslim States. The non-Western world understands the logic behind the West's actions. It is also quite clear that the West is uninterested in the 'niceties' of international law.

It is a familiar story. The first no-fly zone (also illegal) dates back to 1991, imposed unilaterally by the US, UK and France after the first Iraq war. We saw there the demise of the kind of International Law that we associate with the East-West bipolar global divide.

With the founding of ICISS (the International Commission on Intervention and State Sovereignty), a 'new' worldview came to the fore. ICISS was announced to the UN Assembly in September 2000.[156] The initiative, originating in Canada, can be linked to a broad based interest group. According to jurist Luca Baiada,

> To identify the group more precisely, follow the money. Among ICISS's founders we find the Carnegie Corporation in New York, and the Simons, Rockefeller, William and Flora Hewlett, and John D. and Catherine T. MacArthur foundations. ICISS presented its report in late September 2001. The Commission believes not only that, on the

basis of Responsibility to Protect (aka RtoP or R2P), military intervention is to be permitted anywhere, but also that such intervention is legitimized by the UN Charter. To overcome the veto right in the Security Council, the practice of constructive abstention must be reinforced, and regional organizations must be considered (rather as we saw in the case of Libya: abstention of a number of Council members and an unclear line adopted by an African organization). ICISS considers sovereignty as equivalent to responsibility, and it urges the UN to embrace the R2P theory. Only the Security Council embraced it, in part. No corresponding Assembly Resolution was passed, as had been desired [...]. Human rights exist and they're important. When the time comes to define them and to check that they are being respected, the temptation is all too great to demand that they be respected only elsewhere and not at home. The most exalted principles are therefore sullied and the most broad-reaching plans are found to be actually very limited in scope. The entities promoting R2P are not lacking in resources. The International Coalition for the Responsibility to Protect (ICRtoP) and the Global Centre for the Responsibility to Protect (GCR2P) are based in New York. R2P is an institution coming out of a complex geopolitical and symbolic game.[157]

The developing world and real international community (as opposed to the 'international community' that Western media insist on) largely know where all this is meant to lead. R2P works toward the death of the concept of "national sovereignty"—the death of a concept that emerged, in effect, with the Westphalia Treaty of 1648. The proponents of the 'new theory', as described, intend to modify the concept of sovereignty, and their efforts have received the approval even of religious organizations. The theory has been defined by others as "an insidious juridical construct which attempts to introduce into international law the right to meddle in the affairs of others, but the principles of international law firmly reject such interference".[158]

The new approach was illuminated in Security Council Resolution 1973 authorizing the Coalition of the Willing to intervene in Libya, citing as a justification (at least, as a formal justification) precisely "the protection of civilians".[159]

If we look at developments during the Libyan crisis, we see that the approach of the United States and European Union to Libya totally differed from their approach to Tunisia, Egypt, Bahrain, Oman, Jordan, Morocco and Saudi Arabia.

No sanctions were applied against the authorities of Bahrain, for example, whose armed forces, without warning, brutally attacked and fired on the demonstrators in Manama's Pearl Square.[160] The demonstrators were protesting against "religious discrimination, political, social and economic ostracism".[161] They called for an end to the Sunni dynasty in power since 1783. "A war has been launched against the people without a declaration of war", the demonstrators cried. The press reported that the people who took to the streets were absolutely nonviolent. The al-Khalifa ruling family nevertheless ordered the forces of law and order to shoot directly into the crowds.[162]

Shiites, making up 70% of the population of Bahrain, are constantly discriminated against by a hated, unwanted regime foisted upon the people from outside. The political system is without even the mildest and most symbolic forms of democracy. It is ironic that Barack Obama, NATO and the leaders of the European Union should thank al-Khalifa for having immediately joined the coalition against Libya. Bahrain, held up as an example of probity, is a key partner of the USA.[163]

Bahrain hosts America's Fifth Fleet and 2,300 American troops, "of vital importance for the USA in projecting their military power against Iran and in controlling the oil traffic in the Gulf".[164]

We note the blatant hypocrisy of the oil monarchies of the Gulf Cooperation Council (GCC),[165] who were the first to go to the Arab League with the request for a no-fly zone in Libya. Hillary Clinton and her acolytes, the leaders of the European Union, presented these regimes as the overseers and representatives of the Arab masses.[166] A group of Western-originated hereditary monarchs feel they can do what they want. They represent no one. Most troubling is the fact that there is no democratic forum before which their acts can be judged. For many years, the Western and Atlantic powers have been eagerly refining the techniques of application of such double standards.

Bahrain is only a ripple on the surface of this sordid story.

3

WHO WERE LIBYA'S 'REBELS'? WHO BACKED THEM?

Let us now return to the key events and developments of the so called "Arab Spring". While the top brass in the West were wary of the political, economic and military implications of the Tunisian and Egyptian "Springs", the French, Americans and British immediately and unreservedly supported the Libyan rebels both in Cyrenaica (where most of the country's oil wealth is to be found) and in Fezzan. The 'rebels' included many Sanusi Islamists, Egyptians from the Muslim Brotherhood and jihadists from Algeria, Morocco, Tunisia, Jordan, Qatar, Afghanistan and elsewhere.[167] These men were headed by two leading members of the government of Libya, the former Justice Minister, Mustafa Abdel al-Jalil, and the former Minister of the Interior, General Abdel al-Fattah Younis (assassinated on 28 July 2011 by Islamist members of the National Transitional Council). The monarchical conservatives, who wanted to restore the dynasty of King Idris I, joined al-Jalil and Younis in this venture.[168]

Colonel Gaddafi, however, in speech after speech, insisted that the 2011 revolt was dominated by "Al-Qa'ida" elements. It had also come to light that tens of British

MI6 agents, Special Air Services (SAS) and Special Boat Services (SBS) operatives, the CIA and the French *Direction Générale de la Sécurité Extérieure* (DGSE) were secretly on the ground in Libya, working as military trainers and organizers for the rebel cause.[169]

"London had actually sent its special forces to Libya just days before the Cyrenaica revolt erupted, a fact that raises many questions as to the role of the British in detonating the tribal revolt against Gaddafi", wrote one observer.[170] It has also been reported that the French and British provided the insurrectionists with arms and motor vehicles to enable the triumphant march on Tripoli.[171]

So, many military and intelligence operatives were in Libya even before the United Nations passed the no-fly zone order. Governments that authorize deployment of operatives in this manner clearly violate international law.[172]

Although, during those early days, the information reaching the media from the field was anything but clear, "Paris decided to initiate air raids over Benghazi the very night Resolution 1973 had been approved".[173] France thus managed to steal a march on the Coalition of the Willing, made up of the USA and Great Britain (soon to be joined by Norway, the Netherlands, the United Arab Emirates, Jordan, Denmark, Canada, Spain, Belgium, Turkey and Italy).[174]

In order to protect the civilian population of Benghazi and Tripoli from *Gaddafi the bloodthirsty dictator and madman*, the French president, Nicolas Sarkozy, imposed the no-fly zone. Of course, the political reasons for all this, the ousting of a 'dictator', were left unmentioned. This was a humanitarian mission, after all! France thus became the leader of Operation Odyssey Dawn, then was replaced by NATO-directed Operation Unified Protector (thus implementing the military embargo on Libya).[175]

US Admiral William Gortney's first concern was Gaddafi's physical safety and wellbeing. It goes without saying that Gaddafi was not on the coalition's list of targets, although someone might accidentally kill him... Britain's Chief of the Defence Staff, Sir David Richards, was equally insistent that Gaddafi was not to be targeted. Not that killing Gaddafi was such a bad thing in itself in their eyes, but UN law would not permit it.[176]

The coalition was 'willing' to do some things, but less 'willing' to do others. Less willing to admit, for example, that the aim was precisely to assassinate Gaddafi. The coalition was unwilling to admit that it hoped to bury his death under Resolution 1973's 'collateral' carnage. However, in a joint letter, Obama, Sarkozy and Cameron did publicly admit that the Libya mission would not be over until Gaddafi had been removed (he had to "go and go for good").[177] Hence, the repeated targeting of Gaddafi's Bab al 'Aziziyah residential compound (where Gaddafi normally resided with his family).[178]

Too cowardly to admit what this humanitarian mission was really all about, the assassins hoped to present Gaddafi's death to the world as something 'incidental', prevention of which was beyond the powers even of the world's leaders. We heard of an excess of bombs raining down on Libya as though they were part of the weather or climate But then, the West sees itself as the morally superior player because of its advanced arms technology and considerable resources. Claiming to act in the name of freedom and democracy, the West exerts its power to decide who is to live and who is to die. As the self-appointed arbiter of human rights, it dispenses self-interested decisions on who is to enjoy these rights and who must do without. Principles don't come into this picture. Today, as in the past, tyrants are often greeted with open arms and welcomed into our home countries.

Those resisting Western dominion are rubbed out, and the cities of their peoples are obliterated.[179]

But what are the motives, really? While there is much to conjecture about why the West might like to see Gaddafi removed, on 2 April 2011, under the heading "Subject: H: France's client & Q's gold." Sidney Blumenthal (a confidant of the Clintons of thirty years' standing) sent fellow-coward Hillary Clinton a confidential e-mail message concerning "France's client & Qaddafi's gold" that outlined an insider's understanding. Blumenthal reported that

> 1. A high ranking official on the National Libyan Council [the rebels' first council] states that factions have developed within it. In part this reflects the cultivation by France in particular of clients among the rebels. General Abdelfateh Younis is the leading figure closest to the French, who are believed to have made payments of an unknown amount to him. Younis has told others on the NLC that the French have promised they will provide military trainers and arms. So far the men and materiel have not made an appearance. Instead, a few "risk assessment analysts" wielding clipboards have come and gone. Jabril, Jalil and others are impatient. It is understood that France has clear economic interests at stake. Sarkozy's occasional emissary, the intellectual self-promoter Bernard Henri-Levy [sic], is considered by those in the NLC who have dealt with him as a semi-useful, semi-joke figure.
>
> 2. Rumors swept the NLC upper echelon this week that Qaddafi may be dead or maybe not.

3. Qaddafi has nearly bottomless financial resources to continue indefinitely, according to the latest report we have received: On April 2, 2011 sources with access to advisors to Saif al-Islam Qaddafi stated in strictest confidence that while the freezing of Libya's foreign bank accounts presents Muammar Qaddafi with serious challenges, his ability to equip and maintain his armed forces and intelligence services remains intact. According to sensitive information available to these individuals, Qaddafi's government holds 143 tons of gold, and a similar amount in silver. During late March, 2011 these stocks were moved to SABHA (south west in the direction of the Libyan border with Niger and Chad); taken from the vaults of the Libyan Central Bank in Tripoli.

This gold was accumulated prior to the current rebellion and was intended to be used to establish a pan-African currency based on the Libyan golden Dinar. This plan was designed to provide the Francophone African Countries with an alternative to the French. franc (CFA).

(Source Comment: According to knowledgeable individuals this quantity of gold and silver is valued at more than $7 billion. French intelligence officers discovered this plan shortly after the current rebellion began, and this was one of the factors that influenced President Nicolas Sarkozy's decision to commit France to the attack on Libya. According to these

individuals Sarkozy's plans are driven by the
following issues:

a. A desire to gain a greater share of Libya
oil production,

b. Increase French influence in North
Africa,

c. Improve his internal political situation
in France,

d. Provide the French military with an
opportunity to reassert its position in the
world,

e. Address the concern of his advisors
over Qaddafi's long term plans to supplant
France as the dominant power in Francophone
Africa.)

On the afternoon of April 1, an individual
with access to the National Libyan Council
(NLC) stated in private that senior officials of
the NLC believe that the rebel military forces
are beginning to show signs of improved
discipline and fighting spirit under some of the
new military commanders, including Colonel
Khalifha Haftar, the former commander of
the anti-Qaddafi forces in the Libyan National
Army (LNA). According to these sources,
units defecting from Qaddafi's force are also
taking a greater role in the fighting on behalf
of the rebels.[180]

This e-mail points to violation of the terms of
Resolution 1973[181] on Sarkozy's part, and to complacency, at
the very minimum, on the part of Mrs Clinton in particular.

Among the coalition's members there was a diplomatic row as to who was to lead the Libya operation. It was

decided that it should be NATO. Having performed more than 15,000 aerial bombing and naval shelling missions—causing countless civilian deaths, and often using arms with depleted uranium—NATO was the ideal candidate. It had the experience required for missions of this kind.[182]

The international media repeatedly tell us that Gaddafi ordered the Lockerbie massacre that took place on 21 December 1988 (270 victims),[183] that Gaddafi was a 'terrorist'.

If we read the Lockerbie trial records, we learn that on 31 January 2011, the British justice system acquitted one of the two accused, Ali Amin Khalif Fhimah, due to insufficient evidence.[184] The other, 'Abdel Baset Ali Mohamed al-Megrahi, imprisoned for years, was then extradited to Libya in August 2009.[185]

The charges against al-Megrahi remain unsubstantiated. In February 2011,

> Robert Black, the Scottish law professor who devised the format of the Netherlands-based trial, was quoted [...] as saying he was 'absolutely astounded' that Al Megrahi had been found guilty. Mr Black said he believed the prosecution had 'a very, very weak circumstantial case' and he was reluctant to believe that Scottish judges would 'convict anyone, even a Libyan' on such evidence.[186]

Black was not alone. A major Scottish newspaper that had followed up the affair over the years concluded on 28 August 2005 that the evidence against al-Megrahi had been fabricated.[187] Amid the various claims and counterclaims, the Libyans paid a high price: an embargo lasting ten years, and payments in damages in the order of 10 million dollars for each Pan Am passenger who died [188]

The former Libyan Justice Minister, Mustafa Abdel al-Jalil, saw fit to draw "the entire world's attention once more to the responsibilities of Gaddafi over Lockerbie"[189] for which the Libyan government had already paid reparations and accepted responsibility, issues of actual guilt aside.[190] .Mustafa Abdel al-Jalil was Justice Minister until 21 February 2011, when he passed directly into the 'rebel' camp.[191] From his point of view, or from the point of view of those whose interests he represented, if pointing to Libyan responsibility for Lockerbie would galvanize public opinion and justify the upcoming massive attack, so much the better![192]

The Benghazi 'rebels' were the West's new ally. Benghazi was a stronghold of tribal and religious traditionalist tendencies. The 'rebels' were to be encouraged. Photo ops were arranged. For the benefit of visiting TV journalists, the rebels shot their guns into the air and charged around on pickup trucks fitted out with heavy machine guns.[193] Poster boys perhaps they were, but they were not very popular in Libya.

Perhaps they were well armed and had been trained, but they were still at the 'rag tag army' stage. The insurgents repeatedly fell back when faced by the loyalist army, and they received little support from the people of Libya. It takes quite some imagination to see these people, who lacked popular support, as having anything to do with a popular revolt.[194] "It is very likely," concluded Thierry Meyssan, "that there are more NATO Special Forces commandos on the ground than the number of Libyan combatants they are supposed to oversee".[195]

The opposition government appointed itself, presumably at the request of these 'rebels'. It called itself the National Transitional Council. Its existence was announced on 27 February 2011, but it was not clear how it was composed. Mahmud Jibril was appointed executive president.[196] Jibril, who was once Gaddafi's right hand man and the former director of the National Economic Development Board (NEDB) (since 2007), made the arrangements for key operatives from the armed forces of various Western States to come in and train the insurgents.[197]

French President Nicolas Sarkozy was the leader who showed the greatest determination in demanding military intervention against Gaddafi's Libya. He is said to have frankly admitted that "We were the ones who created the rebels' Council [in Benghazi], and without our support, our money and our arms, the Council would not exist".[198]

The opposition forces needed greater credibility. So the media ran stories about the Libyan dictator's tremendous cruelty and brutality. It was claimed (with considerable clamor) that he had hired black mercenaries who committed the most terrible acts of violence.

Bernard-Henri Lévy (the famed à la carte French 'philosopher' also widely known as BHL) was the first to reveal to a stunned world how the pilloried tyrant had hired many low cost mercenaries from Sub-Saharan Africa.[199] No one thought to remind BHL that the tribes of southern Libya are mainly black, or that blacks were to be found at the time at all administrative levels in Libya. As opposed to France, various Libyan functionaries and ambassadors were black.

BHL's misconceptions (if we may call them that…) arise out of his racist mindset, according to which Africans of Arab origin and blacks are held to the Western view of their respective places within the cultural hierarchy. BHL absurdly claimed on television that "Gaddafi's army is a rag tag affair made up of 300 poorly equipped wretches".[200] Did BHL convince *monsieur le président* that the war would be over in three days?

The myth of the black African mercenaries caused quite a stir in the West. Journalist Fausto Biloslavo, an eyewitness, commented,

There surely are mercenaries, but I think very few are professionals or true warriors. I think, and as I personally saw, quite a few were in the area because they were immigrants looking for a job, frequently illegal immigrants and with no embassy to protect them. They were forced to join the ranks of the combatants and were probably never even actually paid. So I wouldn't really call them mercenaries. I'd call them wretched souls who kill so as not to be killed, under the threat of a bayonet behind their backs. In Tripoli, a number of columns of these illegal immigrants who were attempting to leave Libya were blocked, and basically the 'rebels' gave them a choice. They might be considered mercenaries and therefore summarily executed, or they could join the rebels. When I was at the anti-Gaddafi strongholds, as in Zawiya, which has now been wiped out, I saw a black skinned soldier, because he came from the Fezzan region in southern Libya. He was paraded in front of the TV cameras as though he was a foreign mercenary, when in actual fact he was a Libyan policeman. Believe me, in Libya today, they're all mad dogs, and that includes the best among them.[201]

As time went by, various international investigations were conducted to verify the Libyan government's alleged use of 'mercenaries'. According to a number of African governments, black immigrants in Libya, and witnesses interviewed by humanitarian organizations such as the *Féderation internationale des droits de l'homme* (FIDH),

in eastern Libya—controlled by the rebels—
innocent migrant workers were accused
of being 'Gaddafi mercenaries' and were
lynched, tortured, killed or in any case
subject to racist attacks and theft. The rebels,
as a number of videos confirm, executed and
tortured Libyan soldiers, especially blacks.[202]

Over and above the question of whether government
mercenaries existed during the early stages of the war, we
should remember that the Anglo-Americans had already
adopted this ignoble practice of using mercenaries in
Afghanistan and Iraq. It is well known that top officials in
the United States believe that the deployment of mercenaries
has led to progress in management of the war theatres of
the twenty-first century, though the term, 'mercenaries', has
been euphemized. As 'contractors', they do exactly what
is traditionally expected from mercenaries (to fight or to
conduct intelligence operations for pay—unlike the regular
armies who are presumed to be fighting for the cause). The
advantage of hiring mercenaries is that they need no longer
abide by, or have anything to do with, the rules of military
conduct. 'Contractors' is a politically correct, sanitized, term,
and the Anglo-American warmongers know how important
image and media discourse is.

It was also officially announced that the 'rebels'
received arms and other equipment from Qatar, with oil as
the medium of exchange. These arms and equipment had
previously been shipped to Libya secretly.[203] Sheikh Hamad
bin Khalifa al-Thani was the first Chief of State to officially
recognise the Libyan 'rebels'. He was the first member of
the GCC to provide NATO with support, deploying French
Mirage F1 fighters and American C-17 Globemasters. He
also installed the satellite channel Ahrar TV on behalf of

the Transitional Council, shipped in many MILAN missile-launchers, and (not least) he immediately engaged in the overseeing of oil exports from Cyrenaica. Such behaviour was entirely illegal: the Arms Trade Treaty (ATT) and UN Resolutions 1970 and 1973 explicitly prohibit the arming of groups such as the 'rebels', who do not represent the legal government of Libya.[204]

The governments of the West also felt free to ignore these provisions. They recognized the NTC (then renamed National Liberation Army, NLA) as the only legal government of Libya.[205] American government officials told the *Washington Post* (30 March 2011) on condition of anonymity that, "President Obama has issued a secret finding that would authorize the CIA to carry out a clandestine effort to provide arms and other support to Libyan opposition groups".[206]

Public opinion in the USA is familiar with the illegal wars of the infamous Bush era. Obama's bandit war came into being on 21 March 2011. According to the War Powers Act (WPA)—passed in 1973 over Nixon's veto—unless he/she receives approval from Congress, the President must order that all military intervention that has commenced cease within sixty days. The limit rises to ninety days

> if the President determines and certifies to the Congress in writing that unavoidable military necessity respecting the safety of United States Armed Forces requires the continued use of such armed forces in the course of bringing about a prompt removal of such forces.

On 28 May the conservative intellectual, George F. Will, slammed Obama's intention to "degrade the rule of law".

The opinion piece appeared in the *Washington Post* and was republished by other newspapers such as the *New York Post*. At that very time, Dennis Kucinich, a leftist Congressman, submitted a motion to the House demanding that the government cease its operations against Tripoli. Senator Richard Lugar, heading his party delegation on the Foreign Affairs Committee, also wrote Obama a letter reminding the White House of its obligation to consult Congress and to act consistently with the War Powers Resolution (WPR). Lugar complained that Obama had cancelled without explanation a Foreign Affairs Committee briefing on Libya with the chief of the White House military staff and that the government was obstructing all debate.[207]

Congress was concerned over the costs involved and the irresponsible manner in which the war on Libya was being conducted (outside the legal framework set forth in the War Powers Act). Under pressure, Obama sent a 32-page document to John Boehner, the Republican Speaker of the House of Representatives, in which he claimed that the White House did not require Congress approval. *Business Insider* summed up the White House response as follows— "We don't need Congressional approval because this is not technically a hostile action (because we don't have ground troops in Libya)".[208] A close observer of Washington practices remarked, "Obama's flagrant violation of the War Powers Act in Libya would make him subject to impeachment, and this possibility might become more likely if the US economy continues to deteriorate".[209]

Through its indifference toward questions of constitutional legality, the Obama administration showed it was uninterested in the kind of "change" that had been promised after Bush Jr.'s tragic double mandate. Indeed, Obama sent Chris Stevens, formerly second-in-command at the US embassy in Tripoli, to Benghazi, with instructions to "work with the opposition, get a clear idea of what they needed, work out how we can help them and fill in the gaps in what we know about them".[210] While there were many "gaps" in what Western public opinion knew about the Libyan opposition, the American government knew very well who it was dealing with. Let's join a few dots.

4

THE ROLE OF THE SANUSIS IN THE LIBYAN REVOLT

The NTC (National Transitional Council) had thirty-two members. No one knew who these people were. Personal identities were a mere detail, of course, and the lack of names certainly wouldn't prevent the Coalition from recognizing these strangers as the sole legitimate representatives of the entire Libyan nation. The names of about thirty NTC members were kept secret, in order to protect them—it was claimed—from reprisal on Gaddafi's part. Might there have been other reasons for this secrecy?

Firstly, we should note that as a group, the 'rebels' were a military entity, not a civil society entity. Of course, we lack the information possessed by the intelligence services of the United States, United Kingdom or France, but to understand who they might be we can in any case turn to an authoritative study conducted in 2007 by two analysts at the United States Military Academy at West Point.[211]

Joseph Felter and Brian Fishman's study provides a sociological profile and the background of the guerrillas (jihadists, mujahideen and kamikazes) who crossed the border into Iraq from Syria between 2006 and 2007, under the auspices of Al-Qaʻida .

The West Point study is based on detailed analysis of some 700 documents confiscated in Iraq by the American forces during autumn 2007. The results were made public through the efforts of the geopolitical writer and expert, Webster Tarpley. In an extensively documented essay,[212] Tarpley sheds much light on the views and ideologies prevailing in certain circles in northeastern Libya (Cyrenaica). The study illustrates the political and social nature of the anti-Gaddafi revolt in Cyrenaica, the epicenter of the clashes that broke out in February 2011.[213]

The most surprising discovery was that the Benghazi-Derna-Tobruk corridor in Libya had established itself as one of the areas with the highest concentrations of jihadist terrorists in the world, perhaps the main recruiting ground worldwide for kamikaze fighters. Derna provided combatants at the rate of one terrorist per 1,500 inhabitants. They were shipped into Iraq to kill American troops. As an 'exporter' of such fighters, the area surpassed its main 'rival', Riyadh (Saudi Arabia).[214]

Felter and Fishman state that most of the jihadists deployed during the first period considered in the report, who were in Iraq to combat the United States and other members of the coalition, came from Saudi Arabia. With a population of less than a quarter of that of Saudi Arabia, Libya ranked second. While 41% of the combatants came from Saudi Arabia, Felter and Fishman reckon "Libya was the next most common country of origin, with 18.8% (112) of the fighters". Comparable numbers did not come from other considerably larger Arab States. "Syria, Yemen, and Algeria were the next most common origin countries with 8.2% (49), 8.1% (48), and 7.2% (43), respectively. Moroccans accounted for 6.1% (36) of the records and Jordanians 1.9% (11)".[215]

Nearly one fifth of the foreign combatants crossing the Syrian border into Iraq came from Libya, a country with a population of less than six million. In other words, proportionately speaking, more Libyans were ready to fight in Iraq than were the citizens of any other 'mujahideen exporting' nation in the world.[216] Since these Al-Qa'ida 'personnel' files included the addresses and places of origin of the foreign combatants, we can also assess the geographic distribution, within Libya itself, of the places of origin of the volunteers who came to Iraq to kill Anglo-American soldiers. As indicated, the distribution is not uniform within the country. Most came from the environs of Benghazi, precisely the epicenter of the anti-Gaddafi revolt that was hailed by the United States, Great Britain, France, Italy and other allies.

Benghazi was the capital of the new Libyan government—a government that Italy's Foreign Minister, Franco Frattini, came to consider "the only legitimate partner representing the Libyan people".[217] Interestingly, just a few months earlier, on 8 January 2011 (while preparations for the anti-Gaddafi revolt were underway), Frattini stated "If Libya did not exert very strong controls as part of its anti-terrorism policy, the cells of terrorists in Benghazi would be very much closer to us".[218]

Benghazi had sent 21 jihadist combatants to Iraq. Demographically speaking, this figure is high.

Irony upon irony, a week after that January statement, the very same Frattini added,

> I believe we must provide strong support to those countries with Kings or Chiefs of State who have constructed secular regimes and who have kept their distance from fundamentalism. Our first priority is

preventing fundamentalism and embryos of terrorism.

The interviewer then asked Frattini how this was to be accomplished. He replied,

> Take Gaddafi, for example. He has achieved a reform that he calls 'of the provincial Congresses of the people'. District by district, assemblies of tribes and local potentates meet, discuss and submit requests to the government and the leader. Searching for a path between a parliamentary system, which is not what we are considering, and one in which there was no outlet for grass roots feelings, as in Tunisia. Every week, Gaddafi goes there and listens. I see these as positive signals.[219]

There had been some talk of an Islamic Emirate being set up in Benghazi. On 21 February, Frattini "voiced alarm". "Would you imagine," he asked journalists, "to have an Islamic Arab Emirate on the borders of Europe? This would be a really serious threat."[220]

Derna, with a population of about 90,000, accounted for 52 jihadists. Riyadh, the Saudi capital (with a population of 4,500,000!) accounted for 51, Benghazi, 21; Tripoli, none.

Why were there so many anti-American combatants from Derna and Benghazi? The answer seems to lie in the Sanusi Islamist schools located there.[221] As the report from West Point notes, "Both Darnah [Derna] and Benghazi have long been associated with Islamic militancy in Libya".[222] These areas had been the theater of religious and tribal clashes following the 1969 Revolution.

A characteristic feature of the Libyan anti-American guerrillas in Iraq is their eagerness to carry out kamikaze actions. The West Point study notes that, "Of the 112 Libyans in the Records, 54.4% (61) listed their 'work'. Fully 85.2% (51) of these Libyan fighters listed 'suicide bomber' as their work in Iraq".[223] The available data tell us that the Libyans were much more inclined to take their own lives than were fighters from any other country.

The entity that recruited guerrillas in Cyrenaica was associated institutionally with the Libyan Islamic Fighting Group (LIFG), or *Al-jam'a al-islamiyya al-muqatila bi Libya*.[224] This group first appeared in Libya in 1995 during an attempt to oust Gaddafi and set up an Islamic State (establishing *Sha'ria*). Violent clashes broke out between the LIFG and Libyan police. The struggle was to continue over the next three years. Tens of government operatives lost their lives.[225]

According to American intelligence sources, the group (numerous in Cyrenaica) was led by Abu al-Laith al-Liby, an Afghanistan volunteer who had, over time, become one of Osama Bin Laden's closest associates, Al-Qa'ida's third in command.[226] In 2007, both the LIFG and the Salafist Group for Preaching and Combat announced that they had joined Al-Qa'ida. Hence the new name for the local entity: Al-Qa'ida in the Islamic Maghreb (AQIM). Following this union, fighters left Libya for Iraq in greater numbers. Other sources confirm this merger with the mother organization. In a declaration made in 2008, ascribed to Ayman al-Zawahiri, it was announced that the LIFG had merged with Al-Qa'ida.[227]

On 12 March 2011, Abu al-Laith al-Liby appeared in a video issued by as-Sahab.[228] By now, he was one of the top Al-Qa'ida figures, chairing the council šura in the absence both of the figurehead (Bin Laden) and Ayman al-Zawahiri. During his thirty-minute speech, he called upon the Libyan rebels to proclaim an Islamic State in Libya as soon as possible.

The West Point study indicates that Benghazi, Derna and Bayda were the main LIFG/AQIM strongholds.

The leading figure in Bayda was a certain Khayr Allah Bar'asi (another Al-Qa'ida Afghanistan and Iraq veteran). In Bayda, it was reported that the women refused to venture outside their homes because the clerics had imposed radical codes of conduct. The women were told they were not allowed to appear in public unveiled.[229] Under Gaddafi, no specific dress code applied either to men or women appearing in public.[230]

After the merger of these terrorist groups in 2007, Libyan recruits were to play a role of growing importance within Al-Qa'ida as a whole. They took on the burden, so to speak, that had formerly been shouldered, above all, by the Saudis and Egyptians.[231]

Felter and Fishman were of the idea that the former LIFG (now Al-Qa'ida) might be used in Libya. An alliance between the United States and a segment of this terrorist organization might be of use in ousting Gaddafi.

> The Libyan Islamic Fighting Group's unification with al-Qa'ida and its apparent decision to prioritize providing logistical support to the Islamic State of Iraq is likely controversial within the organization. It is likely that some LIFG factions still want to prioritize the fight against the Libyan regime, rather than the fight in Iraq. It may be possible to exacerbate schisms within LIFG, and between LIFG's leaders and al-Qa'ida's traditional Egyptian and Saudi power-base.[232]

This suggests the USA may have wished to *"exacerbate"* the divisions between the two components, while siding with the Libyan Al-Qaʻida militants who wanted to depose Gaddafi. In other words, "the jihadists of Cyrenaica, once the worst among America's foes in Iraq, are now [America's] ideal allies in a war to bring down Gaddafi."[233]

The facts point to the kind of thing America was becoming famous for, right from its inciting the Afghan population to rise up against the Soviet occupation after 1979. Reagan's anti-Soviet strategy included providing Osama Bin Laden's mujahideen with Stinger missiles and other items of modern weaponry. Strategically, this was not an entirely 'win-win' situation.[234]

The former US Secretary of Defense, Robert Gates (former CIA Director and Defense Secretary under Bush and Obama) claimed (in a plausibly deniable way) that to take on the Soviets in Afghanistan, the United States had created Al-Qaʻida as a sort of Arab Legion. Gates boasted of having organized aid for the mujahideen in Afghanistan. The aid grew considerably in the 1980s (approx. 500 million dollars in US and Saudi funds), with Pakistan acting as a transit nation.[235] On 7 July 2005, following the Al-Qaʻida terrorist attack in London, the former Foreign Minister, Robin Cook, published a long article in *The Guardian* in which he stated that, as far as he was aware, the name Al-Qaʻida literally meant "database", listing the names of the mujahideen recruited by the CIA to fight the Soviets in Afghanistan. Prior to his death a month later (officially due to cardiac arrest), Cook had made these extraordinary statements in parliament (March 2003) while resigning from his post in protest against the invasion of Iraq organized by Blair and Bush, which he (rightly) claimed was illegal.[236]

The information available suggests, indeed, that two former Afghani mujahideen and a former Guantanamo inmate of six years played a leading role in the military campaign in Derna. Derna is a key city between Benghazi and Tobruk, which had been taken by the 'rebels'. Here, new recruits were trained for the struggle against the Tripoli government.

In 2002, Abdalla al Sadeq also known as Hakim al-Hasadi (the pseudonym of Abdel Hakim Belhadj, or Belhaj)[237] was captured by the Americans in Pakistan. He was then handed over to the Libyans. Freed in 2010, he supervised the recruiting, training and deployment of about 300 fighting 'rebels' from Derna. Other sources considered him the leader of the Libyan 'rebels'.[238]

Derna boasted the presence of the most famous of Guantanamo's Libyan 'guests': Sufiyan al-Koumi, a veteran who was once employed at a Bin Laden 'branch' concern in Sudan. Sufiyan al-Koumi then joined a charity organization with Al-Qa'ida links. He was arrested by the Americans, extradited to Libya, and freed in September 2010, thanks to the "reform and repent" scheme set up by Gaddafi's son, Saif al-Islam. Sufiyan al-Koumi now spent his time training recruits.[239]

The Italian newspaper correspondent, Roberto Bongiorni, noted:

> Derna is a conservative city. We see this in the religious fervour of its inhabitants, in the Islamic clothing, in the long beards. 'Dear brothers who fought in Iraq and Afghanistan', cries a speaker on the local radio, 'the time has come to defend your own land!' In 2007, the US Army in Baghdad released a list of foreign mujahideen fighting alongside the insurgents. Of the 112 Libyan citizens, 52 (including kamekazis) were from Derna. 'I sent about

25', said al-Hasadi. 'Some have returned and are now on the Ajdabiya front. They are patriots and good muslims, not terrorists. I condemn the September 11 attacks and those against innocent civilians in general. But the members of Al-Qa'ida are good muslims and fight against the invader'. His words are ambiguous. And it is odd to hear someone accused of belonging to Al-Qa'ida invoking a no-fly zone and international bombing raids against the rais's strongholds.[240]

LIFG leader 'Abd al-Hakim Belhadj, the military commander, Khaled Shrif, and the group's official ideologist, Sami Sa'di, made up the élite of the city of Derna.[241]

Between March 2009 and the start of the rebellion in Cyrenaica, the Libyan government released 350 former terrorists.

Over a period of five years, 850 have been released. The latest wave of 110 releases, on 16 February (2011), is surprising, coming as it did one day before the 'al-Mukhtar revolution' or 'Day of Rage'.[242]

These fanatics and criminals (acclaimed as liberators by the mainstream media worldwide) were to form Libya's emerging ruling class. These were the people tasked to ensure a democratic future for Libya. However, the 'rebel' council of Benghazi did what it does best—ensuring chaos for the country as a whole, under a phantom government and a system of local fiefdoms (each with a warlord or tribal chief). This appears to have been the desired outcome all along, and not just in Libya.[243]

DEBKA*file* (a very well informed Israeli intelligence site) noted that the United States, Great Britain and France had sent hundreds of military advisers to Cyrenaica on a delicate mission. Their mission was to enable these 'rebels' to govern the lands under their 'control'.[244] It was equally clear that shipments of large quantities of arms had arrived via Saudi Arabia and Qatar. The arms were shipped across the Egyptian border with the active aid of the new military junta in command.[245]

What do we know about the ethnic makeup of the LIFG base? We find the 'Abaidat tribe, belonging to the Harabi confederation. The Harabi confederation acts as a *trait d'union* among Cyrenaica's various *qabile*, or *qab'ail* (tribal subdivisions). It brings together such tribes as the Zuwaya (more than one third of whose members supported the 'rebels') and 30% of the Bara'asa.[246] Many from the Arabized Mesratha tribe (the name is not to be confused with the name of the city of Misrata, in Tripolitania) also supported the 'rebels', as did 20% or more of the Arabized Fawakir tribe, not to mention the Magharba, various Kawar and 'Awaqir elements and, lastly, an unknown number of clans of the Cyrenaica branch of the Majabra tribe.[247]

The vast majority of the 'rebel' council's members were apparently from the 'Abaidat tribe, including General Abdel al-Fattah Younis (brutally assassinated on 28 July 2011).[248] Mustafa Abdel al-Jalil, heading the NTC, was indicated as a leading member of the Sanusi brotherhood.[249] These facts suggest that the Libyan Islamic Fighting Group, the confederation élite and the rebel council—backed up by the "coalition of the willing"—are actually a single entity. These parties had one thing in common: they all detested Gaddafi. However, some also pursued their own Islamist, tribal or parochial interests.[250]

The most realistic appraisal therefore appears to be as follows, that:

> the clans of Cyrenaica took advantage of the revolts occurring in much of North Africa and the Middle East to win back their losses following the *coup d'état* of 1969 during which a certain number of officers led by Gaddafi ousted King Idris, of the al-Sanusi, who had been installed as the monarch of Libya by the Americans and British in the aftermath of World War II.[251]

In the light of what has emerged about Cyrenaica's LIFG and Al-Qaʻida—not to mention the Salafists and, above all, the Sanusis—we can conclude that the identities of the members of the Council were kept secret not so much out of fear of Gaddafi reprisals as out of a desire to hide the true Al-Qaʻida terrorist nature of the entire initiative.[252]

The questions raised are of the kind that tend not to have answers.

'Who were the groups that started the war in Libya?' 'How unscrupulous and cynical have the Western exporters of democracy shown themselves to be?' 'Given the political and religious background of the Libyan rebels, how could anyone consider them champions of democracy?' The flag they flew, from the very first days, was that of the old Sanusi royal house.

Italian journalist Alberto Mariantoni, concluded that anyone who is at all familiar with Libya

> knows perfectly well that the major, unbreakable 'bond'—which, for at least two hundred years, has brought the variegated and

partial geo-ethno-politico-tribal realities (now openly rebelling against Mu'ammar Gaddafi's regime) into contact with each other—can only be their specific, characteristic and shared religious creed, Sanusiya [...]. It therefore has nothing at all to do with the mantra of 'aspirations for freedom' and 'democracy' of 'the entire population' that we receive daily from most of 'our' politicians and the western mainstream media![253]

Tangible proof of this situation emerged during an exclusive interview with Saif al-Islam Gaddafi conducted by the correspondent in Tripoli of the Italian newspaper, *Corriere della Sera*. Asked by the correspondent about the concrete outcomes of the Libyan crisis, Saif al-Islam replied,

Elections. We could have elections within three months. At most at the end of the year. And as a guarantee that they are transparent, international observers could be called in. We won't be skittish or fussy about who they are. We accept the European Union, the African Union, the United Nations, even NATO. The vital thing is that the polls must be clean and there must be no suspicion of fraud. Then the world over will know that Gaddafi is still popular in his country. I have no doubt that the vast majority of Libyans are with my father and see the rebels as fanatic Islamic fundamentalists, terrorists incited by foreigners, mercenaries acting on the orders of Sarkozy. Our people are perfectly aware that the president of the puppet government in Benghazi, Mustafa Abdel al-Jalil, and likewise the military commander, Abdel al-Fattah Younis, are, like many others, quite simply old guard people who jumped onto the rebel bandwagon at the very last minute, like the miserable opportunists and sellouts that they are. They were ministers with Gaddafi and now they want to play at being the leaders against him. Ridiculous. They are Paris puppets. Without help from others, they can't even stand on their own two feet. [...] During the run-up to the voting, a new constitution would in any case have to be worked out, alongside a truly free media system. I believe in a future Libya made up of strong local autonomies and a weak federal government in Tripoli. The model might be the United States, New Zealand or Australia. Over the last few months, I have come to believe firmly that pre-17 February Libya exists no more. Come what may, military defeat or the politics of the rebels, there'll be no turning back. My father's regime, as it played out since 1969, is now dead and buried. Gaddafi has been completely surpassed by events, but so has Jalil. We must now build something completely new.[254]

Since these democratic proposals were immediately ruled out (even as a talking point), country-wide tribal warfare[255] was guaranteed.

The reply came within hours, and was immediately relayed by press agencies worldwide: "immediate refusal on the part of the rebel leadership and the United States".

Democratic elections within three months? Out of the question![256]

The 'strength' of these self-proclaimed rebels lay entirely in international political and military support.[257] Even the Tripoli correspondent of the firmly anti-Gaddafi *Corriere della Sera* was forced to admit that, "Left to their own devices, the rebels would probably collapse in a fairly short time."[258]

No one, except their Western masters, ever claimed that the 'rebels' were capable of forming a credible alternative government. This is as evident today as it was in 2011.

5

TIMELINE TO
UN RESOLUTION 1973

When exactly did the Libyan crisis flare up? In all likelihood,

> just two days after the start of the protests, when the inhabitants of Benghazi besieged the city's main military base. In order to reach the barracks, a man—a martyr, as a father, the head of a family—drove a car loaded with gas cylinders into a wall. In another city in Cyrenaica, Derna, the police station was torched. Two officers died. The violence spiralled out of control when the demonstrators took over the arms store abandoned by the retreating soldiers.[259]

The situation was becoming increasingly tense:

> On the evening of February 15, the most recent round of demonstrations began when several hundred people gathered in front of the Benghazi police headquarters to protest the arrest of attorney and human rights activist Fethi Tarbel. As the February 17 "day of rage"

neared, protests escalated in Benghazi and
other cities despite reported police attempts
at dispersion with water cannons, tear gas,
rubber bullets, and batons. There were
multiple reports of protestors setting police
and other government buildings on fire.[260]

The US Congressional Research Service's account
of events, issued on 18 February (on the day following the
"day of rage"), acknowledged multiple reports of violent
behavior and incendiary acts in Benghazi and other locations
such as might well lead to the deployment of lethal force in
all states, including those that consider themselves advanced
democracies.

However, Human Rights Watch—also closely
following the events—stressed the entirely peaceful nature
of the demonstrations.[261] A retrospective report drawn up in
2012 at the Syracuse University College of Law cites HRW
reports on the events at this time in Libya but, significantly,
it fails to cite the Congressional Research Service (CRS)
document.[262] This omission is of particular interest, since the
"main purpose" of the Syracuse University report was "to
provide Chief Prosecutor of the International Criminal Court
(ICC), Luis Moreno Ocampo, with research-based legal
analysis under Article 51 Rules of Procedure and Evidence of
the Rome Statute, as well as a resulting framework to inform
imminent prosecutorial decisions". On the vital question of
who actually started the fighting, the findings of HRW and
INSCT, on the one hand, and those of CRS, on the other,
differ somewhat.

A UN Human Rights Council report of June 2011
concerning the same events rather cautiously states that when
lethal force was used to repress demonstrations, "there was
little evidence to suggest that the protestors were engaged in

other than peaceful assembly". Albeit rather ambiguously, the UNHRC actually neither confirms nor denies that the Libyan authorities decided to use firearms against protesters following attacks on government buildings. In this document it was noted that "particular circumstances, leading up to the use of force by security forces against demonstrators, have been contested by the demonstrators and the Government. The Government has stated that its security forces refrained from using live ammunition and instead used instead tear-gas on 15 February. The Government has further stated that demonstrators' violent actions, in attacking police stations, necessitated the use of force by authorities. Protestors have reiterated the peaceful nature of their demonstrations. Estimates of those killed and injured also vary.

On 20 February, human rights groups estimated that approximately 233 persons had been killed. Saif al-Islam Qaddafi made reference to 98".[263] The document cautiously noted that "there is sufficient evidence to suggest that the Government forces engaged in excessive use of force against demonstrators, at least in the early days of the protests, leading to significant deaths and injuries". Why the caution? Evidently, the UNHRC were awaiting their marching orders. Another UNHCR report, issued eight months later, is more forthright in its condemnations of the Libyan government, embattled but still in power at the time, Surprisingly, it contained no fresh evidence.[264] The UNHCR had evidently received its marching orders, at last.

Indeed, the various publications of international authorities and humanitarian organizations generally reflect an unwillingness to get to the bottom of such macroscopic developments as the mid-February incidents in Benghazi, al-Bayda and elsewhere (not to mention the immigration issue before and after 2011).

This reluctance severely undermines the credibility

of such agencies when they have to 'investigate' other less easily researchable abuses (e.g. rape, torture, health repercussions of repeated flyovers and airstrikes in populated neighborhoods, such as stroke, diabetes, miscarriages etc., or arbitrary detention, racial discrimination, executions, denial of freedoms, denied access to medical treatment or relief, airstrike 'errors', events in remote locations, racist attacks, and, not least, the seizure of up to 1,000 children in all, to be sold in all likelihood to organ traffickers etc.).

NATO, for example, repeatedly targeted specific individuals whom they wanted out of the way, together with their families. Assemblies of religious leaders and tribal elders were also targeted. International lawyer Franklin Lamb cites an example of the general unwillingness of humanitarian agencies to step on the toes of key western players, such as NATO. While generally appreciative of the work of Amnesty International, with whom he has worked, he scathingly denounces the low quality of AI's Syria and Libya 'findings'. Referring in particular to the AI report, *Health Crisis: Syrian Government Targets the Wounded and Health Workers,* released on 25 October 2011, Lamb writes "AI's conclusion from its 'research' in Syria, which consisted significantly of collecting Al Jazeera and Al Arabia type media accounts including the dubious reports on the same subject by CNN's Arwa Damon, and sundry anonymous Youtube clips, is virtually identical to what it concluded from its investigation in Libya on the same subject".[265] We note that the AI report Lamb refers to was issued just as NATO's Libyan campaign was closing down. The NGO was clearly manning the guns to provide the West with talking points for its next Responsibility-to-Protect campaign in Syria.

The UN's approach to information, no less amateurish, sets the template. During the initial clashes between armed demonstrators and government forces, the *A/HRC/17/68* report more or less clearly indicated who was responsible for what. However, the 'fog of war' soon sets in when accounts are provided of unjustified acts of violence taking place after the violence spread westward. The perpetrators of abuses, of the kind listed above, were generally not specified at all, unless they could be convincingly ascribed to Libyan government forces. The acts of violence and use of lethal force that the document ascribes to the government in this document arguably account for less than half of the total number of incidents actually listed. Hence, on a superficial reading, one tends, by dint of association, to blame the government (its forces or supporters) also for those actions for which government responsibility is not explicitly indicated. On death tolls, the report provides vague estimates for the February-June period: "It is not certain what the cumulative number of persons killed or injured has been to date, with government officials, National Transitional Council and NGO providing estimates ranging from 10.000 to 15.000 persons killed".

The organizations, Internationale Ärzle für die Verhütung des Atomkrieges/Ärzle in sozialer Verantwortung, Physicians for Social Responsibility, and Physicians for Global Survival (affiliates of International Physicians for the Prevention of Nuclear War (IPPNW)), declared in 2015 that they still await a "serious" estimate of the Libyan death toll in 2011. They cite other "first estimates (...) of at least 50,000 Libyans". The figure cited by IPPNW, in fact, tallies with the initial estimate provided by the victorious National Transition Council (a figure that the post-NTC government, presumably under Western pressure, then halved in 2013).[266]

We note, furthermore, that UNHRC had made no attempt whatsoever, over the space of eight(!) months, to reassess the initial estimates of June 2011. IPPNW notes, likewise, that no further attempts have been made at all between 2012 and 2015, when conditions on the ground permitted hospital records searches and on-site investigations and interviews: there are "no indications that after NATO's war in Libya, that UN organizations will take any serious measures to find out how many Libyans have paid (...) 'for the protection of the civilian population' with their lives".[267]

In Benghazi, on 15 February, Islamic 'students' (most of whom were unknown to the university staff) commenced their 'liberation' movement activities. The protests had hardly gotten under way when Islamists and others associated with the local criminal underworld took advantage of the chaos to attack the maximum security prison near Benghazi, in order to free a number of Islamist leaders.

While anti-government demonstrations were held in Benghazi, Bayda and Derna, calling for the release of the Islamist militants arrested over the previous days, on 17 February, Libyan groups launched the "Libya Now" Facebook account. The only thing known about these groups was that they were based in London. During the night, the government, acceding to the demonstrators' demands, released 110 Islamist detainees. Soon afterwards, groups of individuals armed with pistols, knives, sticks and Molotov cocktails stormed government buildings and police stations and seized many arms. The next morning, the people of Benghazi awoke to find the bodies of police officers hanging from the city's bridges. The disinformation campaign was on. The mass media promptly relayed a story about tens of deaths at the hands of what they called government militias (the militias were responsible for no deaths, but 38 protesters were injured). The 'rebels' attacked African immigrants in Cyrenaica, claiming that they were Gaddafi mercenaries. Many Africans were lynched, tortured and killed. The killings were carried out in a manner said to be typical of the Groupe Islamique Armé (GIA, the Armed Islamic Group of Algeria)—throats slit, eyes gouged out, limbs amputated, bodies burnt. The Minister for the Interior and commander of the Libyan special forces, Abdel al-Fattah Younis, went to Benghazi. Here, he organized the demonstrations to create an open revolt against the government in Tripoli. Only hours before he had been part of that government.

On 19 February, the town of Nalut, to the south of Tripoli, was taken over by a revolutionary committee about which very little is known. The offices of the local radio station in Benghazi were torched. Protesters lynched two police officers in Bayda. Al Jazeera reported that the army had opened fire on demonstrators in Benghazi. The Western media reported that the army was using heavy artillery and RPG (rocket-propelled-grenade) launchers.

On 20 February, Saif al-Islam made a television appearance during which he claimed the existence of an external conspiracy against Libya. The battalion *Faileq 36*, under the rebel general, Ahmad Qatrani, attacked the *Katiba Fadil Bouaamar* army barracks in Benghazi (80 died during the attack). In Derna, a group of rebels attacked an army compound and seized weapons. The *al-Fadhil* brigade based in Tobruk, under General Abdel Aziz al-Busta, sided with the rebels. The coup leaders seized arms depots and T-55 and T-62 tanks, armored personnel carriers (APCs) and light anti-aircraft artillery. Most of the soldiers refused to join the rebels. They abandoned the compound and headed for home. A number of soldiers abandoned the Misrata, Al Khums, Tarhunah, Zelten, Zawiya and Zuwarah bases. To avoid capture by the rebel forces, the *al-Sybil* brigade (5,000 African Legion troops) and the 32nd Brigade, with T-72 tanks, under Khamis Gaddafi, relocated to Sabratha, between Tripoli and the Tunisian border.

The Muslim Brotherhood's *ulema* based in Qatar, Yusuf al-Qaradawi, issued a *fatwa* against Colonel Gaddafi on 21 February. Yusuf al-Qaradawi was a TV personality well known to viewers of the Anglo-Qatari TV channel, Al Jazeera. He issued this *fatwa* to officers and soldiers who were in a position to kill Mu'ammar Gaddafi—to whoever among them was able to shoot Gaddafi and thus liberate the nation. A second *fatwa* was issued by a number of Cyrenaica Sanusis, who branded overthrow of Gaddafi a *fard'ayn*. This meant all Muslims were morally obliged to rebel against Gaddafi's regime. In the meantime, the Benghazi-Benina, Tobruk-Adem, Tobruk-Bumbah and Tobruk-Abraq air bases were taken by the rebels. The rebels now had nine MIG-23 fighters, a number of Mil-24 attack helicopters, a couple of MIG-21 lightweight fighters and various SA-2 and SA-3 anti-aircraft missile batteries, out of commission. The frigate, *al-Hani*, moored in the port of Benghazi at the time of the coup d'état, was also out of commission. Two Dassault F-1AD and F-1BD *Mirage* aircraft, temporarily at El Adem, were deployed to Malta. In all likelihood with the assistance of Anglo-French and Egyptian 'advisors' (who had entered the country over the previous weeks), the 'rebels' managed to recommission a pair of MIG-23s, a MIG-24 and a MIG-21. The aircraft were to be flown by the seven or eight pilots who had joined the 'rebels'. Italy's foreign minister, Franco Frattini, spoke of "a thousand deaths" (he cited no authoritative sources). This was a media call for diplomatic war to be waged on the Jamahiriyya. The United Kingdom's Minister of Defence, William Hague, officially announced that Gaddafi had fled to Venezuela. The report was totally unfounded; William Hague had quite simply lied to the British public. Coming from such an 'authoritative' source (Her Majesty's Government), the lie had a certain effect. The Libyan Minister of Justice, Mustafa Abdel al-Jalil, deserted his office and joined the coup. In Sabhrata, the 32nd Brigade repulsed a rebel attempt to occupy the town. By now, the death toll had risen to 300 (including 58 troops loyal to the government).

On 22 February, Abdel Hakim al-Hasadi proclaimed an Islamic emirate in Derna. Gaddafi made a TV appearance in order to dispel the rumors of his flight to Venezuela. He spoke from the House of Resistance, the presidential residence that was bombed by the USA in 1986. He referred to the 'rebels' as a miniscule group of drug takers attacking police stations and army bases, as rats who received funding from foreign secret services, and as Al-Qa'ida puppets. He also called upon the people to take to the streets in order to re-establish law and order. He declared himself the leader of the revolution, and refused to stand down. He would rather end his days as a "martyr".

On 23 February, the Tubu tribe sided with the rebels. Tripoli lost control of Kufra. The rebels killed a number of loyalist civilians and military personnel. The video images of the bodies were falsely presented by the Western media as evidence of the massacre of 10,000 unarmed civilians, carried out by Gaddafi's black mercenaries. More lies would soon be disseminated. Another video showed "mass graves" on Tripoli's beach. These allegedly shocking images, it was discovered, recorded a routine task—the shifting of remains at the Sidi Hamed cemetery. These two stories were clearly propaganda stunts. This didn't prevent Obama from thundering against intolerable levels of violence on Gaddafi's part. In Brega, one Su-22 fighter-bomber was shot down by rebel militias. The incident led to a number of stories about deserter pilots and the effectiveness of the rebels' anti-aircraft defenses (at the time, this was the only government aircraft downed by rebel anti-aircraft firepower). The rebels formed a transitional government in Benghazi, made up of a team of fifteen. The green flag of Gaddafi's Libya was replaced by the red, black and green flag of Idris' United Kingdom of Libya.

On 24 February, a British frigate, *HMS Cumberland*, landed special force SAS operatives in Benghazi. Libyan TV showed Egyptian passports, CDs and cell phones belonging to persons suspected of planning terrorist actions against the Libyan people (the prisoners confessed). Interviewed by the Swedish daily, *Expressen*, the former Minister of Justice, Al-Jalil, claimed that Gaddafi had personally ordered the Lockerbie massacre. Italian Minister of Defense Ignazio La Russa announced that the flagship, *Cavour*, had been mobilized.

On 26 February, the UN Security Council voted Resolution 1970 decreeing an embargo against Libya and prohibiting Gaddafi and his family from travelling abroad. Al-Jalil formed and led the National Transitional Council of Benghazi (NTC). In Misrata, the *Al-Khuweildi al-Huamidi* brigade and Libyan helicopter-transported units repulsed coup forces threatening the airport. To the south of Tripoli, two RAF C-130s landed other British special forces commandos. The C-130s were guided by the Airborne Warning and Control System (AWACS).

On 27 February, a Dutch navy helicopter with three men on board was captured at Sirte while conducting an intelligence operation (infiltration/exfiltration of agents).

On 28 February, Hillary Clinton made her first reference to the prospect of exile for Gaddafi. Italian Minister of Defense, Ignazio La Russa, announced the cessation of the Libya-Italy friendship treaty. At Ajdabiya, the Libyan government ordered airstrikes against ammunition depots about to fall into enemy hands. The British transferred Divisions of the Black Watch, Third Battalion, Royal Regiment of Scotland to Malta (on their immediate return from Afghanistan). A spokesperson stated that the 200 soldiers would provide only humanitarian aid and would not be involved in any fighting or military intervention.

On 1 March, Ahmad Qatrani assumed command of a military council of coup leaders. 'Abd al-Salam Jallud (Abdessalam Jalloud) received an invitation to join them. He declared that he would remain loyal to the Tripoli government.

On 2 March, 400 marines from the 24th Marine Expeditionary Unit (MEU) arrived in Crete. While the Jamahiriyya forces retook control of Zintan and Gharyan, about fifty vehicles of the people's militia attacked Brega, with its important petrochemical complex (five 'rebels' and 2 militia fighters lost their lives). The air force was still in action over Ajdabiya. The Tuaregs of Mali, Niger and Libya sided with Gaddafi. The British destroyer, *HMS York*, landed eleven British citizens.

On 3 March, economic sanctions were applied to Libya in accordance with UN Resolution 1970. A government Su-22 bombed an ammunition depot in Brega.

On 4 March, eight SAS operatives were captured by rebels. A Libyan with British citizenship was killed in Brega. The rebels advanced on al-Uwayla. Government units took back Zawiya, the location of the country's most important refinery. They pushed on toward as-Sidrah in the vicinity of Ras Lanuf. The first rumors began to circulate of a mass exodus toward Tunisia and Egypt. At Zawiya, a dozen T-72 tanks belonging to the Khamis brigade were deployed at the major intersections of the town. As the battle reached its high point, the rebels realized that they had fallen into a trap. Instead of attacking along the main thoroughfare in the vicinity of the Martyrs' Square, the government forces moved in from the west, behind the 'rebel' forces, killing the 'rebel' commander at an early stage of the fighting. At Ajdabiya, a depot containing anti-tank missiles was targeted by government airstrikes, and an explosion at another depot in Benghazi claimed nineteen lives.

On 5 March, in view of the rapid progress made by the 'rebels', the Italian government decided to send 'aid' to Benghazi by the patrol boat, *Libra*, escorted by the destroyer, *Francesco Mimbelli*. On 6 March, a column of 'rebel' vehicles under the command of General Wanif Bou Hanada was repulsed by government fighter-bombers at Bin Jawad, a hundred kilometers east of Sirte. The 'rebels' beat a hasty retreat to Ras Lanuf. The British in the meantime recovered the commandos who had been captured on 4 March. In Cairo, the French Foreign Minister, Alain Juppé, proposed a no-fly zone for Libya. The 'rebels' called upon the international community to aid them.

On 7 March, the patrol boat, *Libra*, reached Benghazi with a detachment of the San Marco battalion. The 'rebels' were surrounded at Ras Lanuf. On 8 March, they issued an ultimatum to Gaddafi. He had to step down within 72 hours.

On 9 March, government troops took Zawiya back. General Rahman bin Ali al-Said al-Zawi (at the head of the Libyan army's logistics and supply authority) went to Cairo on behalf of his government to receive assurances that the Egyptian army would remain neutral.

On 10 March, the French government recognized al-Jalil as the legitimate representative of Libya. NATO's AWAC planes conducted operations over Libyan airspace. Three tanks and 150 loyalist troops retook control of Ras Lanuf, aided by civilians and oil terminal workers who opened fire on NTC coup forces. A maneuver—deploying four amphibians that landed 180 Libyan soldiers—forced the rebels back to Brega.

On 11 March, the African Union, meeting in Addis Ababa, rejected all external intervention in regard to the Libyan crisis. On the same day, the European Union declared that it no longer recognized the government of Libya. The EU declared that, since Gaddafi had lost all legitimacy, it would enter into negotiations with the NTC based in Benghazi. In the meantime, loyalist troops besieged Misrata and moved swiftly toward Benghazi. In just a few days, they had retaken control of most of the country. Pro-Gaddafi demonstrations were to be seen in many cities. To all appearances, Gaddafi's victory was at hand. In the meantime, France was calling for a no-fly zone, in order to ground Gaddafi's air force.

On 12 March, the Arab League Summit approved the no-fly zone motion. Gaddafi proposed a pact of national reconciliation (on condition, however, that the rebels lay down their arms). The rebels abandoned Brega on 13 March. In the meantime, the Libyan forces had practically reached Benghazi and had retaken al-Uqayla and al-Bicher. The coup forces were losing ground, and tens of rebels were forced to retreat.

On 14 March, government forces took Zuwarah back. Antonov An-26 airborne troops were deployed behind Ajdabiya. Gaddafi promised a general amnesty for all surrendering rebel soldiers. He urged Russia, China and India to invest in Libya. The American attack submarine, *USS Providence*, had meanwhile been deployed off the coast of Libya. Over recent years, wherever the *USS Providence* turned up, you could expect American aggression soon.

On 15 March, during an interview for the Italian daily, *il Giornale*, Gaddafi expressed his "irritation at the stance of the Europeans" and stated that he felt he had been "betrayed" by Italy's PM, Silvio Berlusconi. Government troops retook Zliten. Ajdabiya, the last 'rebel' stronghold before Benghazi, was liberated by the Libyan army after a clash that led to the deaths of three and the wounding of fifteen 'rebels'.

On 16 March, the government air force bombed the Benina air base, destroying the aircraft that had been seized by the rebels. Saif al-Islam, announcing that the operations would be over in 48 hours, called upon the NTC to surrender.

The UN Security Council passed Resolution 1973 on 17 March, imposing a no-fly zone upon Libya. Under the umbrella of this resolution, aircraft could be deployed to "protect civilians". The resolution, which made no provision for occupation, was passed with ten countries voting in favor—France, the United Kingdom, the United States, Bosnia, Gabon, Nigeria, South Africa, Portugal, Colombia and Lebanon. Germany, Brazil, India and the two permanent members of the Security Council, Russia and China, abstained. By means of Obama's Executive Order 13566, a number of Libyan financial assets were also frozen. Frequently referred to by the media as Gaddafi's money, these assets belonged to such institutions as the Central Bank of Libya (CBL), the Libyan Investment Authority (LIA), the Libya Foreign Bank and the Libyan National Oil Company (LNOC). No flights to or from Libya were to be permitted. Soon after, the American Odyssey Dawn operation commenced. Naval units in the Mediterranean launched hundreds of Tomahawk missiles against sensitive targets. Italy, for the time being, limited its role to providing the services of its bases. Responding to the resolution, the Libyan Foreign Minister announced an immediate ceasefire. Up to the time of the resolution, the (failed) coup d'état had cost the lives of 796 people. More than ten times that number (8,800) were wounded or maimed.

6

THE ROLE OF AL JAZEERA AND AL ARABIYA IN GADDAFI'S DOWNFALL

Why was the decision made to topple the government in Tripoli by force of arms? We can rule out "humanitarian" concerns.

The humanitarian 'mother of all lies' concerned an alleged massacre. The satellite TV station, Al Arabiya, spread the news of ten thousand dead and at least fifty thousand wounded or maimed in Libya. First came a tweet, or a twitter message, and then the campaign took off. Reports appeared about Libyan airstrikes against Tripoli and Benghazi. There was talk also of "mass graves". The source of the rumors was a certain Sayyid al-Shanuka, based in Paris. He claimed he was a Libyan member of the International Criminal Court (ICC).[268]

The 'news' went viral. The UNSC was convened. The International Criminal Court flatly denied that Sayyid al-Shanuka was an ICC member:

> Various media sources have published information regarding the situation in Libya attributed to Mr Sayed Al Shanuka (or El-Hadi Shallouf), presented as a 'member of

the International Criminal Court' (ICC). The ICC wishes to clarify that this person is neither a staff member nor a counsel currently practicing before it, and by no means can he speak on behalf of the Court. Any declaration he made is given solely in his personal capacity.[269]

Have we seen any photographs or video footage of the February massacre of thousands of people in Tripoli? None. Images of the Libyan air force bombing three districts of Tripoli? Not one witness was produced, and there were no signs of the kind of destruction that one would expect had such attacks taken place. The Russian armed forces monitoring the skies of Libya reported that they had no evidence of any Libyan airstrikes against civilians, nor did their satellite images indicate any damage of the kind produced by airstrikes.[270]

What about the seaside mass graves story? What we saw was a cemetery, Sidi Hamed, with individual (!) graves. The contents of the graves had been moved well before the crisis erupted. It was a routine operation, of a kind frequently occurring within Jewish, Christian and Muslim societies. The remains are shifted to make room for new graves. Such operations take place every one or two decades, according to country.[271] What of the massacres that Gaddafi is said to have ordered in eastern Libya in February? No evidence of these either. Perhaps the people of eastern Libya are so primitive that not one individual there had access to a camera or cell phone. Not one image of these alleged massacres (not even a shaky, blurred shot) has been produced.[272]

We know that an armed revolt took place. We know that hundreds of people were involved. We know that the focal point was in Cyrenaica.

When the revolt broke out, the police resisted the attacks on their buildings. In similar situations, worldwide, all police forces receive orders to do precisely this: resist attacks on your buildings. The violence escalated. Some of the 'rebel' groups also used heavy arms to attack police stations.[273]

The alarm bells went off immediately in Tripoli, since—well before the period of *rapprochement* between Gaddafi and the Western Powers—the United Kingdom, France and the United States had already covertly (and sometimes not so very covertly) worked toward destabilizing Libya. Even within official circles in the USA, it was acknowledged that Washington had repeatedly attempted regime change in Tripoli.[274]

We should point out that the right to dissent and protest is as sacred in Libya as anywhere else. However, in all countries it is equally clear that the armed forces and the forces of law and order will, if armed persons attempt to seize their arms or besiege their premises, invariably use violence against the aggressor. In this regard, we note fundamental differences between the events in Libya and in Egypt and Tunisia. We must consider the facts, starting out precisely from these differences.

Our aim is not to justify the reaction of Libya's security forces in opening fire upon groups bearing arms and attempting a coup d'état. Our aim, instead, is to understand why France, the United Kingdom and the United States immediately slammed the Libyan authorities for reacting just as they would in similar circumstances.

In a comparable situation, they would order their own police forces to act precisely as happened in Libya.[275] We remember the Kent State University incident (4 May 1970), when the National Guard opened fire on peaceful demonstrators. At various locations—Watts (1965), Newark

(1967), Detroit (1969), Los Angeles (1992)—the democratic authorities of the United States ordered its forces to open fire on crowds. Hundreds died. Western countries, and not just the United States, have all at one time or another had to deal with the threat of armed rebellion.

We owe the military action to a media campaign conducted on a grand scale. To be effective, the flames had to be fanned; the lies had to be repeated incessantly. As pointed out above, it was said that Gaddafi had bombed protestors in Tripoli and killed more than 10,000. This 'news' was immediately taken up by the two most important media outlets of the Arab world, Al Jazeera and Al Arabiya. The two stations are considered the major propaganda outlets of the Near and Middle East. They are the equivalents of other major broadcasters targeting other audiences (Fox News, BBC, CNN etc.). This campaign came directly from a part of the Arab world controlled by the Sunni Wahhabi aristocracies of Qatar and Dubai.[276]

Ghassan Bin Jiddo—director of Al Jazeera's office in Beirut and a former anchor responsible for one of the Arab world's leading political analysis programs—was disgusted at the conduct of his colleagues. He submitted his resignation on 23 April 2011, accusing Al Jazeera of conducting a massive campaign of falsification of the facts. He sharply rebuked the broadcaster (controlled by the Emir of Qatar) for its non-neutral reporting on the revolts taking place in the Middle East.

The Arab daily, *El Shorouk*, reported that, in his letter of resignation, Bin Jiddo claimed that Al Jazeera was not objective in its reporting, preferring to fan the flames of revolt and incite bloodletting.[277] The complaint concerned Al Jazeera's reporting of the people's uprisings in Yemen and Syria, and, previously, the revolts in Egypt and Tunisia. Bin Jiddo's complaints above all addressed the manner in which the reports coming out of Libya were distorted and manipulated.

The Doha TV station has also been accused of having practically turned a blind eye to the popular revolt in Bahrain. Of course, Qatar and Bahrain belong to the Gulf Cooperation Council (GCC). Al Jazeera was rebuked by journalist Abdel Hamid Tawfiq, who also handed in his resignation, accusing the TV station of having manipulated death counts and mass graves stories, first in Libya and then in Syria. He stated that the Al Jazeera death count reports in Syria were vastly different from those actually verified.[278]

Fausto Biloslavo—one of the few Italian journalists reporting from 'ground zero' right from the very start of the conflict in Libya—wrote:

> The information provided to us by Al Jazeera was totally wrong, as in the case of the 'mass graves', which were nothing but old cemeteries [...]. Al Jazeera created the foundations for Western military intervention in Libya. I must add that we see a return of the humanitarian war rhetoric, the 'love thy neighbor' and 'let's hand out sweeties for the kids' rhetoric, even if loving all these people leads to airstrikes. All this while the other side was apparently murdering prisoners, soldiers and agents who had surrendered. There are death squads in Benghazi too. In a live TV appearance, they tore out the heart from the chest of one of the Gaddafi's militia men and placed it like a trophy on top of a tank [...]. It's time to put an end to all this ridiculous nonsense about a humanitarian war. We have to be honest with ourselves.

They wanted change in Libya and Gaddafi was in the way.[279]

Following Bin Jiddo's lead, other colleagues quit their jobs. Zeina al-Jaziji, a key *Al Arabiya* anchor woman, stated that she had to resign after failing in her attempt to change the editorial line.[280] Many other famous news correspondents handed in their resignations, such as Luna al-Shibl, Iman Ayad, the noted Berlin correspondent, Aktham Suliman, and the Paris, London, Moscow and Cairo correspondents. Others were abandoning even Al Jazeera's headquarters in Doha. The Western press failed to relay this story.[281]

We may consider the scandalous conduct of Reuters and, again, of Al Jazeera. A source informs us that the British agency and the Anglo-Qatari TV broadcaster were forced to formally apologize for having transmitted video footage and photographs of protests that were false. The incidents that they reported on had taken place earlier, and had even taken place in other countries, but were presented to the public as anti-government demonstrations in Libya.[282]

The two Arab broadcasters, Al Jazeera and Al Arabiya, fired the first round of accusations. The story of the 10,000 protesters slaughtered by Gaddafi went mainstream globally. The impression for most people was that the story was true, despite the absence of video footage, photographs or other tangible proof.

Despite the lack of convincing evidence, the official voices of the European Union and the United States immediately validated the claims, slammed the dictator for his unprecedented savagery, and called for military intervention to halt the slaughter.

They had not even a second's worth of footage to back them up. However, footage of all kinds was filtering out of Libya. Furthermore, the Pentagon, the European

Union and NATO all have access to a broad set of satellite and intelligence resources. They knew that the airstrikes as described had not taken place. The fact that they did not release the data that they claimed existed can only mean one thing. They had no proof of the airstrikes. The reports were pure propaganda.

The Libyan air force was already weak. Admiral Samuel J. Locklear III, commander of the US naval forces responsible for the attacks that started off the war, informed the press that "Gadhafi's air force before coalition operations was 'not in good repair', and that his tactical capability consisted of several dozen helicopters".[283] The Admiral painted a picture of disarray, and yet others insisted that Libya's air force was still powerful enough to constitute a grave threat to the civilian population.[284]

The Western Powers had images of street demonstrations, false images of 'mass graves', and scenes of alleged night time 'burials' of the bloody dictator's victims, but they had no concrete proof of atrocities.

The footage of workers at the Sidi Hamed cemetery, engaged the routine task of moving remains from one site to another, fired the collective imagination. It evoked the horrors unearthed in the aftermath of World War II, a North African Timisoara.[285]

The spin industry knows that first impressions are crucial, and practically indelible. We have seen the mechanism at work in what will go down in history as an absolute masterpiece of the art of mystification—the 9/11 terrorist attacks (ascribed to Al-Qa'ida).

In the Libyan case, that round figure, 10,000, was useful, as were such words as "genocide", "mad", "bloody", "dictator" and so forth. Reporters worldwide took up the call. Incessant repetition did the rest.[286]

Aligning its actions with Goebbels' famous principle

of perception management, a 'Big Brother' was at work producing a 'Big Lie'. The official storyline had to stand at all costs and despite all the evidence to the contrary. This was not a time for real debate on our media... or for the 'Winston Smiths' of this world. The machine swept all before it. Perplexities were disregarded and written off as malicious gossip or... 'conspiracy theory'.

The behavior of left wingers (whether moderate or extreme) was also a decisive factor. The political and trade union left wings aligned their stances to the mass media narratives, as described. In Italy, in some cases, the leftists were more rabidly pro-war than the war cabinet itself. References were made to Libyan "concentration camps" and "lagers", packed with black immigrants from Sub-Saharan Africa. These rumors were unfounded.

The decision to go to war was defended on 'humanitarian' grounds. One of the key 'humanitarians' was the aforementioned Bernard-Henri Lévy, who immediately went to Benghazi to talk with the 'rebels'. Supplanting Juppé as France's *de facto* foreign minister, Lévy proposed a "war to prevent war": he wanted to aid "the Libyans in their efforts to liberate Libya". He saw war as necessary to stop the "crimes against humanity" perpetrated by a "psychopathic dictator". These claims (appearing in the Italian daily, *Corriere della Sera* on 22 March 2011) reveal to us depths of the thinking of these *nouveaux philosophes*.[287]

Instinct took the place of rational consideration. It has been described as 'the longest knee jerk reaction in history'. People closed their eyes to all alternative interpretations of events. More astonishingly, not once did they wonder who these Benghazi 'rebels' really were. They willingly assented to war, and paved the way for "transnational interest groups" who were determined to bring about a long cherished aim: "establishing a new balance of power in the Mediterranean".[288]

Up to the end of August, the Coalition of the Willing had protected civilians by showering more than 600 Tomahawk missiles on their heads. These 'surgical' or 'pinpoint' arms carry half a ton of explosives, destroying everything within a range of fifty meters of the target and scattering debris over 500 metres. These missiles were launched alongside the more 'normal' airstrike missions, conducted on a massive scale. When the damage was done, it would require very little effort to firmly pin the blame on the victims themselves, and on Gaddafi. In the famous case of the battle for Misrata, fought in mid-April, the organization, Human Rights Investigations, documented the atrocious sufferings of civilians following the NATO airstrikes.[289]

The President of the Italian Republic, Giorgio Napolitano, was, at the very least, embarrassing. Napolitano must surely remember Article 11 of the Italian Constitution, which declares in no uncertain terms that "Italy repudiates war as an instrument of offence against the liberties of other persons and as a means of settling international disputes".

Since Napolitano's role was that of supreme guarantor of the institutions of the Republic of Italy, it was his duty to prevent violation of the terms of the Treaty of Friendship, Partnership and Cooperation between Libya and Italy (concluded on 30 August 2008). Among the principles violated we find the mutual recognition of sovereignty (article 2); the abnegation of the threat or use of force against the territorial integrity or political independency of the other party, or the taking of measures that are incompatible with the Charter of the United Nations (article 3); non-intervention in the internal affairs of the other party, and the commitment to respect the principles of international law, and to abstain from using one's own territories for any hostile act against the other party, or allowing use by others of one's own territories for that purpose (article 4); and, last but not least, commitment to efforts for the peaceful settlement of disputes (article 5).[290]

Frequently, President Napolitano, despite the clearly contrasting evidence, insisted in public that NATO's actions against Libya (actions in which Italy played a key part) were not acts of war but "operations carried out in the name of peace".[291]

Napolitano's stance is best summed up by Leonardo Tricarico, the former Chief of Staff of the Italian Air Force, who noted "lexical madness" in the accounts of the war in progress. He concluded that "Italy's military operations are, as we clearly see in the Libyan crisis, always accompanied by ambiguity and hypocrisy".[292]

Giovanni Lazzaretti observed,

> If you show a kid something real, like an airstrike that destroys Libyan government offices, and you ask him, 'What's that?', he'll say, 'It's war'. This is where granddad Napolitano steps in and says, 'No, young fellow, this is repression of breaches of the peace. These bombs defend civilians'. Poor Napolitano![293]

The most authoritative historian of Italy's colonial past, and a biographer of Gaddafi, Angelo Del Boca, took an equally dim view of the allies' conduct.

> I must confess that what struck me was the conduct of the President of the Republic, who should defend the Constitution but, instead, deletes at least four articles. I am disappointed because I was really a great admirer of Napolitano.[294]

Napolitano parroted the official war party line that was repeated incessantly in the mass media. NATO and US airstrikes are operations carried out in the name of peace. Airstrikes by others are crimes against humanity. After Vietnam, Grenada, Panama, Yugoslavia, Afghanistan, Iraq and Somalia, Libya showed us that George Orwell's *Newspeak* was truly prophetic.

The opposition in Italy's parliament swallowed these stories whole (after all, hadn't the airstrikes been ordered by the UN, and by a Nobel Peace Prize Winner?). We owe these raids, of course, also to Sarkozy. His generosity of spirit in defending the citizens of other countries finished with the fighting. At France's borders, he prevented the very civilians he was trying to save from seeking refuge in France.

This more or less says it all.

7

WHAT WE SAW
WITH OUR OWN EYES
IN LIBYA[295]

There were many reasons for immediately accepting the invitation to visit Tripoli with the group known as the Non-Governmental Fact Finding Commission on the Current Events in Libya. Those of us who did so were a real "coalition of the willing". We were eager to see with our own eyes what had happened and what the prospects were for Libya now.

Our plane from Rome landed in the late afternoon of 15 April 2011 in Djerba. There had been a delay of more than three hours. During our trip through Libyan territory, we had to pass through the hundreds of roadblocks set up between Tripoli and the Tunisian border. On reaching Tripoli, the atmosphere changed immediately. It had been a tense, demanding journey, but life in Tripoli looked fairly normal. It was an orderly, well-maintained, attractive city. There were no signs of an imminent war. These first impressions were completely at variance with what the embedded journalists had been writing in their reports from Tripoli—chaos, the dictator's massacres and so forth.

The next morning, in the streets of Tripoli and as we headed toward the southwest of Libya, my first impression was that Gaddafi enjoyed the strong, sincere, unconditional support of a proud people. I saw no trace of the widespread resentment that the media had been talking about during the previous weeks. One of the unexpected consequences of military intervention in Libya, according to political analyst Mustafa Fetouri, was that it had strengthened the regime's credibility, lending it greater force and legitimacy in the zones under its control. After the aggression, Libya seemed to be responding to the old rallying cry of anti-imperialism.[296]

On our arrival in Bani Walid, about 120 kilometres south of Tripoli, located in an extensive mountainous region, we were warmly welcomed by the staff of the local electronic engineering faculty. This is the territory of the largest of Libya's and Tripolitania's tribes, the Warfalla or Orfella, with 52 clans and roughly a million members. Sixty-six percent of the population of Libya live in Tripolitania (26-27% live in Cyrenaica, and the rest in Fezzan). The Warfalla tribe is present in the district of Misrata and, in part, in the district of Sawfajjn.

We went to the main square where a demonstration was being held against the Western coalition's attack on Libya. The impression I had, of popular support for Gaddafi, was reinforced a thousand-fold. It was a demonstration of very evident, unconditional support for Libya's leader. Everywhere we went, we heard the words repeated like a film soundtrack, *"Allah—Mu'ammar—ua Libia—ua bas!"* ("Allah, Gaddafi, Libya, that's all!"). They particularly condemned Sarkozy ("Down, down Sarkozy!").[297] Other Western leaders of course, also received their fair share of scorn: Obama was called *"Obomba"*.[298]

We were taken to a large walled residential complex to meet the Warfalla tribal chiefs, all dressed in their traditional costumes. We were aided by interpreters and an elderly chieftain who spoke good Italian. They insisted on the point of the strength of the bond between their tribe and Gaddafi, and they claimed that they were all prepared to take up arms in the case of a military invasion—and would fight "to the last man". One clan chieftain clutching a brand new Kalashnikov in his bony fingers said in a resolute tone, "If they decide to invade Libya, they'll find out we're ready". They would not allow their country to go the way of Kosovo, Afghanistan or Iraq. The Anglo-Americans came to Iraq, and Iraq has since become perhaps one of the most dangerous places on Earth—where people die when out shopping, dining at a restaurant, in a bank or quite simply walking down the street. This is the bloodstained future that—with their near decade of experience—the humanitarians, peacekeepers and exporters of democracy were cooking up for Libya.

Wherever we went, in Tripoli or in Tripoli's suburbs, the people we met all wanted to know, "Why are France, Britain and America bombing us? What harm have we done to them? Why did Italy sign a non-aggression friendship treaty with Libya and then do this to us?"[299] They had every right to ask these questions. However, if we look at the record of the conduct of Britain and the United States over the last few years, the questions are naïve. The answers are under our very noses.

Over the next few days, we visited schools for students of all ages in Tripoli and its surroundings. We came across the same manifestations of support for the regime. As I looked at the youngsters, I realized that, far from being "unemancipated"—as the Western press would like us to believe—they were keenly aware of what was happening to their country and what the consequences of an invasion would be. In this they were very different from Italy's masses, and tablet-brandishing teens.

These Libyan youngsters weren't intimidated, and my impression was that they wouldn't resign themselves to defeat. They would fight "by all means". I felt a desire on their part to distance themselves from the grave situation. There was passion, and a desire to share that passion. Insofar as this was possible.

In the suburbs of Tripoli, we met people along the streets, in their homes, at work. We met the doctors who had been injured during airstrikes (some were now hospital patients). We saw groups gather in the very heart of Tripoli. On the questions of their leadership and relating to the current situation (relayed by the anxious news bulletins that came day by day), their views were steadfast.[300]

The only thing that struck me as out of place here (after all, Libya is one of the world's greatest producers of oil) were the cars waiting in line, mile after mile, for petrol. The queues formed at sunset. Just another of the contradictions of war. Over the weeks and months to come, the situation worsened, and transport came practically to a standstill.

As we wandered around Tripoli, we saw no signs at all of the airstrikes that Gaddafi is said to have ordered. These airstrikes, after all, were the pretext for the UN Resolutions that paved the way for the campaign of aggression. If Gaddafi had killed 10,000 people, as has been reported, by bombing them in the streets of a large city like Tripoli, we would expect to come across some serious damage and many clues indicating what had really happened. We looked for them but found nothing. The mainstream reporters, of course, never went out to check the facts for themselves. They were happy to remain in their hotel rooms, writing up fantasy scenarios for their masters.

The only signs of bombing were to be found just beyond Tripoli's suburbs, in Tajura, Suq al-Juma and Fashlum. Here, repeated NATO airstrikes claimed the lives of more than 40 civilians. We checked a farm that had been bombed. The neighboring buildings were also severely damaged. Here, the remains of deflagrating devices were clearly evident. We went to the hospital in Tajura and were shown the official body counts.

Our first-hand impressions were confirmed officially during a meeting at Hotel Rixos, where Moussa Ibrahim, the government spokesman, gave us his point of view. After outlining developments over the last two months, both military and diplomatic, Ibrahim asked us why, before the airstrikes started up, international bodies that were set up precisely for controls of this kind, hadn't sent a mission of enquiry to Libya. Gaddafi had repeatedly called upon these organizations to come to Libya, to investigate and find the answers at least to the following questions: 1) How did the rebellion concretely get under way? The rebels were armed from the very start; 2) What do the rebels really want? Do they also want secession? We note the flag chosen by the rebels, and also their apparent leader, al-Jalil, the former Minister of Justice; 3) Who bombed what?; 4) How well-armed were the rebels? Who did they get their arms from?; 5) How many people died during the airstrikes allegedly ordered by Gaddafi, and how many died during the airstrikes ordered by the Coalition of the Willing?

Ibrahim added, that

> the cost of sending a mission to Libya would have been less than the cost of a single Tomahawk cruise missile, and hundreds and hundreds have been fired at us over the last few days. Why is the West so hypocritical in our regard? Why wasn't a no-fly zone imposed upon Israel when the Israelis bombarded Gaza for more than a month? Not one country complained. Why this double standard, when it has been proved that we have never—I repeat, never—bombed our own people?

Despite the repeated requests of the Libyans, an international commission never turned up to investigate the various claims. In the meantime, accusations were pumped out incessantly, as from a sewer pipe ("crazed, murderous, bloody dictator" "bombing his own people"). The West—or that minority group of countries that believes it can speak for the rest of us—turned down Hugo Chavez's offer to act as mediator for Libya. The Chavez offer received the support of many Latin American countries, of a number of Middle Eastern countries, and, lastly, of the African Union (an organ with greater legitimacy in this area than NATO or the USA could ever have!). Europe, of course, immediately sided with NATO and the USA.[301]

This writer can testify, on having visited Gaddafi's Bab al 'Aziziyah bunker residence, how misleading the news spread by the Western media was, in regard to Gaddafi's popularity or lack of popularity among the people of Tripoli and Libya as a whole. Under the very close scrutiny of security guards, we were the only Westerners to enter the garden facing Gaddafi's bunker.

On entering the garden of his former residence, I saw something that immediately told me that the stories we in the West were told were totally false.

Bombed by the Americans on 15 April 1986, the premises had been deliberately left as they were after the airstrike, as a reminder and warning. The walls were down, the ceilings were crumbling, the armchairs stood where they stood, filled with rubble and debris, the beds were overturned. Only Hana's bed was placed in a display case. She was sixteen months old.

With the airstrikes of 2011, the place became the venue for something like a 'happening'. Families came with their infants (a large kindergarten had been set up to take care of them). Old people parked themselves down in their tents, complete with their hookah pipes and many, many cushions and mats. A large stage was erected before Gaddafi's home, from which musicians played and speakers spoke. The events alleviated the anxiety of a people facing a situation becoming graver by the day.

The true meaning of this initiative, willfully ignored by the Western media, was explained to me by a young, well-educated electronic engineer acting as our guide: "It is our way of being close to our brother Gaddafi"—"a brother and a father" who received the affectionate tributes of his people. Every evening, a human shield was formed against airstrikes (airstrikes such as that of 25 April, during which an office building located within the Bab al 'Aziziyah complex was destroyed by a Tomahawk missile launched by a Royal Navy submarine; the coordinates were provided by British special forces in hiding in Tripoli).[302]

The last of our meetings with members of the government was with the Deputy Foreign Minister, Khaled Kaim, who provided us with a highly detailed account of how the crisis had developed. The Libyan authorities immediately discovered members of the "Muslim Brotherhood" and other foreign jihadists among the 'rebels' of Benghazi. He also pointed out the odd fact that the staff of many embassies had left the country with no plausible explanations. He listed the longstanding geopolitical reasons behind the West's decision to target Libya.

Kaim provided us with video footage and an international press book covering the entire sequence of events, so that we might examine the various incidents and objectively assess what had happened up to that time. Concerning Western public opinion, he pointed to the dangers of becoming hypnotized by the incessant media campaigns of the last few months. He believed we needed to look to look into the substantive issues of the conflict between his government and the 'rebels'. He concluded that NATO intervention in the internal affairs of Libya had complicated matters and had lengthened the time that would be necessary for national reconciliation.

National reconciliation was, of course, the last thing on the minds of Libya's foes. They wanted Gaddafi out, and this was just the latest of innumerable attempts to oust him. Their intention was to take over Libya and seize control of the country's enormous natural resources.

During one operation, a telephone call was intercepted. The enemy thought they'd precisely located Gaddafi. The subsequent bombing took the lives of one of Gaddafi's sons (the youngest), three grandchildren and a daughter-in-law. In this case, depleted uranium was used.

Aiming to protect civilian lives, the coalition slaughtered a son, grandchildren, a daughter-in-law and many, many dignitaries, crushed under the debris caused by massive bombing.

Our next, and last, appointment was with Monsignor Giovanni Innocenzo Martinelli, Vicar Apostolic of Tripoli, one of the few Italians remaining in Tripoli after the outbreak of the crisis. He confirmed the impressions of the fact-finding mission, which tallied also with those of the admirably determined Italian import-export agent, Tiziana Gamannossi.

Martinelli did not believe the Libyan government had bombed its own people, adding,

> The deaths from the airstrikes were caused only by NATO at Tajuri. The only possible solution to the conflict is dialogue, not bombs". [...] the 'rebels in Benghazi' have committed grave crimes and have precipitated chaos throughout the country.

He added that the allied attack on Libya was unjust and mistaken both tactically and strategically, because "the raids will strengthen Gaddafi's hand and will enable him to win". He had thought long and deep before reaching this assessment of the situation—the judgement of a man who had no particular reason to view Gaddafi at all favorably. The future, he believed, was not bright. In an interview of 2008, he objectively assessed both Gaddafi and the manner in which he governed Libya, for good or for ill:

> A man with enormous strength of character and willpower," he noted, "who, on entering the government, favored freedom of movement, political freedom and religious freedom, and who made it possible for as many as five religious creeds to live together peacefully in Libya. [...] Libya's Islam, and, in particular the World Islamic Call Society, is a cultural association open to dialogue— the genuinely 'moderate' Islam that people talk about so much, and seek so desperately, in Europe. Although Gaddafi urges people to abandon the Christian faith, which he sees as a residue of colonialism, he actually fosters dialogue.[303]

Our visit was over. Martinelli observed,

> Over a period of more than forty years, I have never been the object of provocation on the part of anyone, and our community lives peacefully alongside all others. Tell me, where else is such a thing possible?

As we look at today's Near and Middle East, his words are as relevant (and as poignant) as ever.

8

GADDAFI'S JAMAHIRIYYA– FACTS AND FIGURES

We must look beyond the anti-Libya propaganda of recent years. At the beginning of this century, Libyans had a life expectancy of about 75 years—a record-breaking achievement, in a continent in which the index is sometimes as low as approximately 40 years. When Gaddafi seized power in 1969, the country had an illiteracy rate of about 94%. At the time of his downfall, the literacy rate had risen to about 88%. Many Libyan students were attending foreign universities at that time.[304]

Libya's performance as a provider of free education, of support for families and households, and of quality health care was truly impressive. Libyan students could receive 50,000 dinars on graduating, as a loan with which they could buy a home. There was no deadline for repayment, and the loan was interest-free. The money could be returned as and when the beneficiaries thought best.[305]

According to the report dedicated to Libya, drawn up in 2005 by the Federal Research Division of the Library of Congress of the United States,

Basic health care is provided to all citizens.

Health, training, rehabilitation, education, housing, family issues, and disability and old-age benefits are all regulated by the [...] Social Care Fund. The health care system is not purely state-run but rather a mixed system of public and private care. In comparison to other states in the Middle East, the health status of the population is relatively good. Childhood immunization is almost universal. The clean water supply has increased, and sanitation has been improved. The country's major hospitals are in Tripoli and Benghazi, and private health clinics and diagnostic centers, offering newer equipment and better service, compete with the public sector. [...] The number of medical doctors and dentists reportedly increased sevenfold between 1970 and 1985, producing a ratio of one doctor per 673 citizens. In 1985 about one-third of the doctors in the [sic] Libya were native-born, with the remainder being primarily expatriate foreigners. The number of hospital beds tripled in this same time period. [...] Malaria has been eradicated. [...] In 1985 the infant mortality rate was 84 per 1,000; by 2004, the US Agency for International Development estimated that the infant mortality rate had dropped to 25.7 per 1,000. Other estimates report an infant mortality rate of less than 20 per 1,000.[306]

How was all this achieved? Libya's Central Bank was entirely in public hands (in the West, the Central Banks are, instead, practically all controlled by enormous private, economic and financial interests). Thanks to this alternative banking system, the Libyan State could afford to spend profusely, with fewer public debt concerns.[307] Indeed, it has been estimated that, by eliminating public loan interest, the costs of public projects can be reduced by an average of 50%.[308]Mainstream economists might respond with alarm, 'What!? Everything free!? Interest-free loans!? The inflation rate in Gaddafi's Libya must have been very, very high!' It wasn't. It was on a par with the area as a whole (2-5%)—i.e. more or less as in Algeria and Tunisia (and lower than in Egypt or Morocco). Furthermore, Libya's social services were, regionally speaking, far superior.

The World Bank's *Human Development Index* (HDI) is a standard instrument adopted to gauge a country's wellbeing. The index is based on a set of criteria such as life expectancy, education and earnings. Readers of this document, before even reaching the HDI tables themselves, will be astonished by the colorful map of Africa. Libya in 2010 was in fact the only 'green' country of the continent (green denoting a high HDI value). At the 52nd position worldwide, it ranked higher than as many as nine European nations (including Russia, at the 65th position). Tunisia ranked 95th, Algeria 100th, Egypt 116t[h] and Morocco 127th.[309] Libya's per capita GDP was one of the largest in Africa, and the largest in North Africa, comfortably doubling or tripling that of its neighbors (Libya $18,700, Tunisia $8,621, Algeria $8,270, Egypt $5,912, Morocco $4,796). Per capita GDP vs cost-of-living data reflect similar trends.[310]

Let us now consider the percentage of Libyans living under the poverty line. The level stood at 3.1%. This compares favorably to the figures in 2005 for such 'great democracies' as France and the United States, where the percentages are roughly four times higher (12.1% and 12.5%, respectively)![311]

The Italian national institute of statistics, ISTAT, also provides data of considerable interest. The figures for North African immigrants to Italy as on 31 December 2007 were as follows: 365,908 from Morocco, 93,601 from Tunisia, 69,572 from Egypt, 22,627 from Algeria, and, lastly, from Libya, 1,517 (the Libyan immigrants were mainly business people and traders)[312].

Just before the Anglo-French attack, the government of Libya had announced an assisted housing project for which investments were to total approximately 24 billion dollars (647,000 new homes in all zones of a country of about 6 million inhabitants).[313] Needless to say, the project has since been abandoned.

Any report on Libya's performance as a developing nation during the Gaddafi era must include an account of the Great Man-Made River (GMMR). The GMMR project was devised to exploit giant aquifers lying 600-1000 meters below the Sahara Desert. The various basins are located at Kufra, Sirte, Murzuq and al-Hamada al-Hamra'. The project includes four aqueducts buried under the sand, laid to transport the water from the desert to the coast (900 km to the north), to the areas inhabited by 70% of the population. The planned aqueducts are of an aggregate length of about 4,000 kilometers, with provision for a capacity of more than 5,000,000 cubic meters of fresh water per day.[314]

The idea was to provide for all the water requirements of the population and to accumulate food reserves in order to reach as high a level of national self-sufficiency as possible, thus lowering dependence on foreign markets.[315] The idea behind this truly enormous 25-billion dollar project for the largest aqueduct ever built by humankind was to exploit the aquifers to an estimated extent of "the capacity of the Nile, for 200 years".[316] Subsequent hydrological research has indicated the possible presence of water in the Saharan subsoil over an area of 80,000 square kilometers (quantities sufficient to irrigate 40,000 hectares of land for 800 years).[317] It has been estimated that under Libya's soil there is an enormous fresh water lake the size of Germany.[318]

We were led to believe that if the Egyptian people ousted Mubarak and the Tunisians ousted Ben 'Ali, it could only mean that the Libyans would want to get rid of Gaddafi. While Mubarak and Ben 'Ali were plausibly brought down by their cronyism, the comparison does not hold up for Gaddafi's Libya. Libya, after all, had the highest living standards in the entire African continent.

This documented information provided our Fact Finding Commission with a clearer picture of the situation in Libya. We felt that (despite our modest resources) we had all the information we needed to prove that the UNSC Resolutions 1970 and 1973 had been extorted under false pretences. The conduct of the Jamahiriyya (the legitimate government in Libya) was not to blame for the rebellion.

The actions of the "Libya Contact Group" were aimed essentially at looting the country. Then came the actual initiatives of The Hague's International Criminal Court (ICC), whose aim was facilitate these efforts to loot the country. The ICC intervention encouraged the members of Libya's ruling élite to defect as soon as possible. This would facilitate the NTC's seizure of power. Furthermore, by its actions, the court also sealed off all routes toward a political solution to the crisis.[319]

On 5 May 2011, the ICC issued a formal accusation against Gaddafi, Gaddafi's son Saif al-Islam and Libya's intelligence chief, Abdullah al-Senoussi. The charges were said to be based on evidence acquired by thirty missions of eleven nations and through interviews with a considerable number of persons, including insiders and eyewitnesses.[320]

The prosecutor, José Luis Moreno Ocampo announced that the court had even gathered "direct evidence". We shall now look at just how "direct" it was.[321]

The final draft of the official charge of 27 June[322] was based entirely on hearsay and indirect sources. These sources were the International Federation for Human Rights (funded by the National Endowment for Democracy and the Tides Foundation) and media players—the Al Jazeera and *Al Arabiya* television stations of the feudal oil monarchies, Britain's *The Guardian*, the BBC (run by the British government), Fox News, *The New York Times*, and Voice of America (under the State Department's Broadcasting Board of Governors).

The ICC apparently places great hopes on its international standing, its fine logo, its prestigiously appointed headquarters and the polished look of its website. This is so because it has little more to commend it. We must seek out the people who ordered the ICC to act as it did, and who cherry-picked the facts behind the court's accusations. We must seek out the people behind certain government-funded and corporate-funded 'non-governmental' organizations. The most gross accusations regarded rape:

> On June 8 in New York City, Luis Moreno Ocampo, chief prosecutor of the International Criminal Court (ICC), said there were indications that Libyan dictator Muammar Gaddafi had ordered the rape of hundreds of women during his violent crackdown on the rebels and that he had even provided his soldiers with Viagra to stimulate the potential for attacks. The ICC will most likely add rape to the list of war-crime charges already levied against Gaddafi. Rape, Moreno-Ocampo told

reporters, is a new weapon for Libya's regime. 'We had doubts at the beginning,' he said, 'but now we are more convinced. Apparently, [he] decided to punish, using rape'.[323]

This particular nail in Gaddafi's coffin attracted attention after a highly dubious incident[324] and an Al Jazeera interview with a doctor from Benghazi who reported that he found Viagra pills in the pockets of a number of Libyan soldiers.

During the Al Jazeera interview, the doctor insisted that this clearly indicates that Gaddafi was using rape as a weapon of war. It has also been claimed that Gaddafi himself was a rapist.[325]

If nothing else, such gruesome stories surely helped newspaper sales![326]

The activists of Human Rights Watch and Amnesty International found no rape victims.

Donatella Rovera, senior crisis response adviser for Amnesty, who spent three months in Libya after the start of the uprising in February, said of systemic mass rape: **'We have not found any evidence or a single victim of rape or a doctor who knew about somebody being raped'.**[327] [Emphasis added]

Liesel Gernholtz, head of women's rights at Human Rights Watch, was forced to admit that "we have not been able to find evidence" of mass rape.[328]

The evidence leads us to other conclusions. Cherif Bassiouni, heading the commission of enquiry that contributed to the UN report on Libya, told the Agence

France-Presse agency that the rape and Viagra story was circulated by the authorities in Benghazi as "part of a 'massive hysteria'".[329]

The rape accusations—and various other stories that we were able to investigate during April 2011—were circulated in order to demonize Gaddafi. The media in general and the ICC accepted these allegations at face value.[330]

According to analyst Chris Marsden,

> the hypocrisy of the proposed investigation is glaring. It comes amid the more than 5,500 sorties, including 2,204 strike sorties by the NATO powers on Tripoli and other locations with civilian populations. These operations include the deliberate targeting [...] of Gaddafi for assassination [...]. While supporting legal trials for war crimes against the regime they are seeking to oust, Washington, London and Paris are carrying out massive war crimes of their own.[331]

We have yet to hear of ICC investigations of crimes against humanity or genocidal acts committed by French, British and American forces, despite the many allegations made and documents produced.[332] The ICC has in fact initiated no proceedings in regard to crimes against humanity committed by British and American forces in Afghanistan, Somalia or Iraq. Yet, starting in October 2001, George W. Bush, Tony Blair and others opened up preventive campaigns (ongoing to this day) that have claimed the lives of hundreds of thousands of people while shattering entire nations.[333] In October 2015, for example, Blair's falsehoods concerning Iraq again hit the headlines. Andrew MacKinlay, a member of the foreign affairs select committee of the British parliament told LBC Radio "that a new memo shows Tony Blair 'duped' him along with the rest of the country". MacKinlay added:

> One assumed that even allowing for exaggeration or inaccuracies in intelligence, I never thought it would be one hundred per cent untrue, but it was and myself and the British people, all of us, were duped.[334]

On 3 June 2011, the National Conference of Libyan Tribes, with its 2,000 members—the true voice of Libya—rebutted the accusations of the International Criminal Court against Gaddafi and others. The conference ended with total adhesion to the principle of Libya's unity, unshakeable condemnation of the war of aggression and unconditional support for Gaddafi.

For the benefit of public opinion in the countries that sustain the ICC, Sheikh Ali (the spokesman for the tribal chiefs) gave the concluding document of the conference to JoAnne Moriarty and the other members of the international commission of enquiry. The document from the National Conference of Libyan Tribes reads as follows:

> The Libyan people have the right to govern themselves. Constant attacks from the skies, at all hours of the day have completely disrupted the lives of the families of Libya. There has never been any fighting in Tripoli, yet we are bombed every day. We are civilians and we are being killed by the British and NATO. Civilians are people without guns, yet the British and NATO protect only the armed crusaders from the East by acting as their attack army. We have read the UN resolutions

and there is no mention of bombing innocent civilians. There is no mention of assassinating the legitimate authorities in all of Libya.

The Libyan People have the right to select their own leaders. We have suffered occupation by foreign countries for thousands of years. Only in the last 41 years have we Libyans enjoyed property ownership. Only in the last 41 years have we seen our country develop. Only in the last 41 years have we seen all of the Libyans enjoy a better life, and know that our children will have a better life [than] we have had. But now with the British and NATO bombings of our country, we see the destruction of our new and developed infrastructure.

We leaders see the destruction of our culture. We leaders see tears in the eyes of our children because of the constant fear from the 'rain of terror' in the skies of Libya from the British and NATO bombings. Our old people suffer from heart problems, increased diabetes and loss of vigor. Our young mothers are losing their babies every day because of the stress of the British and NATO bombings. These lost babies are the future of Libya. They can never be replaced. Our armies have been destroyed by the British and NATO bombings. We cannot defend ourselves from attacks from anyone.

As Tribal Leaders of Libya, we must ask why have the British and NATO decided to wage this war against the Libyan people? There are a small percentage of dissidents in the east of Libya that started an armed insurrection against our legitimate authority. Every country has the right to defend itself against armed insurrection. So why cannot Libya defend itself?

The Tribal Leaders of Libya demand that all acts of aggression, by the British and NATO, against the Libyan People stop immediately.[335]

What could our Fact Finding Commission add to this appeal, undersigned by 2,000 Libyan tribal chiefs? Instead, the following became evident: that the ICC has become merely the tool of brute force. This truth lies in the fact that the NATO countries have yet to be brought to The Hague to answer for their conduct in Libya or anywhere else. They—the United States, France and the United Kingdom, for example—would insist on justice and countermeasures if their families and loved ones had been targeted in this manner. The world can no longer tolerate double standards, with the 'top dog' countries savaging defenseless States, secure in the knowledge that they will never be called to account for their actions.

David Roberts, the spokesman for British Civilians for Peace in Libya, was entrusted with the task of drawing up a detailed account of the findings of our mission. The document was presented at a press conference open to the world's media at Tripoli's luxury Rixos Hotel. The very capable British video reporter and activist, Ishmahil Blagrove, put up the screen in record time. The press conference was an occasion for informing the media of the documents, the probatory findings and the evidence collected by the Fact Finding Commission. After presenting its findings, the Commission recorded all the media omissions and manipulations from the very start of the war.

A number of journalists and 'talking heads' from major British and American media corporations attended the meeting. They were not pleased. They protested bitterly, claiming that they had scrupulously provided all of the information in their possession, that they were innocent of any deceit.

We proved they were lying, with a fraction of the resources they enjoyed. Their stories, in effect, had been written for them months before they even arrived in Tripoli.

On the return flight from Tunis to Rome, there she was! One seat behind me. This was my chance! The Italian senator, Angela Finocchiaro, a key figure of the anti-Berlusconi 'opposition' and the *Partito Democratico*'s chief representative at the Senate (a key supporter also of the war on Libya).

I wondered, "Should I give her the tongue lashing she deserves?" I paused, "What good would it do? None". Four years later, she is still one of Italy's most important 'left wingers'. In 2011, she and her faction had insisted on intervention. They are aware that wars such as these may be disastrous also for Italy.

A brilliant Italian author, Mario Mariani, once wrote, "if journalists and politicians want to create the impression that they know it all, they are well advised to know nothing."[336] "Know nothing", we clarify, except "which way the wind blows".

9

THE REAL REASONS
FOR GOING TO WAR

Having come into direct contact with what was actually going on in Libya, and having visited many web sites and blogs that provided information as opposed to propaganda, we now saw the real reasons for the war. It had been planned a long time ago.

Libya's oil reserves are, of course, enormous (an estimated 60 billion barrels). This oil is one of the cheapest to extract, worldwide. The quality is very high, and it is easier to refine than the denser Gulf crude. Italy was Libya's prime client (24% of exports).

Then we have Libya's large natural gas fields. Up to the present, only 25% of the country's territory has been prospected. Libya ranked fourth, after Nigeria, Algeria and Egypt, as a gas producer in Africa (an estimated 1,500 billion cubic metres). It is thought that the total quantity in Libya may double that figure. "80% of the reserves are in Western Libya, onshore and offshore. These are the figures that count".[337]

The authoritative *Wall Street Journal* examined the various interests involved.[338] After the sanctions were lifted in 2003, the Western oil giants homed in on Libya. They expected more benefits than Gaddafi was prepared to give them. The Libyan government granted licences to foreign companies on the basis of a system known as EPSA-4. According to this system, most of the oil extracted was to go to Libya's National Oil Company (NOC). Furthermore, the portion due to NOC rose as the competition between foreign companies increased. The levy came to as much as 90%. According to Bob Fryklund, former chairman in Libya of the American company, ConocoPhillips, EPSA-4 oil contracts were the toughest worldwide.[339]

The National Transitional Council created its own Libyan Oil Company—an authority for the control of oil production and policies. The company was founded because Washington, London and Paris wanted it. Not Benghazi. The Libyan Oil Company was headed by the minister for oil and finance, former opposition activist Ali Tarhouni. Tarhouni returned from exile (in the United States) in March where he had been a senior lecturer at Washington University, Seattle, and was well known as an implacable foe of the pro-Gaddafi oil lobby in the USA.[340] The Libyan Oil Company—merely a 'turnkey' concern—took over NOC's interests.

Tarhouni became the Benghazi Council's head of financial affairs. His ideas on finance and oil were simple and clear—obtain credit and use as security the assets of Libya's sovereign fund (frozen by the banks abroad). His job also entailed stipulating extremely advantageous contracts for British, French and American oil concerns.

The losers were the companies operating in Libya before the war. Italy's ENI, was a big loser (it had paid a billion dollars for rights up to 2042). Germany's Wintershall also lost out. The biggest losers, however, were the Russians and Chinese. On 14 March 2011, they had received Gaddafi's promise that they would enjoy the oil rights withdrawn from the Europeans and Americans.

The plans of the Coalition of the Willing included privatizing the NOC. This condition would be imposed by the International Monetary Fund (IMF): NOC was to be sacrificed in exchange for 'aid' distributed by the West for reconstructing the industries and infrastructure destroyed... by the West.

Researchers on this topic are indebted to the American "McClatchy Company" and the WikiLeaks site founded by Julian Assange, who agreed to publish nearly 24,000 documents (from the more than 250,000 diplomatic cables in WikiLeaks' hands). Many of these documents indicate that the keystone of the foreign policy of the United States consists in ensuring its control of all energy resources worldwide. A major question dealt with in these WikiLeaks-released cables concerns diversification of supply routes to Europe. In a cable to the State Department dated 24 April 2008, Ronald P. Spogli, US Ambassador in Rome from 2005 to 2009, discussed ENI's recent agreement with Gazprom according to which the former would facilitate Russian access to North African gas fields—i.e. Libyan gas fields—while the Russians would open up their own fields to ENI.[341]

American diplomacy failed to prevent Gazprom's entry into Libya and North Africa. An attack on Libya may therefore have been seen as necessary. Diplomatic efforts had failed to block Russian advances, and NATO bombs were seen to be more effective. Within a month of the commencement of the bombing campaigns, the top management teams of ENI and Gazprom decided to temporarily suspend their agreement. The agreement would have enabled Gazprom to undertake considerable investments in technical assistance and oil production, notably in the Elephant field in deepest Fezzan (which is apparently the largest and most promising of all Libya's fields, capable of fully meeting the country's considerable crude oil export requirements for decades).

Furthermore, the agreement with Gaddafi also included large scale arms deals. With these supplies, the

Jamahiriyya would have become the strongest military force in Africa after Egypt, South Africa and (by a hair's breadth) Bouteflika's Algeria.

An assessment of the documents published by WikiLeaks tell us that an attack on Libya by French, British and American forces was practically inevitable. The United States had been planning it since 2008, at the latest.[342]

But it was more than just a question of oil and gas. Gaddafi had managed to circumvent the projection of himself as a rogue and Libya as a rogue State.[343] Gaddafi had become a diplomat, repeatedly paying visits to Europe's major capitals and receiving dignitaries in Tripoli.

With the embargo suspended, Italy's Prime Minister, Massimo D'Alema was the first Western head of government since 1992 to pay an official visit to Libya (1-2 December 1999). His declared aim was to create a partnership (representing, for Italy, business interests totaling 7,242 billion liras).[344]

In April 2004, it was British PM Tony Blair's turn.[345] In that same month, Romano Prodi, President of the EU Commission, invited the redeemed Gaddafi to Brussels as guest of honour.

The increase in foreign investments in Libya was unprecedented (4 billion dollars at the close of 2004, up 6 times on 2003).[346]

In December 2007, Sarkozy rolled out the red carpet for Gaddafi, in the park of the Hôtel de Marigny where the esteemed visitor erected his tent. Sarkozy had been elected President of France just months before, and was the first Chief of State to extend such a welcome. Many believe Saif al-Islam's claim that Libya contributed enormous sums to Sarkozy's election campaign.[347] Sarkozy repeatedly pointed out that he was the first Chief of State of a European or Western country to invite the Libyan leader to his capital in an official capacity. Gaddafi was there to ratify a Memorandum of Understanding previously negotiated by the two parties regarding one or two nuclear reactors for desalinization plants, and also concerning support in prospecting for uranium and exploitation of the uranium fields of southern Libya.

During the meeting in Paris, the two leaders also agreed upon a Memorandum of Cooperation on the basis of which Libya would commit itself to "exclusive negotiations with France for purchases of [military] equipment". According to this document, Libya was to purchase 14 Rafale fighters, 35 combat helicopters manufactured in France, various items of materiel, and 21 Airbus aircraft. Price tag? 10 billion euros.[348]

According to one Italian observer, Franco Bechis,

> despite pressure from the Elysée, the agreement with Libya bore no fruits whatsoever. Every preliminary agreement reached with France in 2007 was annulled as Gaddafi, replacing French firms, repeatedly reached out to the Russians and Italians. Sarkozy was livid [...]. So, in late November [2010] [he] went on the counter-offensive, against Gaddafi. He found an ideal accomplice in an individual who could reveal many of the regime's secrets. One of Gaddafi's right hand men, Nouri Mesmari, had just arrived in Paris with his entire family. He officially came as Gaddafi's chief of protocol, on a delicate mission. But this was only a pretext—as Gaddafi immediately realized when he signed off an international arrest warrant with Mesmari's name on it. Formalities required

that the French police detain Mesmari. In early December, Mesmari appealed to Sarkozy for political asylum for himself and his family, and thus became France's most precious asset. Mesmari proceeded to reveal all Libya's military and economic secrets. In a word, he'd handed over to France the keys to his own country. In return, he wanted France to rid Libya of Gaddafi and his courtiers.[349]

Gaddafi (again) became the villain of the piece. Why the smiles, handshakes and red carpets? Why did we sell him all that military equipment, if we wanted him out of the way?

In regard to relations between Italy and Libya, as pointed out earlier, the two countries signed a Friendship Treaty in August 2008. The treaty brought to an end the tension that had existed between the two countries since the close of World War II.

In 2010, a Libyan, H.E. Dr. Ali Abdussalam Treki, was then elected as President of the General Assembly of the United Nations. The country had at last been 'rehabilitated'. During the following months, Libya became a member of the United Nations Human Rights Council.

Then came the change. Great Britain, France and the United States again began calling for Gaddafi's head. Why now?

We find the answer in the United States. A story appeared in the *Washington Times* in March about the 200 billion dollars of the Libyan Investment Authority (LIA) held by banks in London, New York and Paris—and also Italy.

Libyan shareholdings in the Italian bank, UniCredit Banca, totalled 7.582% (4.988% held by the Central Bank of Libya and 2.594% by LIA),[350] Libya held the largest share package in Italy's top banking concern.[351] In January 2011, with a 2.01% share, Libya also became a major partner in one of Italy's key industrial concerns, Finmeccanica.[352] This "alarmed the White House, also because Finmeccanica, having taking over the American company, DRS, is one of the Pentagon's top suppliers".[353]

The Pentagon had "orders for a value of 6 billion dollars from Finmeccanica for the construction of 145 army and air force aircraft".[354] For 2011-2016, "Finmeccanica was awarded a £570 million contract by Britain's Ministry of Defence".[355] The Anglo-American military-industrial complex had good reason to be concerned.

In the meantime, a financial storm had broken, on an unprecedented scale. France, Great Britain and the United States (not to mention Italy…) were keen to recapitalize. Libya's sovereign funds were a tempting 'morsel'. According to Nourredine Leghliel, an Algerian stock market analyst residing in Sweden, this was the real reason for war on Libya. Among the various expert observers, Leghliel was one of the first to raise this issue. The 200 billion dollars—referred to only fleetingly or behind closed doors—were made up of assets 'frozen' by European banking interests.[356] The excuse for freezing the funds would be that the money was in some way held by Gaddafi's family itself. According to Leghliel, this was a mere pretext for seizing these assets.[357]

Here, perhaps, we find a solution for the British, who were struggling under their own financial crisis. Perhaps not. The Americans had their own very good economic and geopolitical reasons for installing themselves in the Sahel. France would be more than willing to act as a subcontractor for American interests there. Among the French, after all, there are some who feel they have a kind of historic claim to the region.[358]

A document published by the IMF points to another reason for the Libya mission. Since the Americans were (and are) in a state of rapid decline as actors on the world stage—and since IMF analysts believe the USA will soon be economically superseded by the Chinese—Washington may have decided it should also impede China's progress in Africa to keep the Chinese 'dragon' away from as many sources of energy and raw materials as possible.[359]

The seizing of Libya's sovereign funds and hydrocarbon resources had grave consequences for Africa as a whole. The Libyan Arab Investment Company had ploughed considerable funds into more than 25 countries, the vast majority, 22, being Sub-Saharan. The intent was to plan growth over a period of five years, above all in the sectors of mineral resources, manufacturing, tourism and telecommunications.

This was the contribution that 'Gaddafi the African' wished to make over the years, as part of his efforts to create a single political and economic continental bloc. As a senior Italian statesman remarked, "This alone would be enough to have him qualify as one of the leading figures in the history of that continent".[360] His efforts received some recognition internationally. Despite some opposition, he was appointed Chairperson of the African Union (UA) between 2 February 2009 and 10 May 2010.[361]

In 2005, in keeping with his overall plan for a changed social and political scene in Africa, Gaddafi proclaimed that nation-states no longer had a useful role to play in the new world picture. A vast continental bloc had to be constructed. He also urged the Arab States to join forces with the existing African Union to form a new Arab-African Union, open also to Iran.[362]

Within the context of the imminent strategic plan for Africa, as described, Libyan investments played a fundamental part in construction of the first telecommunications satellite of the Regional African Satellite Communications Organization (RASCOM).

Up to 2007, Africans had paid an exorbitant price for foreign telecommunications services of all kinds (500 million dollars). Africa didn't have this sum, so the burdens of debt of the countries involved, already unmanageable, snowballed. However, a satellite of the kind they required cost only 400 million dollars. The choice was between a down payment, so to speak, of 400 million dollars or an unending yearly tithe of 500 million dollars.[363] Not one bank was prepared to lend the sum at less than usurious interest rates. Libya therefore stepped into the breach with 300 million dollars. The African Development Bank provided 50 million dollars and the West African Development Bank provided 27 million.[364]

The RASCOM-1 satellite was launched on 26 December 2007. Despite a few technical hitches, the program was at last up and running. New Chinese and Russian technology flowed in. Nigeria, South Africa, Angola and Algeria launched satellites. The second African satellite (RASCOM-1R) was ready on the launching pad on 4 August 2010.[365] Africa had finally shrugged off the burden of this (largely unreported) form of 'telecommunications colonization'. Libya was the most active partner. The Libya Africa Investment Portfolio took on 63% of the costs.

However, Gaddafi would receive little praise. He was soon to be reviled once again as a "madman" and "criminal", then assassinated.... and his country shattered and bombed.

Libya invested in three financial bodies instituted by the African Union. These were the Africa Investment Bank, with headquarters in Sirte (Libya), the African Monetary Fund (AMF), with headquarters in Yaoundé (Cameroon), and the African Central Bank (ACB), with headquarters in Abuja (Nigeria). The fund was to be financed primarily by African nations. Algeria's planned contribution reportedly amounted to 14.8 billion US dollars, and Libya's to 9.33

billion (Nigeria: 5.35 billion; Egypt: 3.43 billion; South Africa: 3.4 billion).

The new fund was considered a vital step in ensuring the continent's monetary and financial independence. According to the United Nations, Africa's balance of payments as a world trading entity has shrunk considerably over the last quarter century, from 6% to 2%. The UN links this development to the fact that Africa's fifty or so national currencies cannot be exchanged among themselves, leading to the shrinking of Africa's importance as a world trading entity. Hence the AMF's role as a stimulus to trade through the creation of an African common market. This would be a necessary step for financial stability and economic progress, and for Africa to rid itself of the CFA franc (14 former French colonies are currently forced to use the CFA franc).

Perhaps the CFA had something to do with Sarkozy's particularly bellicose behavior. According to Isabelle Lasserre, writing for the French pro-government daily, *Le Figaro*, the French operations

> against Libya have revealed the excellence and technical perfection of our materiel, whether Rafale fighters or Scalp cruise missiles. The operations have also revealed the reactive capacities of the forces deployed [...]. 'In Libya, France has shown that it is still a world power. In an increasingly dangerous world, a country's appeal is determined above all by its military capacity', commented a General from France's Defence Staff.[366]

Sarkozy's *Armée del l'air* struck targets with no regard for the 'rules of the game'. The media turned a blind eye. As an Italian observer, Pierluigi Magnaschi, pointed out, "for the French, the war against Gaddafi allows them to show off their saleable arms to the world after demonstrating how effective they are against the civilian population of Libya".[367]

The French arms sector was quick to respond to these new opportunities.

> The Le Bourget international arms fair opened not in Paris on 20 June but in Libya on 19 March [...]. Prospective customers were faced with a bewildering array of merchandise. How can I be sure this is the right fighter or attack helicopter for me? Easy! Look at the label and see if it says 'combat-proven in Libya'.[368]

The 'humanitarian intervention' pretext was set up in order to quash re-emerging African efforts towards independence. The projects in question were gaining popularity throughout Africa and were especially dear to the heart of the Libyan *Qa'id* ("leader"). Tiring of 'Western aid', with its hefty price tags, Africans were experimenting with the idea of autonomous development. However, the pacifists, the 'peace brigade' and the moderate left in the West yet again failed to oppose their governments' efforts to block this development.[369]

The African Union was working on another key project proposed by Libya—the creation of a single currency (the gold dinar). Again, Libya's intention was to have Arab countries align themselves with the United States of Africa.[370] South Africa and the leaders of the Arab League were the only powers to oppose this project.

Gaddafi's plan was officially announced in Addis Ababa four days before the 'humanitarian' attacks on the

Jamahiriyya began. The plan foresaw the creation of a single currency for about a billion people. Gaddafi hoped to draw many oil producing countries into his own sphere of influence. Libya's gold reserves totaled 143.8 tons. As the ninth oil and gas producer worldwide, maybe Libya really had the resources to make this plan work,[371] failing Western interference.

In the mid or long term, it might have become *the* reference currency for traders in the African world and perhaps even in the Arab world. The plan was to allow payments with the gold dinar even for energy imports, such as oil and natural gas. The United States, Great Britain, Italy and France, and many other commercial partners, might have found themselves obliged to hold reserves in this new currency for trading purposes with African Union countries.[372]

Sarkozy is reported to have said that Libya is a "threat to the financial security of mankind".[373] As noted above, Hillary Clinton was fully aware that France's involvement was dictated not by humanitarian concerns at all, but by the threat the Jamahiriyya's very existence was beginning to pose to the "financial security" of France in francophone Africa.[374] Why should a single currency be a good idea in Europe, but a bad idea in Africa? The idea that local African currencies, the dollar and the CFA franc[375] might soon be replaced in Africa by the gold dinar was intolerable for the West. Dollar payments for oil, and the dollar's standing as *the* global economic benchmark, are what allow America to continue to survive as it is today.

Indeed, the dollar would probably sink like a stone were oil prices to be quoted via a basket of currencies. It was a vague idea at the time. The Saudi oil minister, Sheikh Zaki Yamani, was receptive to it... and was replaced within the month. Saddam Hussein and Gaddafi were more forthright.

Hussein—the old ally of the United States during his struggle against Iran—was also in favour of alternatives to the dollar, and instantly became the Hitler of the Gulf. The West's *mantra* for Iraq was recited again for Libya. Peace and democracy could return to Libya only when Gaddafi was gone. After Hussein fell, did we not see the dawning of an era of peace and democracy for Iraq? Why not in Libya too?

The economic motivations may have played a part, perhaps a big part, in recent developments. Armed intervention, initially covert, was soon brandished openly like a sword. The old colonial powers in Africa—France, the United Kingdom and the United States—were 'back in business'. In the meantime, the freezing of Libya's assets dealt a body blow to the monetary and trade confederation of the African Union.[376]

The jury is still out as to whether the war on Libya was fought on behalf of fossil fuel interests or on behalf of banking interests. Many say the former. Others, the latter. Perhaps both. Maybe the war was also waged with an eye on Libya's enormous reserves of 'blue gold' (fresh water). A country endowed with such energy resources, plus the windfall of its massive underground lake, doesn't really need international creditors. It can develop the infrastructures required to turn these resources to best account with no outside investments at all. Libya's very good luck, however, is perhaps why it has been so unlucky. Gaddafi's greatest sin was that, over the years, he had consistently demonstrated what can be done without recourse to the world's great financial institutions.[377]

On 19 March 2011, the 'rebels' formally incorporated the Central Bank of Benghazi (CBB). Significantly, they did so before even forming their own provisional government! Such a top-down 'bank revolution' is surely unique in the history of humankind! CBB was clearly incorporated to manage Libya's sovereign funds once the United States and the major European powers decided to unfreeze them. The funds, however, remain frozen.[378]

The operative word here is 'formally'. As reported by Italy's financial press, the British banking giant, HSBC (the custodian bank responsible for all Libya's frozen investments) appointed a team of top managers who worked together with the 'rebels' to create the new banking institute. The bank was founded under a puppet Governor, Ali el-Sharif. HSBC aimed to manage Libya's investments in accordance with the goals foreseen by their own strategists.[379]

10

THE CURTAIN DROPS

Five months had gone by. The NATO campaign had advanced the 'rebels' only so far, despite the considerable enthusiasm with which it had been conducted—with its constant 'humanitarian' airstrikes, a siege, sabotaged pipelines and a naval embargo, leading to shortages of gas, foods, drugs, petrol, electricity and water.

The turning point came on 20-22 August. Tripoli came under a concentric sea and land attack. During the spring and summer period, the NATO-sponsored 'rebels' had been faring badly on their various fronts. If they finally reached Tripoli it was only thanks to the umbrella of British airstrikes, guided by Pentagon satellite data, and the firepower of British, French, Qatari and Jordanian special forces.[380]

Some six months into the crisis, a coalition of 42(!) countries had still not overcome Gaddafi's stubborn resistance. NATO decided it had had enough. Hence the final Tripoli offensive.

Saving Benghazi, the original call to arms, had come to mean besieging other locations.[381] The encircling of Benghazi, of course, was quite simply a response on the part of a legitimate government to the mid-February attempted coup d'état organised by Libya's Sanusi Islamic fundamentalists. The 'rebels' received the aid of other radical Muslim groupings, and their actions were planned and directed for them by an omnipotent 'triad' of great powers (UK, France, USA).

Some months had gone by, and the campaign to 'save' civilian lives had turned into a bloodbath. *Human rights*? In this war, fought in the name of *human rights*, there wasn't a right that hadn't been violated.[382]

There were no independent sources on the ground to report on events, so the embedded media and journalists of the aggressor nations (including, of course, Italy) presented to the world a totally fact-free reality. It was said that the rebels had "liberated" Tripoli without encountering resistance; that the people had come out onto the streets to welcome them (a lie accompanying all US-NATO wars); that Gaddafi had fled to Venezuela; that three of his sons (including Saif al-Islam) had been captured by the rebels; and that a fourth son (Khamis) had been killed (the Khamis story appeared three or four times in the media over the preceding months, and was disproved each time, though apparently he did ultimately die, but the time and circumstances of his death have still not been fully confirmed).

We watched TV broadcasts with live coverage of the 'rebel' advances. Mixed in, however, we found pre-recorded sequences edited to convince us that Tripoli in its entirety had been taken, and that Gaddafi's forces had fled the scene. In the meantime, NATO was brutally bombing Tripoli's various urban districts, including hospitals and schools. Many innocent civilians were killed, and the carnage went on for days.

The "international community" looked on approvingly. Ironically, as opposed to Tripoli (now crushed by the West), the leaders of the European Union warned that Benghazi was untouchable—off limits even to its own central government! The rule of the National Transitional Council, intolerant of all forms of dissent, was imposed upon Libya's people in the name of democracy.

The German general, Egon Ramms, saw the operation as entirely dependent on NATO's infinitely greater firepower. He considered this war totally unprecedented. In any case, as we have repeatedly noted, the world's media played a massive role in numbing public opinion.[383] To use an image adopted by Eugène Ionesco, the public was reduced to the state of the "rhinoceros" (an animal open to control by others, a willing slave of the fashions and falsehoods of others). Lies accompanied this war from beginning to end. Of course, one might object: "What's so surprising or new about that? Doesn't this happens in all wars?"

Not quite...

In this case, the role of mass communications went far beyond what we may generically call 'war propaganda'. Nowadays, mass communications play a more sophisticated (but rougher) game: *human rights as a religious tenet* furthered by the idea of *airstrikes as a humanitarian measure.*

While something of the kind took place during NATO's intervention in Yugoslavia, Libya was a game changer. Here, the mass media played the part of a military vanguard. The cart, as it were, had been put before the horse. Rather than obediently repackaging and relaying the news that had been spoon fed to them by military commanders and Secretaries of State, the media were called upon actually to provide legitimation for armed actors. The media's function was military. The material aggression on the ground and in the sky was paralleled and anticipated by virtual and symbolic aggression. Worldwide, we have witnessed the affirmation of a Soviet approach to information, enhanced to the *nth* degree. It effectively produces a 'deafening silence'— an information deficit. The trade unions, the parties of the left and the 'love-thy-neighbor' pacifists did not rise to this challenge and demonstrate against the rape of Libya.

However, there was another surprise in store for us all... at least for the people who had already fallen for the rhetoric of a chimerical ten-year "war on terror".

Thanks to the courageous, ethical and professional commitment of a handful of journalists, we learned that the Commander in Chief of the Tripoli Military Council was none other than General Abdel Hakim Belhadj.[384] The general had assumed a new identity, calling himself Abdel Hakim al-Hasadi (or Hasadak). This veteran Al Qa'ida leader became Derna's notorious "Emir of terror". A former inmate at Guantanamo, in 1995—together with Salim Hamdam (Osama Bin Laden's chauffeur at one time) and Mohamed Barani— he formed the Libyan Islamic Fighting Group, sending many Libyan *mujahideen* to Afghanistan and Iraq.[385]

During the war against the Soviets, Belhadj had been personally trained by Osama Bin Laden in the province of Khost, Afghanistan. Belhadj admitted that he had imported Libyans into Afghanistan on behalf of Al Qa'ida. He was detained for a period in Pakistan.

According to journalist Pepe Escobar, Belhadj organized the offensive against Tripoli from the mountains to the southwest, in the Berber zone. He was the military commander of the offensive from the very start. He provided the coordinates for NATO airstrikes and for the ground operations of Qatar's special forces and Britain's SAS divisions. He joined his men on their march from Misrata to Tripoli. The CIA were on his trail. But it was the UK that captured him in Malaysia in 2004. He was then subjected to torture in Bangkok (as part of the extraordinary renditions operation), he was then handed over to the Libyans. Following a deal struck with Saif al-Islam, he was released six years later, in 2010.[386]

Webster Tarpley also reported on Belhadj's role as Commander of the Military Council in Tripoli. This Council, of course, owed its existence to NATO's Mermaid Dawn operation, and the massive *humanitarian* airstrikes on Tripoli, not to mention the special foreign forces that had landed in the port of Tripoli under the command of the British and French special divisions.

After civil war had been deliberately fomented in March, Al Jazeera's lies, commissioned by the government of Qatar and NATO, served as a pretext for UN approval of a Libyan no-fly zone. This was when Belhadj joined a group of Libyan government dissidents (the National Transitional Council) and was appointed commander of the anti-Gaddafi forces. It was then that he assumed the *nom de guerre*, Abdel Hakim al-Hasadi.

> He is now exercising powers of life and death over the inhabitants of Tripoli. And, of course, he's been brought into town on a carpet of NATO bombs. He's going to be receiving billions of dollars from the United States, the most modern weapons, diplomatic support, recognition, media support, moral support, Special Forces support and everything else.[387]

On 23 August, assisted by British, Franco-Jordanian and Qatari special forces, Belhadj's brigade captured Gaddafi's former stronghold, the Bab al 'Aziziyah complex. On 27 August, the brigade took control of southern Tripoli (Abu Salim, a district inhabited by civil servants and Libya's élite class, namely the bureaucrats of the Jamahiriyya State machinery). The streets ran with blood. The inmates, most of whom were linked to Al Qa'ida, were released from the local jail.

French, British and American special forces had distributed arms to the NTC 'rebels'. These 'rebels' now obligingly handed them over to Belhadj's forces. Sophisticated arms were now in the hands of the extremists. In addition, after taking Tripoli, Belhadj's brigade had access to Gaddafi's own arms depots.

In a word, in an unprecedented manner, NATO handed over part of Libya's territory to Al Qa'ida.[388] The West aided Al Qa'ida's occupation of the Arab capital of a sovereign State, Libya—the wealthiest of all African nations in terms of its oil, gas and gold reserves.

A number of Western media were quick to report on tensions among the anti-Gaddafi groupings. Clearly, local fighters affiliated to Al Qa'ida would not voluntarily leave Tripoli (the capital city of a nation "classified as a high human development country among [sic] the Middle East and North Africa region").[389] It was also unlikely that Al Qa'ida would voluntarily abandon the strongholds it had created in central and western Libya. So, the war looked set to continue.

"Another country with a modern, developed infrastructure reduced to a pre-industrial age [...] Another 'Liberation', another unimaginable, international, Criminal Tragedy", commented American journalist Felicity Arbuthnot.[390] Following the removal of Gaddafi, the rival factions were now left to settle accounts among themselves, in the Afghan manner.[391]

The Libyan tribes would contribute to the "geopolitics of chaos", which American strategists find so conducive to their aims. They would act as a destabilizing force in an energy-rich nation that, during the four decades of Gaddafi's rule, had enjoyed a considerable degree of stability.[392]

Libya was set to become an Iraq/Somalia on the shores of the Mediterranean, its natural resources taken over by others.[393] As Mireille Dellamaire points out, further military and 'humanitarian' intervention may be required in the near future. This time to "liberate Libya from Al Qa'ida".[394]

The transitional outcome in Libya in 2011 provided a clear benchmark with which we can gauge the moral consistency of the West today. This moral bankruptcy is supremely embodied by NATO, an icon signifying the moral bankruptcy of American diplomacy and, above all, of the diplomacy of the European Union. The Western media's mask of political independence has fallen to the ground—no surprise there. Some were surprised at Al Jazeera's conduct, too. The movements, unions and political players of the left in Western nations also abdicated their responsibilities. Many militants even called upon NATO to assassinate Gaddafi.

Having profited for 42 years from sales to Gaddafi of all the arms and logistical equipment that he might need, the nations of the West assured us that this "Bedouin from Sirte" had always been and would never not be a tyrant, a criminal, a terrorist of the worst kind imaginable.

Doesn't all this sound rather familiar?

Once upon a time, there was a country that went by the name of Libya.... once upon a time.

It was 'liberated'. The banners and flags of 'Libyan democracy' are those of the Sanusi kingdom under Idris (an Anglo-American protectorate).

ONCE UPON A TIME... LIBYA

The UN Resolution of 19 March 2011 unleashed the NATO forces, which conducted an estimated 9,700 raids against Libya. Many of the attacks were directed against inhabited areas and civilian infrastructures.

> Mr Ibrahim, one of the few members of the former regime—along with Gaddafi and his son Saif al-Islam—who has continued to make public statements (...) maintained that "in the past 17 days, more than 2,000 residents of the city of Sirte were killed in Nato air strikes".[395]

NATO denied all such accusations, repeatedly and insistently.

The capacity for resistance of Gaddafi's forces was unexpected. NATO may therefore have been pushed toward subjecting Libya and her people to more extensive attacks than had originally been planned. In other words, the struggle overshot its expected date of cessation. The budgets had to be revised. Upward. As the summer approached, cracks appeared and the alliance was beginning to fear 'mission creep'. It was a humiliating prospect for "the world's premier military alliance and the three most formidable militaries in the world" to be unable to swiftly dispatch a puny "third-rate despot" and his sandbox of a country. It was observed that "without significant support by the US", Europe could not have defeated Gaddafi. Nor is Europe "likely to make any progress in attaining these capabilities anytime soon".

The gloves had to come off. Defeat was unthinkable, but NATO was running out of steam:

> OUP [Operation Unified Protector] exposed significant limitations in the alliance's military ability. Many European leaders want to emphasize the fact that NATO played a lead role in the mission with the US only supporting by providing 'unique capabilities'. The role played by the US, though, was critical in filling gaps in ISR [Intelligence, Surveillance and Reconnaissance], air refueling, and unmanned drones. So, while the US only flew 25 percent of the sorties in OUP, it still provided half of the aircraft deployed, eighty percent of the air refueling and ISR missions, and augmented airborne C2 [command and control] providing 25 percent of the coverage and control. The remaining ISR capability was mostly provided by the UK and France, who also accounted for half of the strike forces, reiterating the lack of burden sharing amongst participants. NATO also depended on the US for nearly all its suppression of enemy air defense missions and for combat search and rescue. Quite simply, Europe could not have conducted this operation without significant support by the US. Additionally, Europe is

not likely to make any progress in attaining these capabilities anytime soon. (...)

By early June, reports surfaced that several nations were running out of weapons, requiring the US to replenish their depleted stockpiles. Soon after this came out, Norway, who had contributed 17 percent of the strike missions with just six aircraft, announced that it would be withdrawing its forces because of the excessive burden on its small force. The 26,500 sorties launched over the campaign may appear significant until one considers that in the mere 78 days of OAF [Operation Allied Force, of the Balkans campaign of 1999] more than 38,000 sorties were flown with non-US members flying 15,000 of those. An even greater concern amongst the coalition was that the air operations were designed 'for an effort of 300 sorties a day but was struggling to manage 150'. That the alliance's capability was strained on what is considered 'a very small operation' is troubling (...)

Most theorists figured early on that Qaddafi's regime would crumble fairly quickly once it faced coalition attack, yet it endured for seven months. The regime certainly appeared to be heading for quick defeat when the US had knocked out the Libyan air defense, grounded the Libyan Air Force, and was flying unopposed within the first few days. But then 'the world's premier military alliance and the three most formidable militaries in the world' barely prevailed 'over a third-rate despot.' If the Libyans, whose defense spending was one eight hundredth that of the opposition, nearly forced a stalemate with the Western alliance, then this campaign may not be the exemplification of airpower's promises. To address accusations of airpower not having been decisive, proponents claim that it did not attain overwhelming results against Libya because of military and political limitations. Airpower was relegated to tactical choices, rather than strategic targets. Many lament that this waste of potential, turning [sic] 'an air force into an exceedingly expensive artillery branch'".[396]

A stalemate with the West would have galvanized an entire continent.

It is to be remembered that submarine-launched Tomahawk missiles were also used[397] and that Western special forces had already been active on Libyan ground since February.

By September 2015, the UN had been repeatedly called upon to assess the 'collateral damage'—the losses and injuries of civilians, refugees, cumulative effects, internally displaced persons, the homeless, damage to infrastructures, people's homes and sites of cultural interest, etc.—caused by the years of civil war (or, if one prefers, of the two civil wars). Reluctantly, it seems, the UN produced a brief, decidedly superficial account of the impacts of explosive weapons. The report is based not on its own research but on estimates provided by third parties (including assessments made incidentally and not for this specific purpose). Indeed, one key source had only a marginal interest in collecting data on

Libya. The basic data presented in the UN's report can thus be compressed quite satisfactorily into a single paragraph:

Every year since 2011, Libyan civilians have paid the highest price for the use of explosive weapons, particularly in populated areas. Data collected by AOAV [Action on Armed Violence] indicate that between January 2011 and June 2015, civilians comprised about 79 per cent of all reported casualties (people killed or physically injured) from explosive weapon attacks in populated areas in Libya. This compares with 34 per cent when explosive weapons were used in other areas in Libya. The use of explosive weapons in populated areas was a major cause of civilian deaths and injuries across Libya in 2014 and the first half of 2015, including in the three most populous cities (Tripoli, Benghazi and Misrata) and in Derna, Wershafana and Al Qubbah. In 2014, AOAV recorded 36 incidents of explosive weapons use in Libya resulting in 549 people killed or injured, including 306 civilians. When explosive weapons were used in populated areas in 2014, civilians comprised 86 per cent of the resulting casualties, compared with just 19 per cent in other areas. In addition, between January and June 2015, AOAV recorded 38 incidents of explosive weapons use in Libya, with 419 civilian casualties. When explosive weapons were used in populated areas during this period, civilians comprised 81 per cent of the casualties, compared with 45 per cent in other areas. 2012 and 2013 were marked by more stability relative to 2011 and 2014-15, but there were still a large number of civilian casualties due to explosive weapons use. AOAV counted 299 civilian casualties from explosive weapons use in 2012 and 306 civilian casualties from explosive weapons use in 2013. When explosive weapons were used in populated areas, civilians comprised 81 per cent of the casualties in 2012 and 97 per cent of the casualties in 2013. In December 2013, Libya experienced its first suicide bombing, which killed seven people at a checkpoint in Benghazi. The most violent of the past five years was 2011, the year of the popular uprising and NATO air campaign. AOAV counted 134 incidents of explosive weapons use in 2011, resulting in 2,108 civilian casualties. Civilians comprised 75 per cent of casualties when explosive weapons were used in populated areas, compared with just 25 per cent in other areas. The vast majority of recorded civilian casualties in 2011 were reported in the first few months of the conflict in Libya. AOAV's data clearly illustrate the disproportionate loss of civilian life due to explosive weapons use in populated areas in Libya. However, these figures alone do not capture the devastation that explosive weapons have caused to civilian lives and communities across the country.[398]

The most widely cited press report on the effects of the NATO sorties and missile attacks on the civilian population is most surely that of *The New York Times*. In "Strikes on Libya by NATO, an Unspoken Civilian Toll", conveniently published after NATO's direct intervention had ceased. The article is truly a fine example of 'embeddedness':

> While the overwhelming preponderance of strikes seemed to have hit their targets without killing noncombatants, many factors contributed to a run of fatal mistakes. These included a technically faulty bomb, poor or dated intelligence and the near absence of experienced military personnel on the ground who could help direct airstrikes. The alliance's apparent presumption that residences thought to harbor pro Qaddafi forces were not occupied by civilians repeatedly proved mistaken, the evidence suggests, posing a reminder to advocates of air power that no war is cost or error free. (...)
>
> Elements of two American led air campaigns in Iraq, in 1991 and 2003, appear to have been avoided, including attacks on electrical grids. Such steps spared civilians certain hardships and risks that accompanied previous Western air to ground operations. NATO also said that allied forces did not use cluster munitions or ordnance containing depleted uranium, both of which pose health and environmental risks, in Libya at any time.[399]

This account fails to address the reasons why, according to OCHA (the United Nations Office for the Coordination of Humanitarian Affairs), the "vast majority of recorded civilian casualties in 2011 were reported in the first few months of the conflict in Libya". In other words, it fails to ask why most civilian losses were recorded during the time of the alliance's early airstrikes and missile attacks. While defending NATO against accusations that it had used cluster bombs or DU (depleted uranium) munition in 2011, Franklin Lamb—an international lawyer specializing in crimes against humanity, and a member of the legal team defending Saif al-Islam and other detained Jamahiriyya officials—notes that the alliance was much more aware of the civilian nature of certain targets than it is prepared to admit. The press, OCHA and many other agencies and NGOs clearly decided it was best not to look too hard into questions such as these.

In the early hours of 20 June 2011, NATO attacked a residential compound in Sorman, a town 45 miles west of Tripoli. Lamb reports,

> Just before the bombs hit, eye witnesses, reported seeing red specks in the sky and then flashes of intense light, immediately followed by thunderous ear splitting blasts as eight American bombs and rockets pulverized their neighbor's homestead. In an instant Khaled El Hamedi's family was dead.

Khaled El Hamedi—away from home when the missiles struck—is "the 37 year old President of the International Organization for Peace, Care & Relief (IOPCR), one of Libya's most active social service organizations". His home

> was not what NATO labels a 'time critical target' so there was plenty of time for its staff to transmit information about the site

from unmanned reconnaissance aircraft to intelligence analysts. Almost certainly, according to a source at *Jane's Weekly*, NATO UAV's [unmanned aerial vehicles] watched the Hamedi compound over a period of days and presumably observed part of the birthday party being held for three old Huweldi [Khaled El Hamedi's son], the day before the order to bomb was issued. NATO Rules of Engagement for Operation United Protector, constitute a set of classified documents which present specific and detailed instructions about what is a legitimate target and who can approve the target, whether preplanned or 'on the fly' when a pilot happens upon a target of opportunity. The Sorman attack on the Hamedi home was planned as part of what NATO calls its 'Joint Air Tasking Cycle' (JATC). A target development team put the Hamedi home on the June 20 daily list of targets. The team used a report from NATO intelligence analysts who determined that retired officer Khaled al Huweldi Hamedi, one of the original members of the Gadhafi led 1969 *coup* against King Idris in 1969, and a former member of the Al Fatah Revolution's Revolutionary Command Council, was living on the property. His assassination had been ordered by NATO because they hoped to weaken the regime in some way even though the senior Hamedi was retired and had no decision making role in Libya. On June 19, the day before the bombing attack on the Hamedi family at Sorman, NATO was obliged by its own regulations and by the international law of armed conflict to conduct a 'potential for collateral damage review' of this mission. There is no evidence that this was every [sic] done. A requested US Congressional NATO Liaison Office review of the Sorman bombing, initially requested from Libya on August 2, was completed in early September 2011 and found no documentary evidence or other indication that anyone in NATO's Target Selection Unit, evaluated, discussed, or even considered the subject of potential civilian casualties at the Hamedi home in Sorman. Following the green light to bomb the Hamedi home, the coordinates were fixed at 32°45'24"N 12°34'18"E. Specific aim points on the Hamedi property were chosen and eight bombs and missiles were readied and attached to the strike aircraft. At Sorman, NATO used a variety of bombs and missiles including the 'bunker busting' BLU109 (Bomb Live Unit) which is designed to penetrate 18 feet of concrete. NATO also used the American MK series of 500 lb, (MK 81) 1000 lb, (MK82) and the 2000 lb (MK84) that Israel used so widely during its 2006 invasion of Lebanon. Following the inferno at Sorman, NATO denied responsibility but the next day NATO admitted carrying out an air strike somewhere in Sorman but denied that there were civilian deaths even as its drones filmed the scene close up. NATO's media office in Naples issued a statement claiming 'A precision air strike was launched against a high level command and control node in the Sorman area without collateral damage'. NATO spokespersons also told Amnesty International and Human Rights Watch that 'the facility was a legitimate military target and that all necessary precautions were taken before conducting the strike which minimized any potential risk of causing unnecessary casualties'. (...)

Oddly, NATO records for June 20 as well as subsequent reports of bombing attacks listed for June 20th and June 21st in its daily logs have never included the bombing attack on Sorman or the attack on the Al Hamedi residence which indisputably killed 15 civilians.[400]

The socially cohesive role of the noted Al Hamedi family was perhaps the key factor of this fatal "mistake" insofar as Khaled El Hamedi is a noted relief worker and Khaled al Hueldi was one of the founders of the Libyan republic. Other close associates of Gaddafi have also lost their lives and families in a similar manner.

NATO, the USA and the United Nations are fundamentally uninterested in the question of the human toll. A FOIA document reveals, for example, that Mrs. Clinton was aware already in March 2011 that, on a routine basis, the rebel militias in Libya summarily executed captured fighters as pro-government mercenaries.[401] Gaddafi's death is a case in point:

NAPLES—Now that NATO has had the opportunity to conduct a post strike assessment of yesterday's strike, we are able to provide a more comprehensive picture of events. At approximately 08h30 local time (GMT+2) on Thursday 20 October 2011, NATO aircraft struck 11 pro-Qadhafi military vehicles which were part of a larger group of approximately 75 vehicles manoeuvring in the vicinity of Sirte. These armed vehicles were leaving Sirte at high speed and were attempting to force their way around the outskirts of the city. The vehicles were carrying a substantial amount of weapons and ammunition posing a significant threat to the local civilian population. The convoy was engaged by a NATO aircraft to reduce the threat. Initially, only one vehicle was destroyed, which disrupted the convoy and resulted in many vehicles dispersing and changing direction. After the disruption, a group of approximately 20 vehicles continued at great speed to proceed in a southerly direction, due west of Sirte, and continuing to pose a significant threat. NATO engaged these vehicles with another air asset. The post strike assessment revealed that approximately 10 pro-Qadhafi vehicles were destroyed or damaged. At the time of the strike, NATO did not know that Qadhafi was in the convoy. NATO's intervention was conducted solely to reduce the threat towards the civilian population, as required to do under our UN mandate. As a matter of policy, NATO does not target individuals. We later learned from open sources and Allied intelligence that Qadhafi was in the convoy and that the strike likely contributed to his capture. NATO does not divulge specific information on national assets involved in operations.[402]

One observer, a supporter of the US and NATO operations, noted:

> For anyone concerned to see the rule of law established after Qaddafi's overthrow, the manner of Qaddafi's own death was an ominous portent. Videos made from cell phones recorded his last minutes after his capture by rebel forces on October 20, 2011. Young rebels fighting in the informal militias were shown assaulting a dazed and disheveled Qaddafi after he was found cowering in a large sewer pipe—a last minute attempt to escape in a convoy from his Sirte hiding place having gone awry. The jerky videos, in which what is happening to Qaddafi is often obscured by those crowding around him, do prove that Qaddafi was screamed at, repeatedly pummeled, and roughly dragged about. Soon there was blood copiously streaming down the left side of his head and onto his chest. With looks of terror and bewilderment alternating on his countenance, he seemed to struggle to understand what was happening to him. How he died is not shown in the videos and remains uncertain. A subsequent investigation by Human Rights Watch uncovered evidence of brutal beatings and summary executions of captured members of Qaddafi's convoy, including his

son Mu'tasim, but, on receiving the NGO's report, the Libyan authorities maintained that the deaths were battle-related, which was indicative of their disinclination to prosecute the perpetrators.[403]

It is also to be remembered that the henchmen not only shot Gaddafi but also sodomized him with a bayonet.[404]

Mrs Clinton's joyous exclamation on hearing the news of Gaddafi's death sums up the recklessness and irresponsibility of an entire political class—an unrepentant class that has wreaked havoc around the world on a truly unprecedented scale. In the presence of the journalist who was about to interview her, she exclaimed, "We came, we saw, he died", evidently believing the cameras and microphones were off. Unable to hide her joy at having triumphed in an apparently personal war, she drew a parallel between herself and Julius Caesar. Perhaps she is not a great scholar of ancient history. Did she really see herself and her government covered in glory even remotely comparable?[405]

The death toll specifically for 2011 is no doubt higher than the official figures released in 2013 suggest:

> Libya's new government has drastically reduced its estimate of the number of people who were killed in the revolution against Muammar Gaddafi's regime, concluding that 4,700 rebel supporters died and 2,100 are missing, with unconfirmed similar casualty figures on the opposing side. Miftah Duwadi, the deputy minister of martyrs and missing persons, told the *Libya Herald* newspaper that the numbers for revolutionary losses were still being checked but officials did not

expect any major changes. (...) Initially rebel officials believed that some 50,000 people had been killed, a figure that was revised down to 25,000 dead and 4,000 missing in October 2011. The latest statistics have been compiled after research by the ministry, though they do not include the final figure for fatalities on the Gaddafi side.[406]

Readers may be forgiven if they learn little from such sloppy reporting as this. It is a fact that Western media generally refer only to cumulative death tolls (initially presented to the world via such agencies as Reuters or AP, or the Gulf TV companies). These sources rarely, if ever, provide a breakdown for losses among, for example, government and opposition forces, the presence amongst the casualties of foreign fighters, immigrants or mercenaries, civilian victims, missing persons, including detainees, losses assessed by age group and sex, ethnicity, location, distance from front lines, location in densely populated areas, or following treatment, not to mention specific causes of death such as explosive devices, the collapse of buildings etc. Data in more detail would help us to more concretely assess the developments on the ground. While hospital records might be a prime source of information, they are only rarely mentioned.

In September 2011, shortly after the taking of Tripoli,

Libya's interim health minister in the country's new leadership, Naji Barakat said that at least 30,000 people have been killed and 50,000 more wounded, including some 20,000 with serious injuries, during the over six month conflict that began in mid February in Benghazi. (...) Speaking to the *Associated*

Press on wednesday [sic], the interim health
minister said that at least 4,000 people are still
missing, either presumed dead or held prisoner
in remaining Al Qathafi strongholds (...)

In an attempt to get a more detailed figure,
Barakat said that next week, worshippers
in local mosques will be asked to report the
dead and missing in their families. Barakat
went on to say that of the estimated 30,000
dead, about half are believed to have been Al
Qathafi fighters.[407]

The scandalously poor quality of the information
provided by NGO and mass media sources cannot be
overstressed—the failings of these agencies are too constant
not to be systemic. Claudia Gazzini, senior analyst for
Libya of the International Crisis Group (ICG), expressed
the opinion that, if the casualty figures provided by Libya's
National Transitional Council in 2011-12 were accurate,
then "the death toll subsequent to the seven-month NATO
intervention was at least ten times greater than the tally of
those killed in the first few weeks of the conflict".[408] Gazzini
seems to consider NTC minister Naji Barakat's early 'body
count' more accurate than the revised figures provided in
2013, which was relayed uncritically by *The Guardian*.
President Obama, of course, explained the entire campaign
away with a lie. Gaddafi, he said, was planning a massacre
of his own people:

We knew that [...] if we waited one more day,
Benghazi, a city nearly the size of Charlotte,
could suffer a massacre that would have
reverberated across the region and stained the
conscience of the world.[409]

An American public affairs academic at Harvard, Alan J. Kuperman, reminds us that by the time the decision had been made to attack Benghazi, Gaddafi's forces had already retaken two cities in the west, Zawiyah and Zuarah, as well as Ajdabiyah in the east, and, for the main part, Misrata (some 120 kilometers to the east of Tripoli). The government forces had done so without bloodbaths, and therefore, according to Kuperman, there was little reason to believe these forces would massacre the civilians of Benghazi, as Obama had suggested (hoped). Gaddafi's forces were "extremely careful to target only militias", Kuperman asserts. The best evidence of this came from Misrata, "the city that had the most intense fighting". The Libyan government was immediately accused by the UN of the worst crimes: "Using imprecise weaponry such as cluster munitions, multiple rocket launchers and mortars, and other forms of heavy weaponry, in crowded urban areas will inevitably lead to civilian casualties," stated the UN High Commissioner for Human Rights, Navi Pillay. "There are also repeated reports of snipers deliberately targeting civilians in Misrata, as well as in other Libyan towns where street fighting has taken place".[410] Kuperman's reference to Human Rights Watch's conclusion that the casualty rate among women and children in Misrata stood at 3% exposes the Commissioner's bias in one fell swoop. He considers this 3% figure extremely low for combat situations in heavily populated areas[411] and reminds us that HRW—although it provides this decidedly positive assessment of the Jamahiriyya defence forces' performance against a highly dangerous foe in 2011—is certainly "no defender of Gaddafi".

Indeed, the *coup* forces found in 2011 that the civilian populations of the centers that they had captured were useful human shields. Leaving aside foreign intervention for a moment, had it not been for the Jamahiriyya's policy of protecting the lives of innocents—adopted at great cost to its chances of victory—Gaddafi's forces might have successfully routed the rebels throughout Libya in a matter of weeks or days (and Gaddafi himself might have survived the onslaught). We can therefore quite safely deduce that Gaddafi's forces used very few explosive weapons in Misrata, and that Benghazi was not necessarily under any greater threat than Misrata had been shortly before.

The State Department and Obama were fully aware that the US-backed 'rebel' forces had no such regard for the lives of innocents.[412] In 2016, following the publication of many of Mrs. Clinton's e-mails (released by the State Department within the terms of FOIA), the worst suspicions concerning the methods and activities of the upper echelons in Washington were all fully confirmed. Hillary Clinton was fully aware of developments as these unfolded in early 2011. She had been informed, for example, that Western and Egyptian special forces were intervening in Libya in violation of Resolution 1973:

> An extremely sensitive source added that the rebels are receiving direct assistance and training from a small number of Egyptian Special Forces units, while French and British Special Operations troops are working out of bases in Egypt, along the Libyan border. These troops are overseeing the transfer of weapons and supplies to the rebels (...)
>
> French, British and Egyptian Special Forces troops are training the rebels inside of western Egypt, and to a limited degree in the western suburbs of Benghazi.[413]

Likewise, she knew that the 'rebel' forces whose

cause she was aiding carried out summary executions of all persons that they considered (or chose to consider) pro-government mercenaries. Her informant, Sidney Blumenthal, informed her that "Speaking in strict confidence, one rebel commander stated that his troops continue to summarily execute all foreign mercenaries captured in the fighting".[414]

The Benghazi massacre threat story, of course, had been put about by the Islamic militants (or by their foreign advisors). It was a desperate last-minute fabrication designed to get the West into Libya at all costs. For the benefit of Western audiences, a vaguely plausible justification was required. The 'rebels' claimed that the killing in Benghazi would be comparable to that in Rwanda. To avoid a Benghazi defeat at Gaddafi's hands, they now required Western air support.[415]

On 14 March 2011, Reuters and the international news networks passed on the militia's message. 'Charlotte' was about to be destroyed. The airstrikes targeted precisely those cities that had remained loyal to the legitimate government. The war was on. As planned.

British SAS operatives were training many of the 'rebels' already some months before the campaign got under way. The *Daily Mirror* noted that the presence of foreign operatives was "an incredibly sensitive subject as the UN security council resolution in March authorising the use of force against Gaddafi specifically excludes 'a foreign occupation force of any form on any Libyan territory'". The Mirror added that the "elite soldiers are experts in going into conflict zones and launching what is known as 'train the trainer' programmes in which they teach officers and NCOs how to prepare their troops".[416]

These militias would then take their British expertise with them to what would become the infamous ISIS and similar groupings active in Syria and Iraq, also responsible for the video transmitted worldwide of the beheadings of 21 Coptic Christian workers seized in Sirte (February 2015).

Obama, Cameron, Hollande, Hillary Clinton, Anders Fogh Rasmussen (Secretary General of NATO), Ban Ki Moon and the Canadian premier, Charles Bouchard, claim Gaddafi was the real criminal.[417] Sarkozy, with a hand on his purse, is reported to have claimed that Gaddafi was a threat to the financial security of mankind. As pointed out above, Navi Pillay, the UN High Commissioner for Human Rights, eagerly joined the chorus.

Why?

Gaddafi had successfully achieved Libya's economic independence, and was on the point of concluding agreements with the African Union that might have contributed decisively to the economic independence of the entire continent of Africa.

Not least, Gaddafi had brazenly declared that he no longer wished sell the oil of Africa's largest fields for US dollars.

Sarkozy was right. Gaddafi was a real threat…

The petrodollar is a vital global power resource for America. Its imminent demise is widely predicted by friend and foe alike, and Gaddafi's efforts to introduce the gold dinar into Africa as a common currency might well have looked very like the final nail in its coffin. Eager to make its mark on the continent by offering military collaboration deals (and by corrupting the various countries' leaders), the USA was appalled at just how popular Libya's plans for an African bank and economic union were among Africa's poverty-stricken but resource-rich nations. For some observers, Libya's more ambitious outreach was a most disturbing development.

Following the NATO attack, under the umbrella of the Security Council, "in August 2011, President Obama confiscated $30 billion from Libya's Central Bank, which

Gaddafi had earmarked for the establishment of the African IMF and African Central Bank".[418] As we shall see presently, the Libyan state's assets abroad (above all in Italy) are estimated at 200 billion dollars.

This was not the first time the 'humanitarian' pretext had been deployed to further Western interests. In 1999, Mrs. Clinton's husband and Tony Blair had ordered NATO airstrikes against Milosevic, guilty of genocide against the ethnic Albanians of the secessionist province of Kosovo. The notorious US diplomat, David Scheffer, lied to reporters at NATO headquarters on 18 May 1999. He claimed that "more than 225,000 ethnic Albanian men between the ages of 14 to 59 were unaccounted for".[419] Hands on hearts, the Clinton and Blair duo evoked the "Holocaust" and the spirit of World War II. In 1999, the West backed the Kosovo Liberation Army (KLA, or UCK)—a drug-running, terrorist grouping whose crimes were deliberately ignored at the time, and have been largely ignored since.

The West's desire to militarily act against Libya at all costs, even in violation of international law, was even rebuked by an American group of analysts of some standing, who (belatedly) concluded that "The war in Libya was unnecessary, served no articulable US national security objective, and led to preventable chaos region-wide". This group, the Citizens' Commission on Benghazi (CCB), comprised of former top military officers, CIA insiders and think tankers, claimed that it had discovered

> that the ensuing civil war may well have been avoided, had the US chosen to permit it. Within days of [the] declaration of US government support for the Libyan rebels, Qaddafi sought to enter into negotiations with the US Africa Command (AFRICOM) under

a flag of truce for the purpose of discussing his possible abdication and exile.

CCB adds,

On 21 March 2011, Rear Admiral (ret.) Chuck Kubic began email and telephone contact between Tripoli and AFRICOM Stuttgart regarding the possibility of talks under a white flag of truce. Over the following days, Qaddafi expressed interest in a truce, and possible abdication and exile out of Libya. He even pulled his forces back from several Libyan cities as a sign of good faith. RADM Kubic telephoned LTC Brian Linvill, the US AFRICOM point of contact for all military matters regarding the Libyan situation, to advise him of Qaddafi's desire to enter into military-to-military discussions. General Carter Ham was advised immediately on 21 March 2011 of these communications and conveyed them up his chain of command to the Pentagon. After two days of back-and-forth with the Libyans, however, General Ham had received no positive affirmation of consent from Washington, D.C. to pursue Qaddafi's offer [...]. Despite the willingness of both AFRICOM Commander Gen. Carter Ham and Muammar Qaddafi to pursue the possibility of truce talks, permission was not given to Gen. Ham from his chain of command in the Pentagon and the window of opportunity closed.[420]

The "window of opportunity", of course, was never meant to be opened.

Gaddafi was willing to negotiate. He had reportedly pulled his forces back from many Libyan cities in an effort to ward off foreign aggression. Shortly before the exchanges described by CCB, Britain's Minister of Defence, William Hague claimed Gaddafi had fled to Venezuela. Gaddafi publicly declared the next day (22 February 2011), and repeatedly thereafter, that he would rather die than abandon Libya to its fate. If supported by verifiable evidence, news of the Colonel's purported willingness at a certain stage to abandon Libya would have been of enormous military and propaganda value to the Coalition at that time. Why was the alleged "window of opportunity" not used to demoralize the Jamahiriyya's armed forces? Incompetence?

It was reported that Gaddafi had been willing to renounce certain powers, as opposed to going into exile. However, he insisted that he must be granted a free hand against the jihadists on Libyan soil. This was unacceptable to the 'all or nothing' West.

PART III

RECIPE FOR DISASTER

1

THE UNENDING
TRANSITION BEGINS

The situation in late 2011 and early 2012 was one of relative calm, but change was in the air. A bomb was thrown at a convoy accompanying the head of the UN mission to Libya (April 2012). The Red Cross was hit with a rocket (May 2012). A diplomatic convoy was attacked, as a result of which the British abandoned their Benghazi consulate (June 2012). A program to train Libyan police in Jordan met with considerable difficulty when the recruits decided to fight it out among themselves, as a result of which many of the trainees were sent back home (July 2012). A bomb exploded in front of the US consulate (August 2012).

Even in its early days, the transitional leadership's role was weakened by a conflict between 'Abd al-Jalil, initially the head of NTC, and Mahmoud Jibril, heading the NTC's executive council. In March 2012, the NTC announced that it would allocate 60 seats in the national assembly to the east, and over 100 to the west (the west being more populous than the east). As a response to this reasonable decision, a group known as the Barqa Council declared itself the interim government of Barqa (the Arabic word for Cyrenaica).[421] The specter of secession raised its head once more.

The country was awash in small arms and light weapons, including MANPADS, anti-tank missiles, Grad rockets, and mortars. France, Qatar, and other countries had also supplied the rebels with weapons during the war, with Qatar contributing more than 20,000 tons of weapons, including assault rifles, rocket-propelled grenades, and other small arms. Qatar and France both also supplied the rebels with Milan anti-tank missiles. More important were Qaddafi's own weapon stocks, most of which had been let loose during the war. The UN estimated that, at the time of Qaddafi's overthrow, Libya's armed forces held between 250,000 and 700,000 firearms, the majority of which (70-80 percent) were assault rifles. MI6 estimated that there were a million tons of weaponry in Libya, more than the entire arsenal of the British army. These weapons now threatened Libya's security. Large numbers of MANPADS [man-portable air defense systems] and the remnants of Qaddafi's nuclear weapons program, meanwhile, posed a threat beyond Libya. Qaddafi had purchased as many as 20,000 Soviet MANPADS, a stunning number that would be a major challenge to track down and collect. The United States funded the program to recover the MANPADS, although it was reportedly run by South African contractors. Libya also had not completed the process of destroying its chemical weapons stocks, and only 51 percent of its original mustard gas stockpile of 24.7 metric tons had been destroyed by the time the regime was overthrown.[422]

This flood of arms provides the backdrop for the dramatic events of this period.

Sub-Saharan Africans on Libyan soil and Libyans of sub-Saharan descent were attacked. The ethnic cleansing of the loyalist town of Tawergha (30-40,000 residents) has remained a key node of contention. Because of the poor performance of Islamist candidates during the July 2012 elections, a *coup* looked likely already in 2012.[423]

On the economic front, prospects in 2012 were decidedly grim. "Libya is heading toward bankruptcy", said Claudia Gazzini in February 2012. "It's running a budget deficit of about 3 billion dollars a month (...) There's a risk that in 18 months the country could be penniless".[424]Needless to say, "The €61bn Marshall Fund promised at the G8 meeting in 2011 never materialised".[425]

2

BENGHAZI-GATE

US Envoy Christopher Stevens had been deployed to the area specifically to coordinate the actions of the jihadists, synchronizing their moves with the coalition airstrikes. He came to Benghazi on 5 April 2011, where he resided during the period of the NATO Libya raids. On the strength of his efficient service, experience and contacts, he was formally appointed Ambassador to Libya in May 2012.

Following Libya's destruction at the hands of NATO, Stevens had to leave the American Embassy because the *"Tahloob"* (or pro-Gaddafi Green Resistance) had burned it down. He moved into a hotel in Tripoli. When Gaddafi loyalists attempted to assassinate him with a car bomb outside his hotel, Stevens moved again to Benghazi where he shared the American Consulate premises in Benghazi with the CIA. Many of the inhabitants were pro-American; Benghazi was the center of Sanusi jihadi fundamentalism. Stevens' task in Benghazi, now, was to oversee shipments of Gaddafi's arms to Turkish ports. The arms were then transferred to the jihadi forces engaged in terrorist actions against the government of Syria under Bashar al-Assad.[426]

Many Islamists came from the ranks of the mujahideen who had previously fought for the West's allies in Afghanistan in 1980, and then joined Al-Qa'ida (supposedly opposed to the West).[427]

Stevens enjoyed jogging in the streets of Benghazi. Perhaps he underestimated the capabilities of the *"Tahloob"* loyalist resistance.[428] Everyone knew who he was and where he lived with his staff. One pro-NATO terrorist, Ahmed al-Abbar, said of Stevens that "He was loved by everybody" in Benghazi.[429] The ambassador's popularity among the militiamen of Benghazi, of course, incensed the pro-Gaddafi resistance forces, who decided once more to seek his death, via an attack on the American consulate.

The Western media painted a false picture of the incident, which is still the subject of controversy.

Safety and security issues at Benghazi again draw our attention to the central role of the ever-destructive Hillary Clinton:

> Republicans have claimed that Clinton refused to offer increased security upon request of diplomats stationed in Libya prior to the Benghazi attack. Clinton has denied she ever received word of such requests.[430]

Had she not "received word" of Stevens' shady dealings in Benghazi either? If she was aware of the nature of his mission, was it not also clear to her that Stevens was placing his life at risk every second of his existence?

In April 2014, the CCB

> declared in Washington that a seven-month review of the deadly 2012 terrorist attack has determined that it could have been prevented—if the U.S. hadn't been helping to arm al-Qaeda militias throughout Libya a year earlier.[431]

While of considerable interest, especially in view of the mammoth sum mentioned (half a billion dollars), this grave accusation is also misleading. It suggests that, on this occasion, Al-Qaʻida had bitten the hand that feeds it.

During the morning of 12 September 2012, immediately after the Benghazi attack, a number of local papers in Libya inadvertently revealed a different picture. They complained that NATO was not doing enough to crush the opponents of the new status quo. These opponents were not the Islamists but pro-Gaddafi militants. During a press conference in Benghazi, broadcast by *al-Jazeera*, the Libyan Deputy Interior Minister (and a former LIFG militant), Wanis al-Sharif, pinned the blame for the attack on the Green (Jamahiriyya) resistance movement.[432] The Prime Minister, Abdurrahim el-Keib, Libya's President, Mohammed al-Magariaf, Ali Aujali (Libya's Ambassador in Washington) and Ibrahim Dabbashi (Libya's Ambassador at the United Nations) also reluctantly admitted that Gaddafi loyalists were responsible for the Benghazi attack. However, the Libyan authorities soon changed their tune (their Western masters were evidently not amused).[433] From now on there was to be mention only of extremists.

Al-Magariaf, the newly designated president, went to Benghazi three days after the attack and accused Al-Qaʻida.[434] However, the Prime Minister, Abdurrahim el-Keib, insisted that pro-Gaddafi activists had been responsible for the attack, and was forced to resign the next day. Mustafa Abushagur tok his place. Abushagur had, of course, spent much of his life in the United States as an openly declared anti-Gaddafi militant.[435]

The attack on Stevens in Benghazi was not a spontaneous action, as relayed by the media. It was a seven-hour military action, planned in detail and well ahead of the date. Many observers claimed it came in response to a blasphemous film said to offend Islam, *The Innocence of Muslims*, that had appeared on the Internet at about that time. The USA and its allies enthusiastically sustained the 'local color' scenario of a spontaneous uprising.[436] A Libyan militia leader, Ahmed Abu Khatallah, was accused of the attack. Without informing the Libyan authorities, a US special unit apprehended him near his Benghazi home (in June 2014) and transferred him to the USA.[437]

During and following regime change, family feuds erupted, and rivalry broke out among the various Arab and Berber militias. However, the pro-Gaddafi resistance stood aloof, attacking NATO targets and eliminating traitors who had supported the foreign invaders.[438]

Before Stevens' death, the media occasionally mentioned the presence of Gaddafi loyalists in Libya. After the incident, all mention of these loyalists disappeared from the Libyan and international press. The reports now focused on Al-Qaʻida, Islamists, *terrorists and protesters. No one was to mention either Gaddafi... or his ghosts.* Many other details on the attack had emerged by 2013:

> four star General Carter Ham, head of US Africa Command, had a rapid response unit ready to go into Benghazi to rescue Ambassador Stevens and the other Americans in both the consulate and the CIA compound a mile away. Rear Admiral Charles Gaouette, head of the US Navy Carrier Strike Group 3 was prepared to assist in the rescue. Former Navy Seals, Tyrone Woods, who was providing security at the CIA annex a mile from the consulate, and Glen Doherty, who had arrived on a rescue flight dispatched by the CIA station chief in Tripoli, were ordered

to 'stand down', as the 7 hour battle raged on. A recently published CIA timeline, obviously an expurgated confession of a failed operation, disputes this.[439]

Stevens, staffer Sean Smith, and the CIA operatives Woods and Doherty all died, perhaps precisely because of the reluctance of other forces to move against the attackers and/or the confusion on the ground following this unusual stand down order. Secretary of Defense, Leon Panetta, announced the resignation of General Ham on October 18th, 2012. It was rumored that General Ham had intended to ignore the stand down orderbut was then arrested by his second in command and removed from his post. It is claimed also that Admiral Gaouette was removed from command and that he has been investigated for having mishandled operations.[440] These cracks in the official versions, hastily pasted over, provide us with fascinating glimpses into how the allied military machine works.

3

THE INSOLUBLE
DISORDER

Before examining the situation to the south of Libya's densely populated coastal strip—also with regard to the immigration situation—we must briefly look at some of the major political, social and military developments of the post-Gaddafi years, above all along the more densely populated Mediterranean seaboard.

Not a day went by without some major upheaval. The violence in Libya escalated after the 2012-13 lull. Elections were held. The NTC handed over the reins of power. A Prime Minister was kidnapped and fled the country. A *coup d'état* devastated Libya's economy (paralyzing oil production). Two rival governments were formed. IS has established a mini-Caliphate in Benghazi... and the feuds continue.

Trafficking in immigrants had been blocked by the signing of the Treaty of Friendship, Partnership and Cooperation between Libya and Italy in 2008. It now took off on a grander scale. Hundreds of thousands of people made their way to the coast of Libya where they were herded onto unseaworthy craft and sent off across the Mediterranean. This was an extremely profitable line of business, providing ready cash to the fundamentalist militias and their allies. It has been estimated that, since late 2001, about one million people (most but not all of whom were Africans) have crossed from Libya into Southern Italy. HRW estimates that 40,000 crossed from Libya into Italy in 2014 alone. The immigrants pay thousands of dollars per passenger.[441]

Italy's neighbor to the south has become a perfect 'Balkan powder keg'. Many observers had accurately foreseen what would happen after Gaddafi's fall. From day one until late 2015, events have played out almost exactly as predicted (not least by Gaddafi himself), in the event of the downfall of the Jamahiriyya, as the various parties to the conflict struggle to expand their own possessions and territorial outreach.

Foreign intervention created a "failed State". Western diplomats quietly packed their bags and left the country. Libya's Tunisian, Egyptian and Algerian borders, open to terrorists and gunrunners, were sealed off. Within the country, gang warfare reigns supreme. Murders in the streets, torture, and robbery became everyday occurrences. In a word— chaos. Not one of the militias or tribes has sufficient power to impose peace upon the others.

Given the large numbers of immigrants setting out on rafts and rubber dinghies, there have been many accidents at sea. More than 3,400 immigrants died in 2014.[442] The humanitarian project, *Mare Nostrum*, was operational as such between October 2013 and 1 November 2014. Thanks to *Mare Nostrum*, the island of Lampedusa, a popular Italian holiday resort, became a focus of attention for the immigrant traffickers (hence the large 'deliveries' there). In view of the failure of *Mare Nostrum*, its enormous costs and the impossibility of directly managing the massive flow of immigrants on Libyan soil, the EU decided to upgrade *Mare Nostrum* in 2014, now renamed *Triton* (originally denominated *Frontex Plus*). The upgrade failed too (this more costly operation has proved equally ineffective).[443]

Knowledgeable observers may have been surprised when the *coup* began, but the likely outcome was immediately clear to all—Gaddafi's victory or a new Somalia. Current developments, both internal and international, are probably best illustrated by a letter of 15 August 2015 issued by Ibrahim O. A. Dabbashi, the Permanent Representative of the internationally recognized transitional government of Libya, based in Tobruk. His superiors instructed him to protest against the international community's and Security Council's decision to prevent the Libyan army "from acquiring weapons and strengthening its capabilities" to face off an unwelcome guest—the Islamic State. Dabbashi's letter graphically underscores the international community's approach to Libya and the chaos the international community is determined to perpetuate. Dabbashi wrote,

> On instructions from my Government, I wish to draw the attention of the Security Council to the grave security and humanitarian situation in the city of Sirte, where the organization Islamic State has committed unprecedented crimes against the population.
>
> Since Wednesday, 12 August 2015, the organization Islamic State has been massacring the civilian population. More than 30 civilians have been killed and a large number have been injured in an effort to suppress the inhabitants' uprising against Islamic State. The latter has carried out a series of assassinations and human rights violations targeting civilians, particularly moderate religious leaders and political activists.
>
> The transitional Government of Libya expresses its outrage at the negative attitude of the international community and the Security

Council, which has looked on at the suffering of the civilian population of Sirte and other Libyan cities all the while preventing the Libyan army from acquiring weapons and strengthening its capabilities. It is also outraged that the necessary measures have not been taken in order to protect civilians in accordance with Security Council resolution 2214 (2015), particularly paragraphs 3 and 7.

I should be grateful if the present letter could be brought to the attention of the members of the Security Council and issued as a document of the Council.[444]

The international community formally recognizes this transitional Government of Libya. Why should it refuse to unfreeze the funds required by it to acquire arms to combat IS? A similar request had already been made in February 2015. The official reason was simple. The arms might fall into the wrong hands. In other words, the government based in Tobruk may have been internationally recognized but it was not to be helped in its struggle against a lethal threat. Why was this government recognized in the first place? The answer is disarmingly simple: in order to buy time. The decision to block the flow of arms to the Tobruk government, furthermore, was reached above all at the insistence of the United States.

The West ("the United States in particular") needed time to organize the next stage in Libya's disaggregation. The UNSC obliged.[445]

When militants looted Gadhafi's arm depots and state institutional authority largely dissolved following his fall, it left Libya awash with weapons and its army weak, fragmented and outgunned. The Tobruk government has subsequently been unable to quash an Islamist uprising that seized much of Benghazi, and it left an Islamic State outpost in Darnah largely untouched—with only hardline Islamist militias and local tribal groups remaining to root the militant group out from the coastal town earlier this year. Thus, the international community has continued to balk at Libya's request to lift the arms ban, even with Arab League support for Tobruk. The United States in particular has led efforts to keep the ban in place, citing the high likelihood of arms delivered to the government being stolen by, or, as in several cases in the past, distributed to various armed groups outside the government's control. Libya last made a concerted effort to lift the arms ban in February 2015, succeeding only in gaining the opportunity to have requests reviewed by a board on a case-by-case basis with the possibility of granting waivers.[446]

Given its record of lavish distribution of arms to all and sundry in Syria, the USA's warning that, in Libya, arms might reach "armed groups outside the government's control" is beneath contempt.

What of the EU? In her response to a written question from the EU parliament of 4 August 2015, the EU foreign affairs chief, Federica Mogherini, remarked,

The EU recalls that the UNSC, in its Resolution 2214 (March 2015), expressed grave concern about ISIL/Da'esh threat in Libya, and called upon the UN Sanctions Committee— established pursuant to resolution 1970 (2011)—to consider expeditiously requests for the transfer or supply of arms and related materiel to the Libyan Government for use by its official Armed Forces to combat ISIL/ Da'esh and its supporters.

Curiously, she added,

The EU supports the UN-led dialogue process, which is now in a decisive phase and should lead to the creation of a government of national accord. The EU stands ready to support this new government with all its instruments to address key concerns, including the fight against terrorism.

The EU Commission declared—in the sly, underhanded manner typical of such authorities—that until the self-declared government of Tripoli and the elected government of Tobruk shake hands, no one gets the arms they need. The EU's Mogherini, in other words, fully sustained the line laid down by the USA. The empty ballot box and the full one were placed on the scales and were found to be of equal weight. The USA's waiting game, apparently, is to allow Libya's chaos to mount until public opinion, at least in the West, clamors for foreign intervention. If the price for this arrangement includes the permanent presence of the IS on the Mediterranean coastline—a stone's throw from Sicily, positioned like a wedge splitting Libya down the middle— so be it. Like the USA, the European Commission believes that the immediate security concerns of certain EU member states, such as Italy, are of secondary importance to other (undeclared) longer-term clearly transatlantic geopolitical priorities.

There is little reason to believe that the violence shall cease in the near future.

In a cable released by WikiLeaks in 2009—referring to one of the US's two closest allies in the Near East—Clinton remarked:

> donors in Saudi Arabia constitute the most significant source of funding to Sunni terrorist groups worldwide. [...] more needs to be done since Saudi Arabia remains a critical financial support base for Al-Qa'ida, the Taliban, LeT, and other terrorist groups.[447]

In brief, Clinton, Obama's Secretary of State for nearly four years, claimed that America's key Arab partner funded the very same terrorist groups that America has allegedly been fighting since September 2001. "Donors," she said—leaving room for the Saudi government to adopt the 'plausible deniability' tactic. As noted above, JCS seems to have (belatedly) awakened to the United States' complacency or active participation and encouragement of such practices (as in the case of Stevens' mission). Despite the flood of warnings circulating internationally, the Department of State sees the chaos as being incomplete and therefore insists that the unelected jihadists of the Tripoli faction must participate in the formation of the new Libya.

Because of the poor performance of Islamist candidates during the July 2012 elections, a *coup* looked likely already in 2012.[448] The women's quota was dropped from the electoral law of January 2012 (polygamy was also introduced, with no consultation required from the husband with his first wife). The *coup* took place in 2014. The voter turnouts for the 2012 and 2014 elections were 60% and 18%, respectively. The Libyan masses, who loathe the armed groups, had clearly had enough. From now on, they will vote with their feet. The GNC's mandate expired in February 2014. It was extended until the end of 2014. Saif al-Islam Gaddafi's captors refused to turn him over to the ICC (Melinda Taylor, an ICC lawyer assigned to defend him, and three colleagues were also detained in Zintan and then released).

The terms of the Political and Administrative Isolation Law (a law designed to bar officials from the previous regime from participation in public life) have dominated much of Libya's political life since 2013. 'Isolation' of persons with ties with the previous Jamahiriyya is a highly divisive issue (the criteria for exclusion could impact as many as half a million people, severely limiting the career prospects and political and civil rights of a large portion of Libya's six million citizens, perhaps not permanently but 'only' for a decade). The measure may also lead to a skills deficit within the State administration.[450] It is highly reminiscent of the program of de-Ba'athification unleashed upon Iraq post "shock and awe" in 2003 by U.S. Ambassador Paul Bremer, responsible not just for the dissolution of the Iraqi army, but for the removal of senior administrators and ordinary members from public positions.[451] In any case, oil sales appear to have averted Libya's immediate meltdown:

> Oil production restarted quickly in the aftermath of the war and has allowed Libya to (...) fund reconstruction and pay salaries to many groups, including militias. With the armed takeover of many of Libya's oil facilities in the summer of 2013, however,

the stability of Libya's economy—including the ability of the government to continue to pay salaries indefinitely—was drawn into question (...) Notably, it [Libya] can foot much of the bill for its post-conflict needs— even if it currently lacks the administrative capacity to manage complex payments to foreign entities.[452]

The General National Congress (GNC) was besieged on 5 March 2013, forcing the legislative body to temporarily suspend its activities. The vehicle carrying the President of the GNC, Mohammed El-Magariaf, was attacked on the same day. Media outlets were assaulted. A siege on various ministries (including foreign affairs, the interior and justice) lasted two weeks (April-May 2013). The tensions flared because the government wished to suspend payments to armed groups. Equally disconcertingly (for these militias), the government wished also to administer Libya's prisons directly (i.e. without the 'assistance' of former rebel groups).

The Amazigh, Touareg and Tebu ethnic groups felt their interests were underrepresented in the draft of Libya's new constitution. The Transitional Council of Barqa, representing the pro-federalists of the east, unilaterally declared eastern Libya a federal region (1 June 2013). Clashes took place in March-April 2013 between the Mashashiya and Guntrar tribes. Many of Libya's oil facilities were sequestered that summer. The UN Security Council's report S/2013/516 documented the situation:

20. Following a series of incidents involving kidnapping, armed robberies and other criminal activity, the General National Congress adopted on 20 March a Decision,

instructing the Ministries of Defence and the Interior to remove from the capital all "illegitimate armed formations", and ensure transfer to the army of all illegal arms and military equipment in the city. Notwithstanding broad public support for the decision, its implementation has proven to be quite difficult, partly owing to the conflicting political and regional agendas on the part of the various brigades.

21. As tensions grew between rival revolutionary units in Tripoli, major clashes erupted on 26 June between Zintan brigades affiliated with the Ministry of Defence and others affiliated with Tripoli's Supreme Security Committee. The two-day clashes left at least 10 dead, and on 27 June, the Minister of Defence, Mohammad al-Bargathi, was dismissed. The restoration of a fragile calm to the city's streets was interrupted by the remote detonation of four car bombs on 16 July.

22. A tribal gathering in Zintan issued a statement strongly criticizing the General National Congress, the Government and political parties for the continued failure to build an effective army and police force. On the opposing side, a number of local councils convened in Tripoli and condemned the actions of those military groups which they perceived as threatening the capital's peace and stability. Amid objections from a number of General National Congress members, on 27 July General National Congress President

Abu Sahmain assigned a coalition of revolutionary brigades the task of protecting Tripoli, citing the inability of the army and the police to do so. Following a decision by the General National Congress on 5 August authorizing the President to take urgent measures to uphold security in all parts of the country, Libya Shield units from the central and western parts of the country began deploying in Tripoli on 8 August as part of an emergency plan to secure the city.

Eastern Libya

23. Benghazi and other parts of eastern Libya witnessed mounting opposition to the revolutionary brigades, particularly those formations referred to as Libya Shields, which are comprised largely of revolutionary units falling under the operational control of the Chief of General Staff of the Libyan army. Political differences regarding their long-term status precipitated a fatal clash on 8 June, when a demonstration outside the barracks of one such Libya Shield brigade deteriorated into an exchange of fire between brigade members and protestors, with some 30 dead.

24. Responding swiftly to the violence in Benghazi, on 9 June the General National Congress passed Decision 53, in which it called on the Prime Minister to present a proposal for the integration of armed brigades into the military and on the judiciary to conduct an investigation into the incident. In the wake of that decision, the General

National Congress accepted the resignation of the Chief of General Staff of the Army. Simultaneously, the Ministry of Defence called on military units in Benghazi to assume control of the barracks belonging to the four Libya Shield components stationed in the city. Although the deployment of Special Forces units from the military throughout Benghazi was welcomed by the city's population, and appeared to go some way towards meeting their demand for the army to be deployed, the move did not fully address the central issue of the Libya Shield brigades and their future.

25. In what appeared to be a related incident, on 15 June unidentified armed elements attacked the police force at the National Security Directorate in Benghazi. They subsequently engaged nearby military units, including from the Special Forces, leading to the death of several soldiers.

26. The tense security situation in Benghazi continued to evolve amid a discernible campaign of assassinations targeting members of the security forces in eastern Libya. Several current and former security officials were killed in Benghazi and Derna by unidentified elements. Similarly, police installations in Benghazi and Derna continued to come under attack.

27. The assassination on 26 July of prominent activist Abdelsalam al-Mesmari, the highest-profile political killing since the revolution, triggered a wave of protest demonstrations in Benghazi, Tripoli and other cities, in a

number of cases accompanied by attacks on the offices of political parties.

Southern Libya

28. The security situation in the south remained mostly fragile despite efforts by the Government to assume greater control over its southern border areas and smuggling routes. The reporting period witnessed a spate of security incidents, including armed attacks on 30 March on the security directorate in Sabha and a military base in the region; and three car bombs in downtown Sabha on 26 June, resulting in four deaths and many others wounded.

29. The population in the south has expressed fears, based on unverified information or unconfirmed reports, regarding the infiltration into the south of members of extremist armed groups coming from, or through, neighbouring countries.[453]

Other explosive situations monitored by the UNSC include the abduction of Prime Minister Ali Zeidan for several hours in Tripoli on 10 October 2013.

Mass demonstrations took place in Tripoli, Benghazi and Derna against both "the political process" and the so-called revolutionary brigades. A car bomb exploded outside the French Embassy in 2013 in what was believed to be a reprisal against French intervention in Mali (two guards were injured and the building was destroyed). On 15 November 2013, protesters marched on compounds in Tripoli held by revolutionary brigades from Misrata with 46 people killed and 516 injured. Faced with considerable public pressure, the Misrata and other brigades had to leave Tripoli. There was also a wave of anti-brigade protests in Benghazi, calling for a new police force and army. The protests were occasioned by the insecurity of the previous few weeks (assassinations and abductions of security and State officials in both Benghazi and Derna).

> The authorities appointed a military commander for Benghazi charged with the task of restoring stability to the city and its surrounding areas, followed by a large-scale deployment of Libyan army units (...) On 18 November, Benghazi's military commander survived an assassination attempt (...) Heavy fighting erupted in Benghazi on 25 November between special-forces units and the Ansar Al-Sharia brigades.[454]

The Jordanian ambassador was abducted in April 2014. He was then released in exchange for a Libyan prisoner detained in Jordan since 2007 on a charge of terrorism. A further cause for concern is Libya's stockpile of yellowcake (a product of uranium ore milling). The UN had been informed that 6,400 barrels "are stored in a non-functioning former military facility close to Sabha, in the South. They are under the control of a Libyan army battalion".[455] Economically speaking, of course, Libya's prospects remain grim. Alan Kuperman noted in 2014 that Libya was producing "one sixth as much oil" as it produced before the troubles began.[456] A major problem arose when oil export terminals in eastern Libya were blockaded by pro-federalist (or secessionist) militias (August 2013).

The United States captured the alleged terrorist, Nazih al-Regaei, also known as Abu-Anas al-Libi, in Tripoli and transferred him to New York where he was detained for his alleged involvement in the 1998 Embassy bombings in East Africa. Most of Libya's political leaders considered this unilateral initiative an affront to Libyan sovereignty. In late 2013, protesters in Benghazi opposing the presence of armed groups forced the Ansar al-Sharia brigade to abandon its headquarters in Benghazi. Government and security premises and protesters were then attacked. In early 2014,

> The absence of an agreed strategy and lack of a clear division of national security responsibilities between the President of the General National Congress, the Prime Minister, the General National Congress security committees and the executive ministries continue to impede the direction and coordination of security sector reform in Libya. The continuing absence of a comprehensive national security architecture has meant that individual efforts by ministries or other agencies has been sporadic, dispersed and poorly resourced.[457]

In early 2014, violence and lawlessness were on the increase nationwide—as will happen anywhere around the world in the absence of, to phrase it euphemistically, "an agreed strategy and lack of a clear division of national security responsibilities". In this case, the situation was complicated by the presence of increasing numbers of IS militants. A report published by the *Mirror* newspaper details the manner in which the Libyan government, unable to rule over the land with its regular forces, hires militias (both Islamist and anti-Islamist) to ensure security.[458] Post-coup Libya has spawned about 1,700 armed groups, some large and others, of course, microscopic (to a great extent through government funding).

The Islamist group, the Ansar al-Sharia brigade declared 300 men in 2014; its linkages have fluctuated, including to Al-Qaʻida and then to Islamic State. Others have reckoned it could count on 5,000. Confusingly, two militias in Libya were named the Libyan National Army.

The peak in violent deaths (since 2011) was officially recorded in July 2014 (estimated at 469). Tripoli International Airport was destroyed together with a number of civilian airliners.

These are just some of the impressive achievements of Libya's post-coup élite! This élite is no doubt also proud of the fact that, by 2015, "Anywhere between one and two million Libyans have fled out of a population of six million".[459]

4

THE SHIPPING NEWS
AND THE BODY COUNT

Libya, with a land surface area equivalent to six times that of Italy, has a population of about six million.[460] Many thousands of Asians and sub-Saharan Africans pass through every year on their way to Europe. In 2008, before the signing of the Treaty of Friendship, Partnership and Cooperation between Libya and Italy, it was estimated that 37,000 boat people came to Italy. After the treaty was signed, the figure fell to 9,600 and 4,400 in 2009 and 2010, respectively.[461]

The post-Gaddafi era brought with it a boom in the migrants trade and the proliferation of Islamist groups backed by Qatar and Turkey (these groups then decided to take over the sector). Qatar turned southern Libya over to Abdel Wahab Qaid, also known as Abu Idris al-Libi. Six months after Gaddafi's death, Doha's emissaries gave him 100,000 euros and a fleet of pickup trucks. A veteran of the Libyan Islamic Fighting Group (LIFG), he was a top 'revolutionary' commander. LIFG merged into Al-Qa'ida in 2007. Born in 1968 and a former student of the University of Cyrenaica, Qaid fought in Afghanistan. He also founded LIFG in Pakistan and Tunisia.[462] He was arrested shortly after returning to Libya in 1995. His death sentence suspended, he was jailed for life, and then released on 16 February 2011. Interestingly, his elder brother, Mohammed Hassan Qaid, an Afghanistan veteran of the late 1980s, had been captured by the Americans. Mohammed Hassan Qaid 'escaped' from jail at the Bagram airbase in Afghanistan in July 2005. He then called himself Abu Yahya al-Libi and became one of Al-Qa'ida top commanders.[463] On his release in 2011, Abdel Wahab Qaid was ready to return to the battlefield (with the full blessing, by the way, of the people who were about to kill his brother). In 2012, Mohammed Hassan Qaid—who had risen to the post of Al-Qa'ida's deputy leader—died following an American drone attack in Pakistan. Thanks to the generosity of Qatar—an ally of the elder Qaid brother's assassins— Abdel Wahab ruled over the drug, arms and migrants dealers of southern Libya, including Tebu and Touareg operators, active along the more than 1,800 kilometres of the borders between Sudan, Chad, Niger and Libya.

While Gaddafi had been able to control the Touaregs, the post-2011 Touaregs embraced the Islamist agenda and took part in the civil war in Mali (using arms plundered in Libya). Human trafficking was one of Libya's growth industries, so Qaid got himself elected to Libya's National Congress, with the backing of the Muslim Brotherhood. As a congressman he founded the al-Wafa Bloc (*al-Wafa li dimaa Al-Shuhadaa*) by means of which he hoped to unite all the militias that had contributed to Gaddafi's downfall. In 2012 and 2013 he set out to seize control of the human trafficking trade on behalf of his Islamist allies (this trade had been managed, until then, only by Tebu tribes).[464]

While the Islamists and their allies, Touareg groups, engaged in a violent struggle against the Tebu tribes, the migrants continued to flow in. Inexhaustible supplies of 'raw material' for this highly profitable trade could be procured. The 'production chain' was unified. The 'goods' were to be shipped to ports under the control of the Islamists, the Muslim Brotherhood, and, ultimately, Turkey and Qatar. A key figure in this business, identified by the Libyan authorities in February 2014, is Ahmad Hasnawi (a militiaman close to Qaid). Hasnawi and his men then began to route the migrants from Sudan and Chad to Kufra, at the expense of Ghat, located in the west of the country.[465] The business was 'industrialized', hence the prices were lowered and better 'services' could be provided. Larger and safer boats were made available, for example, in the Benghazi or Sirte areas. The Italian Ministry of the Interior was kept fully informed of these developments through functionaries sent to Tripoli to monitor the situation.[466]

This more 'modern' approach to human trafficking paid off. In 2012, 1,267 migrants disembarked in Italy. Following reorganization by Wahab Qaid and his partners, the figure grew to 42,925, to be eclipsed in 2014 and 2015 with a reported average 'turnover' of 50,000 new 'passengers' every six months. The figures provided by *The Economist* and the *Daily Mail*, cited above, are much higher.

Following the very low (18%) voter turnout, the losing faction in the 2014 election, the Muslim Brotherhood-backed Libya Dawn movement, occupied the capital. The GNC became the New General National Congress. The vast majority of the elected congressmen supported the elected government, which moved to Tobruk. Islamists from the Shura Council of Benghazi Revolutionaries took control of Benghazi. Benghazi was then seized back by the Libyan National Army. In the meantime IS took over Derna.

5

MONEY MATTERS

The rush to establish Libya's new central bank (CBL) in 2011, while the barricades were still up and the blood was still flowing, is certainly worthy of note.[467] Actually, two rival central banks were founded and battles also raged over access to the country's sovereign fund, the Libyan Investment Authority (LIA).

The LIA is worth at least 100 billion dollars (full accounts are unavailable). The portfolio was revealed in 2011 by the French-Tunisian billionaire, Tarak Ben Ammar. During the 'revolution', it was discovered that one of Tarak Ben Ammar's companies, based in Malta, had dealings with the LIA and with Trefinance. Trefinance is a Luxembourg company controlled by the Italian holding company, Fininvest, run by Silvio Berlusconi's family. Libya's enormous funds were frozen by international order and were then unfrozen. The unfreezing was apparently a fairly safe move, since no one knows exactly who has the right to access these unfrozen assets.

LIA has a 3.2% share in Pearson (the group owning the *Financial Times* and a co-owner of *The Economist*). It holds shares in US defense suppliers such as Halliburton, and the oil giants, Chevron and Exxon Mobil, not to mention the French aerospace corporation, Lagardère, various top-ranking Italian groups such as Italy's flagship hydrocarbon energy company, ENI (probably 1%), Unicredit (Libya's central bank holds 2.92%, as fifth largest shareholder), and Finmeccanica (Finmeccanica is a defense supplier controlled by the Ministry of the Treasury in Rome, with a LIA shareholding of 2.01%). Libya had also invested in smaller companies such as the Milanese technology and communications concern, Retelit (Libya's postal and telecom company holds a 14.8% share, as the major shareholder). Libya's share in the Juventus football team has fallen to 2%.

The assets of Libya's central bank (CBL) are even greater than LIA's and are far more liquid. These assets include bank accounts totaling about 100 billion dollars, in Italy, Europe and America (e.g. Unicredit, Intesa Sanpaolo, BNP Paribas, Société Générale, Credit Agricole, HSBC, Barclays, Lloyd and Bank of New York Mellon).[468] Controversy over the status of the CBL (or the two 'CBLs' held by the respective rival 'governments') has greatly hampered Libya's oil export trade. Following the financial storm of 2008, France, Great Britain and the United States (not to mention Italy...) were (and are) keen to recapitalize. Libya's sovereign funds, her gold, and the business openings for post-war reconstruction could represent valued assets for a financially troubled West. According to Nourredine Leghliel, an Algerian stock market analyst residing in Sweden, financial pillage was why the war on Libya came about in the first place. Among the various expert observers, Leghliel was one of the first to raise this elephant in the room. The 200 billion dollars—mentioned only fleetingly or behind closed doors—consisted of assets 'frozen' by European banking interests.[469] The excuse for freezing the funds was that the money was in some way held by Gaddafi's family itself. According to Leghliel, this was merely a pretext for robbery.[470] Of what? Libya's money? Her sovereign fund shareholdings? Her gold? All three? Or, precisely by these means, had the West aimed at depriving Libya of her most valuable resource—her financial sovereignty?

Ellen Brown (a noted American financial reform activist) considers the question of nationalized central banks (such as Libya's) and draws our attention to an article by Erica Encina posted on *Market Oracle*. Encina writes,

> One seldom mentioned fact by western politicians and media pundits: the Central Bank of Libya is 100% State Owned ... Currently, the Libyan government creates its own money, the Libyan Dinar, through the facilities of its own central bank. Few can argue that Libya is a sovereign nation with its own great resources, able to sustain its own economic destiny. One major problem for globalist banking cartels is that in order to do business with Libya, they must go through the Libyan Central Bank and its national currency, a place where they have absolutely zero dominion or power-broking ability. Hence, taking down the Central Bank of Libya (CBL) may not appear in the speeches of Obama, Cameron and Sarkozy but this is certainly at the top of the globalist agenda for absorbing Libya into its hive of compliant nations.

Ellen Brown adds,

> Libya not only has oil. According to the International Monetary Fund (IMF), its central bank has nearly 144 tonnes of gold in its vaults. With that sort of asset base,

who needs the BIS [Bank for International Settlements], the IMF and their rules?

She also cites the renowned economic leader-writer, Henry Liu.

> BIS regulations serve only the single purpose of strengthening the international private banking system, even at the peril of national economies. The BIS does to national banking systems what the IMF has done to national monetary regimes. National economies under financial globalization no longer serve national interests. (...) FDI [foreign direct investment] denominated in foreign currencies, mostly dollars, has condemned many national economies into unbalanced development toward export, merely to make dollar-denominated interest payments to FDI, with little net benefit to the domestic economies.

Brown then considers the costs of private, as opposed to public, central banking. She debunks the mainstream theory that State central banking leads inevitably to uncontrollable inflation.

> The presumption of the rule against borrowing from the government's own central bank is that this will be inflationary, while borrowing existing money from foreign banks or the IMF will not. But all banks actually create the money they lend on their books, whether publicly owned or privately owned. Most new money today comes from bank loans.

Borrowing it from the government's own central bank has the advantage that the loan is effectively interest-free. Eliminating interest has been shown to reduce the cost of public projects by an average of 50%.[471]

In exchange for large reductions in taxation levels thanks to greatly lowered costs of public works, one might be prepared to tolerate a little inflation anyway! That said, the inflation rate for Libya in 2010 was on a par with the area as a whole (2-5%)—i.e. more or less as in Algeria and Tunisia (and lower than in Egypt or Morocco).

6

DIPLOMACY
AND SCIMITARS

At least one UN diplomat personally profited economically from the chaos and from the prospects of a Libyan Caliphate.

After a number of months of fruitless negotiations, in early October 2015, UN mediator, Bernardino León (rather prematurely) announced the birth of a unity government.[472] The idea was to build a bridge between the two 'capital cities' and 'governments' (the Islamist and secular forces based in Tripoli and Tobruk, respectively), and thus enable a single front that could request international aid against both ISIS and the immigrant traffickers. León's motives, however, were apparently less transparent and noble than one might hope from a UN envoy. One authoritative observer notes that "There has been complete silence—no reaction at all, let alone an official investigation—to leaked emails showing that Bernardino Leon [sic] was secretly advancing the interests of his future employers the UAE while working as UN special envoy (....). A letter of complaint from one of the parliaments, the General National Congress, was ignored. The news was buried on the day of the Paris attacks. A rival peace initiative in Tunis was also ignored. But 'Leongate' did not stop the plan the former envoy was working on. It was pushed ahead regardless".[473] Officially, León's mission was to facilitate the creation of a government that would be recognized by the rival factions. Instead, he covertly pushed the agenda of the UAE as it shipped weapons to Libya in violation of the UN arms embargo.[474]

None of the outstanding problems seem to have been resolved. Recent UN-brokered agreements (Skirhat, Morocco) failed to provide for talks with key armed groups, and aroused considerable anger among all the parties involved:

> Based on the signatures of individual members of the two rival parliaments in Tobruk and Tripoli, the UN appears to have gone over the heads of both bodies. The anger was such that it forced the rival leaders of the two institutions, the Western-backed HOR in Tobruk and the Tripoli-based GNC to meet each other for the first time in Malta. They jointly rejected the UN push to sign the deal. 'We came here to announce to the world that we are able to solve our problems ourselves with the help of the international community, but we will not accept foreign intervention against the will of the Libyan people,' said GNC President Nouri Abusahmain.

In attempting to decipher the situation, a well-qualified observer, David Hearst—former chief foreign leader writer of *The Guardian*—pointed to the Mediterranean Dialogues conference in Rome, organized by the Italian government (10-12 December 2015). He was struck by the warning made there by Alison Pargeter, the North Africa expert at the Royal United Services Institute (RUSI).[475] Pargeter downplayed the role of Libya as "a fall-back position for

IS". IS presence in Libya is countered, she claimed, by "the role of the tribes, the presence of other armed groups and the inherent Libyan suspicion of outsiders". Pargeter warned the international community against conflating IS with rival jihadi Libyan groups (Benghazi Revolutionary Shura Council, Derna Mujaheddin Shura Council, Ajdabiya Revolutionary Shura Council). These groups, she claimed, had distanced themselves from IS. In other words, she took up the line of 'if you can't beat'em, join'em':

> Perhaps we have to accept that some of these elements cannot be beaten militarily and like it or not, they are going to have to be part of the solution for Libya, and they are an uncomfortable part of the jigsaw puzzle that needs to be dealt with if Libya is ever to achieve peace.

Russia Today reported that Britain, France and Italy have already moved against IS in Libya (early January 2016).[476] Such an outcome, says Hearst,

> is what Egypt and the UAE have been pushing for ever since the military coup in Cairo two years ago (…) Before bombing can start, Britain and France need to be invited to intervene by Libya itself. That cannot happen unless there is a nominal government of national unity. It does not have to meet. It simply has to exist as a virtual entity. Here then lies the answer to the rush to create a national unity government. Its first act would not be to start a process of national reconciliation. Nor indeed embark on the quest for national

security. It would be to rubber stamp another foreign intervention. Interventions form a perfect circle—from Libya to Mali to Iraq, to Syria and now back to Libya. Each intervention provides the pretext for another. And none of them end".[477]

The UN intended to go over the heads of both parliaments. But 'the best-laid plans of mice and men go often askew'. Martin Kobler—the UN envoy who had in the meantime replaced the disgraced León—postponed the signing and flew to the al-Marj military installation (near Tobruk) where he met General Khalifa Haftar, eastern Libya's strongman, who opposed talks at this stage. The presidents of the two parliaments rejected the UN-brokered agreement. As noted above, Nuri Abu Sahmain (from the Tripoli Congress, GNC) and Aguila Saleh (from the HOR parliament in Tobruk) unexpectedly agreed to meet in Malta.

New fighting ended the truce, with pitched battles in the area of Tripoli airport. At Ajdabiya, a key oil node to the east of Sirte, the army loyal to Tobruk announced that it was ready to conduct a vast anti-ISIS offensive. In Benghazi, Libyan fighter jets conducted five raids against the positions of jihadi groups.

The Shkirat agreement, with so much occurring on the ground, is the fruit of the imagination of the UN and of the other powers that have brought Libya to its knees. The agreement lacks the support of the two key clans of Libya operating out of Tripoli and Tobruk, not to mention (a mere detail) all the country's militias. The personage that the 'international community' is banking on as PM is a certain Serraj Faiez, an unknown who now heads the presidential council. Meanwhile, it was believed he would be "unable to set foot in or survive his stay in Tripoli for more than a few days.[478]

While "[a] lone, he would be unable to set foot in or survive his stay in Tripoli for more than a few days",[480] this was hardly an impediment to his appointment. He was installed not to govern Libya but to request "international protection" in Libya's name. If he does so, the UNSC might quickly rubber stamp the order for foreign-armed intervention. The 'international community' would like to see intervention under Italian leadership (despite the fact that Italy has been one of the great losers in this affair from the very start).

If an Italian-led attack takes place, groups such as the Benghazi Revolutionary Shura Council, Derna Mujaheddin Shura Council and Ajdabiya Revolutionary Shura Council may find, despite past antagonisms, that they can make common cause with IS and therefore strengthen the latter considerably. One wonders whether Egypt has taken this eventuality into consideration, since such an Islamist union could in turn strengthen the hand of the ousted Muslim Brotherhood in Egypt itself (which after its electoral victory in 2012, was unseated by Abdul Fatah al-Sisi).[479] The Islamist fighters in Syria have frequently re-grouped over recent months, many joining ISIS.

Might Libya—Fezzan, Tripolitania and Cyrenaica—go down the same "deconstruction" road as the foes of the current Syrian state, who have frequently expressed a desire to see that country "deconstructed" into a number of quasi-State entities, each hosting its own predominant ethnic or religious group, and led by a militia that knows how to be strong with the weak... and weak with the strong?[480] If so, the scenario will play out over a number of years. Many of those jostling for power today shall no doubt be rapidly eclipsed by upcoming developments, absorbed into larger groupings, or wiped out.

The tears and blood still flow copiously.[481] Many

Libyans have fled the country. They may decide to stay away for the duration of these struggles. If they return to Libya some years from now, whatever the outcome, they probably won't recognize the place as their own.

Will Libya implode yet further?

Broadly speaking, Libya, the Sahara Desert and the Sahel—if not the entire continent—are all at stake.

ENDNOTES

1   For sources and diplomatic reports, see *The Middle East and North Africa in World Politics* (2 vol.) ed. J. C. Hurewitz (New Haven & London: Yale University Press, 1975-1979), vol. I, pp. 552-553.

2   F. S. Nitti, *Scritti politici* (16 vol.) (Roma-Bari: Laterza, 1959-1980), vol. I, p. 73.

3   The name Libya is a derivation from *Libu*, a most ancient Berber tribe known even to the Greeks. The Greeks occasionally used the name "Libya" to refer to the continent we now call Africa. At the time of the Arab incursions into North Africa in the seventh century, the name, Libya, had fallen practically into disuse. In the early twentieth century, it was revived by the Italian geographer, Federico Minutilli (1846-1906), and led Italy's Prime Minister, Giovanni Giolitti, to designate the two Ottoman provinces of Cyrenaica and Tripolitania as "Libia".

4   There can be no doubt that the most determined opposition to the Libyan adventure came from Gaetano Salvemini. Firstly in Prezzolini's *La Voce* and then in *l'Unità* (the weekly that Salvemini himself founded and edited as from December 1911), he was unrelenting in his campaign against the "libicisti" and their pro intervention campaign.

5   During the late afternoon of 29 September 1911, the *Agenzia Stefani* news agency issued the following official announcement: "Since the Ottoman government has not acceded to the demands contained in the Italian ultimatum, as of 14:30, today, 29 September 1911, Italy and Turkey are at war".

6   Cf, G. Candeloro, *Storia dell'Italia Moderna* (11 vol.), *La crisi di fine secolo e l'età giolittiana: 1896-1914* (Milano: Feltrinelli, 1956-1986, vol. VII), p. 318.

7   G. Salvemini, *La politica estera dell'Italia (1871-1914)* (Firenze:

Barbèra, 1944), p. 178.

8   The most spectacular initiatives saw Mussolini in action on his 'home beat'. He was a native of the Forlì area, where he and others sabotaged the Forlì-Meldola tram line and the railway and telegraph lines between Forlì and Forlimpopoli. The activists also attempted to prevent servicemen from reaching the recruiting station. Leading the actions of the anti-colonialist protest movement, alongside young Mussolini, we find others such as Pietro Nenni, a member of the Republican Party at that time, who was later to become a leader of the Socialist Party. The future *Duce* was arrested on 14 October. Nenni, too, was tried and jailed for sabotage and sent to the local castle prison, Rocca di Forlì. They shared the same cell. On his release (March 1912), Mussolini was no longer just a provincial agitator. He had set his sights on conquering the socialist congress in Reggio Emilia (7-10 July 1912) and on the post of editor in chief of the socialist newspaper, *Avanti!*.

9   B. Mussolini, *Lo sciopero generale di protesta contro l'impresa di Tripoli*, in *La Lotta di Classe*, no. 88, 30 September 1911, in Mussolini, *Opera Omnia*, ed. E. and D. Susmel, (44 vol.) (Firenze-Roma: La Fenice-Volpe 1951-1980, vol. IV), pp. 72-73.

10   A. O. Olivetti, *Sindacalismo e nazionalismo*, in *Pagine Libere*, 15 February 1911.

11   A. Carteny, *Il 1911 e l'intverento italiano in Libia: dalla relazione breve dello Stato Maggiore Esercito Italiano*, in A. Biagini (ed.), *C'era una volta la Libia* (Torino: Miraggi Edizioni, 2011), p. 23.

12   Cf. A. Del Boca, *Gli italiani in Libia*, (2 vol.) (Roma-Bari: Laterza 1968-1988), Vol. I, *Tripoli bel suol d'amore*, pp. 98, 126.

13   G. Pesenti, *Le guerre coloniali* (Bologna: Zanichelli, 1947), pp. 261-264.

14   E. E. Evans-Pritchard's *The Sanusi of Cyrenaica* (London-Oxford: Clarendon Press, 1949) is the classic study of the Sanusi brethren. Cf. N. Ziadeh, *Sanusiyah. A Study of a Revivalist Movement in Islam* (Leiden: Brill, 1958); K. S. Vikør, *Sufi and Scholar of the Desert Edge. Muhammad b. Ali al-Sanusi and his Brotherhood* (London: Hurst & Co., 1995).

15   The 'school' of followers of the religious teachings of the Arab theologian, Malik ibn Anas (711-795). The other Sunni 'schools' are the *Hanafi* school—of the Arab-Persian theologian, Abu Hanifa (699-765) –, the *Shafi'i* school—of the Palestinian-Egyptian theologian, Abū ʿAbdullāh Muhammad ibn Idrīs al-Shāfīʿī (767-820), and the *Hanbali* school—of the Arab theologian, Ahmad ibn Hanbal (780-855).

16   A. M. Hassanein Bey, *The Lost Oases* (London: Thornton Butterworth,

1925).

17 Wahhabism is a doctrine that came into being within the *Hanbali* 'school'. Founded in 1745, it was led by Muhammad ibn Abd al-Wahhab (1703-1792), an Arab sheikh of the Banu Tamim tribe, who was to ally himself with Muhammad bin Sau'd, also known as Ibn Saud (1710-1765), the progenitor of today's Saudi royal family. Wahhabism thus became, and is to this day, the official religious movement of Saudi Arabia.

18 Followers of Zaid ibn 'Ali (a Muslim religious reformer of the eighth century, a great grandson of al-Husayn, a son of the fourth Caliph 'Ali, and hence related to the Prophet). These followers belong to one of the most important currents among the *Shi'ite*. The affiliates to this brotherhood still possess centers of political and religious power in the highlands to the south of the Caspian Sea, and in Yemen and certain parts of Africa.

19 This is the "effort" or "diligence", originally of the first *'ulama* (theologists), of the first *Mufti* (officers capable of providing definitive responses in regard to disputes; they divulge the truth by means of a juridical reply), and of the first *Fuqaha* (jurists) among the Muslims. The effort is exerted to interpret as objectively as possible the founding texts of Islam and to derive from these texts the *Shar'ia* (Muslim law). This "effort" or "diligence" is directed solely toward informing the faithful of that which is *lawful, unlawful* or *forbidden* in their conduct.

20 Cf. E. De Agostini, *Le popolazioni della Cirenaica. Notizie etniche e storiche raccolte dal Colonello Enrico De Agostini*, (2 vol.) (Bengasi: Azienda tipo-litografica della Scuola d'arti e mestieri, 1922-1923).

21 *Taleb* or *t'aleb* is Arabic for "student" (the plural is *tolba*). These *tolba* are frequently referred to by Westerners as "Taliban", a term propagated by the mass media as equivalent to 'warrior' (against whom a "war for peace" has been raging in Afghanistan for the last 14 years).

22 Cf. A. B. Mariantoni, *Libia: evviva i «buoni»!*, in *Civium Libertas*, 21 March 2011.

23 E. d'Armesano, *In Libia. Storia di una conquista* (Buenos Aires: Maucci, 1912), p. 65.

24 The real emergency of those early days was a cholera epidemic. During the first three months following the landing, the cholera took the lives of "7 officers and 369 soldiers, while 34 officers and 432 soldiers died in combat. The epidemic peaked in December" (A. Del Boca, *Gli italiani in Libia*, (2 vol.) (Roma-Bari: Laterza 1968-1988), Vol. I, *Tripoli bel suol d'amore*, p. 106).

25 For a reconstruction of this battle (which for generations of Italians

represented a sort of tragedy of mythical proportions), see L. Del Fra, *Sciara Sciat: genocidio nell'oasi. L'esercito italiano a Tripoli* (Roma: Manifestolibri, 2011).

26   E. E. Evans-Pritchard, *The Sanusi of Cyrenaica* (London-Oxford: Clarendon Press, 1949), p. 110.

27   A. Del Boca, *Tripoli bel suol d'amore*, cit., p. 166.

28   J. Wright, *Libya: A Modern History* (Baltimore: The John Hopkins University Press, 1981), p. 28.

29   On this specific question, see F. Malgeri, *La guerra libica (1911-1912)* (Roma: Edizioni di Storia e Letteratura, 1970).

30   A. Del Boca, *Tripoli bel suol d'amore*, cit., p. 196.

31   Cf. M. A. Vitale, *L'Italia in Africa*, in *L'opera dell'Esercito*, (3 vol.) (Roma: Istituto Poligrafico dello Stato, 1960-1964, vol. III), pp. 62-68.

32   Cf. L. S. Anderson, *The State and Social Transformation in Tunisia and Libya, 1830-1980* (Princeton: Princeton University Press, 1986), pp. 117-121.

33   E. E. Evans-Pritchard, *The Sanusi of Cyrenaica*, cit. p. 122. On 29 April 1990, Gaddafi announced the publication of a small anthology of his short stories to celebrate the 75th anniversary of the destruction of Miani's column, an action in which Gaddafi's own father played a part. [An edition of the anthology, *Escape to Hell and Other Stories*, was published in English by Hushion House in 1998—*translator's note*].

34   D. Vandewalle, *A History of Modern Libya* (Cambridge, New York: Cambridge University Press, 2012; second edition), p. 27.

35   Cf. A. Pelt, *Libyan Independence and the United Nations. A Case of Planned Decolonization* (New Haven: Yale University Press, 1970), pp. 16-24. The Sanusi brotherhood was disbanded in 1930 and its assets were seized. The Sanusi resistance leader, 'Omar Al-Mukhtar, was captured and executed in 1931.

36   The U-turn was formalised in Law no. 1013 of 26 June 1927. This law established the new political, administrative and judicial order of Tripoli and Cyrenaica. The new arrangement removed the notion of equality between, on the one hand, the Italian and Libyan nationality, and, on the other, Italian nationality *tout court*. Italian and Libyan nationality was "sharply distinct from, and, in terms of juridical content, inferior to Italian nationality", G. Mondaini, *La legislazione coloniale italiana nel suo sviluppo storico e nel suo stato attuale, 1881-1940*, (2 vol.) (Milano; ISPI, 1941, Vol. II), p. 644.

37   Constitution of the Italian colony of Libya was declared by Law no. 2012 of 3 December 1934.

38   A member of the pro-Nitti camp [See Part I, Chapter 1—*translator's note*]

39   Cf. R. H. McGuirk, *The Sanusi's Little War* (London: Arabian Publisher, 2007).

40   A. Del Boca, *Gli italiani in Libia, Gli italiani in Libia*, (2 vol.) (Roma-Bari: Laterza 1968-1988), Vol. II, *Dal Fascismo e Gheddafi*, p. 67.

41   Colonel Malta's detailed report, drawn up once the Cyrenaica operation had been completed, is a document of considerable interest to students of twentieth-century anti-guerrilla techniques. Excerpts of this unpublished work are to be found in G. Breccia, *Controguerriglia in Cirenica. 1931: come catturammo Omar al-Mukhtar*, in "Quaderni Speciali di *Limes*", no. 2, April 2011, pp. 136-144.

42   The execution took place in public, at Soluch. Over the following days, the entire Arab press reported that 'Omar al-Mukhtar's last words were, "And after my death, the rebellion against iniquity shall continue" ("El Alam", 5 December 1931). A star-packed epic action movie by Syrian-American director Mustafa al-'Aqqad, *Lion of the Desert* (1981), tells the story of 'Omar al-Mukhtar and the Libyan resistance from the Arab point of view.

43   Cf. E. Salerno, *Genocidio in Libia. Le atrocità mascoste dell'avventura italiana (1911-1931)* (Roma: Manifestolibri, 2005). Between 1911 and 1931, the population of Cyrenaica, where Italy's repressive actions were particularly brutal, fell from 198,000 to about 138,000. Egypt saw the arrival of 20,000 Libyan refugees. 40,000 Libyans perished as a result of the war and deportation, or while in prison camps. See G. Rochat, *La repressione della resistenza in Cirenaica*, in the collective work, *Omar al-Mukhtar e la riconquista fascista della Libia* (Milano: Marzorati, 1981), p. 161.

44   Cf. L. Federzoni. *A.O. Un posto al sole* (Bologna, Zanichelli, 1936) [The acronym A.O. stands for *Africa Orientale—translator's note*]; E. De Bono, *Le mie idee sulla colonizzazione*, in "L'Oltremare", no. 8, 1928, pp. 292-298; L. Bongiovanni, *Demografia, metodo e credito*, in "L'Oltremare", no. 3, 1928, pp. 102-105.

45   Balbo's Libya policies received the backing of the government in the form of a significant measure—Law no. 2012 of 3 December 1934. Article 1 reads, "Tripolitania and Cyernaica make up a single Colony denominated Libya. The colony is endowed with legal personality and is ruled over and represented by a Governor General. The seat of government is in Tripoli".

46   R. Reali, *Il mito della «quarta sponda» e il dibattito sulla conquista*, in A. Biagini (ed.), *C'era una volta la Libia* (Torino: Miraggi Edizioni, 2011), pp. 50-51.

47   Cf. C. Segrè, *Italo Balbo: una vita fascista* (Bologna: Il Mulino, 1988).

48   I. Balbo, *La colonizzazione in Libia*, in the review, "L'agricoltura coloniale", August 1939, p. 466.

49   C. Basilici, *L'armata del lavoro*, in the review, "Gli annali dell'Africa Italiana", no. 3-4, December 1938, p. 751.

50   For an in depth analysis of Balbo's colonial policy, cf. F. Cresti, *Non desiderare la terra d'altri. La colonizzazione italiana della Libia* (Roma: Carocci, 2011), pp. 159-226.

51   A. Del Boca, *Gli italiani in Libia*, cit., p. 275 [Del Boca is Italy's leading historian of Italy's Libyan policies and campaigns—*translator's note*].

52   [Badoglio became a prominent politician in Italy, whose name is associated with the flight of the King of Italy from Rome in 1943—*translator's note*].

53   The official history of the BMA is to be found in Lord Rennel of Rodd's *British Military Administration of Occupied Territories in Africa during the Years 1941-1947* (London: His Majesty's Stationery Office, 1948).

54   The French military administration had taken over Fezzan following the Italians' defeat and expulsion from Libya.

55   Cf. H. S. Villard, Libya. *The New Arab Kingdom of North Africa* (Ithaca: Cornell University Press, 1956).

56   The wording of the agreement is to be found in M. Khadduri, *Modern Libya. A Study in Political Development* (Baltimore: The John Hopkins Press, 1963), pp. 363-382.

57   D. Vandewalle, *A History of Modern Libya*, (Cambridge, New York: Cambridge University Press, 2012; second edition), p. 43.

58   B. Droz, *Storia della decolonizzazione nel XX secolo* (Milano: Bruno Mondadori, 2007), pp. 136-174 and 226-230.

59   A. Del Boca, *Gli italiani in Libia*, (2 vol.) (Roma-Bari: Laterza 1968-1988), p. 432.

60   Cf. A. Aruffo, *Gheddafi. Storia di una dittatura rivoluzionaria* (Roma: Castelvecchi, 2011), pp. 13-14.

61   *The New York Times*, 13 December 1959.

62   B. H. Higgins, *The Economic and Social Development of Libya* (New York: United Nations Technical Assistance Programme, 1953), pp. 62-71.

63   Cf. M. Ouannes, *Militaires, élites et modernisation dans la Libye contemporaine* (Paris: L'Harmattan, 2009), pp. 67-69.

64   Cf. R. Farley, *Planning for Development in Libya. The Exceptional Economy in the Developing World* (New York: Praeger, 1971), pp. 44-53.

65   On these political and economic developments, see S. Salaheddin

Hassan (Salaheddin Salem Hassan), *A New System for a New State. The Libyan Experiment in Statehood 1951-1969*, in *Modern and Contemporary Libya. Sources and Historiographies*, ed. A. Baldinetti (Roma: Istituto Italiano per l'Africa e l'Oriente, 2003); see also M. Cricco, *Il petrolio dei Senussi. Stati Uniti e Gran Bretagna in Libia dall'indipendenza a Gheddafi (1949-1973)* (Firenze: Polistampa, 2002), p. 88.

66   J. Bessis, *La Libia contemporanea* (Soveria Mannelli: Rubbettino, 1991), p. 99.

67   For an account of Libya's early days as an oil nation, see A. A. Q. Kubbah, *Libya, its oil industry and economic system* (Beirut: Rhani Press, 1964).

68   Cf. F. C. Waddams, *The Libyan Oil Industry* (Baltimore: The John Hopkins University Press, 1980), pp. 161-170. *AGIP* arrived in 1959, having received concession no. 82 from the Libyan government, in the south-eastern Sahara.

69   Cf. J. Gurney, *Libya. The Political Economy of Oil* (Oxford: Oxford University Press, 1996), p. 39.

70   Cf. R. De Felice, *Ebrei in un paese arabo* (Bologna: Il Mulino), 1978, pp. 41-42.

71   M. Khadduri, *Modern Libya. A Study in Political Development*, cit., p. 9.

72   J. Davis, *Libyan Politics. Tribe and Revolution* (Berkeley: University of California Press, 1987), p. 258.

73   D. Vandewalle, *A History of Modern Libya*, cit., Chapter 4.

74   Cf. M. Ben Halim, *Libya. The Years of Hope* (London: AAS Media Publishers, 1998), p. 328.

75   An analysis of the social origins of the young Free Officers is to be found in M. Cricco and F. Cresti, *Gheddafi, I volti del potere* (Roma: Carocci, 2011), pp. 37-39; cf. O. I. el-Fathali and M. Palmer, *Political Development and Social Change in Libya* (Lexington: Lexington Books, 1980).

76   G. Fasanella and R. Priore, *Intrigo internazionale* (Milano: Chiarelettere, 2011), pp. 32-33. Over a period of some thirty years, Priore handled some of the most important and delicate domestic and international cases that the Italian juridical system has ever been faced with.

77   C. Chianura, *L'Italia dietro il golpe in Tunisia*, in "La Repubblica", 10 October 1999. This *coup* scenario is described by Martini in his book, *Nome in codice: Ulisse* (Milano: Rizzoli, 1999). Martini's description of events is not exhaustive.

78   *Ibid.*

79   M. Cricco and F. Cresti, *Gheddafi, I volti del potere*, cit., p. 43.

80   A. Aruffo, *Gheddafi. Storia di una dittatura rivoluzionaria*, (Roma: Castelvecchi, 2011), p. 30.

81   Cf. R. First, *Libya. The Elusive Revolution* (Harmondsworth: Penguin, 1974), pp. 10-16.

82   H. Barrada, M. Kravetz and M. Whitaker, *Khadafi: «Je suis un opposant à l'échelon mondial»* (Lausanne: Favre, 1984, p. 86.

83   Originally made up of 28 members, then reduced to 6.

84   Cf. "Il Giornale di Tripoli", 15 November 1969. The decree in which the banks were Libya-ised and nationalised also prohibited use of the words *bank* and *banks*, immediately replaced by the Arab words, *Masraf* and *Masarif*.

85   Cf. J. A. Allan, *Libya. The Experience of Oil* (Boulder: Westview Press, 1981), pp. 170-184; M. G. Shukri, *The Pricing of Libyan Crude Oil* (La Valletta: Adams, 1975), pp. 163-188.

86   Cf. C. T. Rand, *Making Democracy Safe for Oil* (Boston: Little, Brown & Company, 1975).

87   *Address delivered by Colonel Mu'ammar al-Qadaffi in Tripoli on 4 Sha'ban 1389 = 16 October 1969*, in M. O. Ansell and I. al-Arif, *The Libyan Revolution. A Sourcebook of Legal and Historical Documents* (Stoughton, The Oleander Press, 1972), pp. 86-93.

88   Cf. M. Cricco and F. Cresti, *Gheddafi, I volti del potere*, cit., pp. 49-52. See also A. Varvelli, *L'Italia e l'ascesa di Gheddafi* (Milano: Baldini Castoldi Dalai, 2009), pp. 64-74.

89   M. Gheddafi, *Discorso del Presidente del Consiglio della Rivoluzione*, Tripoli 16 October 1969, in "Oriente Moderno", no. 9-10, September-October 1969, pp. 570-572.

90   Cit. in M. Bianco, *Gheddafi: messaggero del deserto* (Milano: Mursia, 1977), p. 143; A. E. Mayer, *In Search of Sacred Law. The Meandering Course of Qadhafi's Legal Policy*, in *Qadhafi's Libya, 1969 to 1994*, ed. D. Vandewalle (New York: St. Martin's Press, 1995), pp. 114-115.

91   On Gaddafi's ideas concerning Islam, and Islam's role in contemporary politics, cf. M. M. Ayoub, *Islam and The Third Universal Theory. The Religious Thought of Mu'ammar al-Qadhdhafi* (London: Kegan Paul International, 1987).

92   Gaddafi interview by D. Bartholoni, in "Le Monde", 13 December 1969; in this regard, see also the concise collection of Gaddafi's speeches, *Socialismo e tradizione* (Parma: Edizioni all'insegna del Veltro, 2011).

93   A. Del Boca, *Gli italiani in Libia*, (2 vol.) (Roma-Bari: Laterza 1968-1988), p. 467.

94   Cf. A. Hulerias, *Qadhafi's Comeback: Libya and Sub-Saharan Africa*

in the 1990s, in "African Affairs", no. 100, April 2001, pp. 5-25.

95   E. Santarelli, *Storia sociale del mondo contemporaneo* (Milano: Feltrinelli, 1982), p. 580.

96   D. Vandewalle, *A History of Modern Libya*, cit., Chapter 4.

97   Cf. A. Del Boca, *Gheddafi. Una sfida dal deserto* (Roma-Bari: Laterza, 2010), pp. 45-51; A. Varvelli, *L'Italia e l'ascesa di Gheddafi*, cit., pp. 97-107.

98   Cf. V. Briani, *Il lavoro italiano in Africa* (Roma: Tipografia Riservata del Ministero degli Esteri, 1980), p. 311.

99   Cf. E. Serra, *Un tessuto connettivo tra Libia e Italia*, in "Relazioni Internazionali", no. 20, 15 May 1971, pp. 489-490.

100   A. Del Boca, *Gli italiani in Libia*, cit., p. 481.

101   On 8 July 1975, ENI and the Libyan oil ministry stipulated an economic cooperation protocol for the design and construction of further oil and chemical plants, as well as oil pipelines and refineries. In exchange for its technical assistance in managing the plants, ENI received preferential treatment as a partner in various Libyan development projects (M. Cricco and F. Cresti, *Gheddafi, I volti del potere*, cit., p. 63).

102   M. el Qaddafi, *The Green Book.*

103   Cf. A. B. Mariantoni and F. Oberson, *Gli occhi bendati sul Golfo* (Milano: Jaca Book, 1991), pp. 90-96.

104   V. Parlato, introduction to M. Gheddafi, *Fuga dall'inferno e altre storie* (Roma: Manifestolibri, 2006), p. 14. For further information, see S. G. Hajjar, *The Jamahiriya Experiment in Libya: Qadhafi and Rousseau*, in "The Journal of Modern African Studies", no. 2, June 1980, pp. 181-200.

105   D. Vandewalle, *A History of Modern Libya*, (Cambridge, New York: Cambridge University Press, 2012; second edition).

106   M. Cricco and F. Cresti, *Gheddafi, I volti del potere* (Roma: Carocci, 2011), p. 70.

107   *The Great Green Charter of the Rights of Man in the Jamahiriyyan Era*, Al-Bayda', 12 June 1988, p. 16.

108   A. Aruffo, *Gheddafi. Storia di una dittatura rivoluzionaria* (Roma: Castelvecchi, 2011), p. 101.

109   Cf. L. S. Anderson, *The State and Social Transformation in Tunisia and Libya, 1830-1980* (Princeton: Princeton University Press, 1986), p. 264.

110   D. Vandewalle, *A History of Modern Libya*, (Cambridge, New York: Cambridge University Press, 2012; second edition), p. 125.

111   J. Wright, *Libya: A Modern History*, (Baltimore: The John Hopkins University Press, 1981), p. 187.

112   Cf. B. Etienne, *L'islamismo radicale* (Milano: Rizzoli, 1988), p. 87;
        L'islamisme radical (Paris: Hachette, 1987).

113   M. el Qaddafi, *The Green Book*.

114   Cit. in M. Cricco and F. Cresti, *Gheddafi, I volti del potere*, cit., p. 77.

115   Cf. R. Gunaratna, *Inside Al Qaeda; Global Network of Terror*
        (New York: Columbia University Press, 2002), p. 142. See also the
        declarations of the Secretary of State of the United States, Condoleeza
        Rice: "US-Libya ties 'off to a good start'", *France 24*, 6 September
        2008.

116   Cf. M. Djaziri, État et société en Libye (Paris: L'Harmattan, 1996), pp.
        244-248; A. Del Boca, *Gheddafi. Una sfida dal deserto*, cit., p. 333.

117   The International Monetary Fund estimated that, in 2004-2005, about
        75% of the Libyans worked for the public sector (IMF, *Country Report
        No. 05/83 Libya*, March 2005, pp. 4-6).

118   Cf. M. and Y Brondino, *Il Nord Africa brucia all'ombra dell'Europa*
        (Milano: Jaca Book, 2011), p. 71.

119   M. el Qaddafi, *The Green Book*.

120   In depth analysis of this question is to be found in A. B. Mariantoni's
        doctoral thesis, *La Jamahiryya, A'apparel d'État libyen* (Lausanne:
        Université de Lausanne, Faculté de sciences sociales et politiques,
        1985). Cf. A. Aruffo, *Gheddafi. Storia di una dittatura rivoluzionaria*,
        cit., pp. 92-109.

121   Libya's performance as a provider for its people also once compared
        favorably with that of France and the United States (see Chapter 8).

122   Cf. N. Sarkis, "Les Arabes pauvres et les Arabes riches", in *Le Monde
        diplomatique*, August 1978.

123   On 23 October 1997, Nelson Mandela, free once more after his twenty-
        seven years in prison, decided to violate the United Nations embargo
        against Libya. As a result of this "total" embargo, not one airplane had
        landed in Libya for five years.

124   G. Fasanella and R. Priore, *Intrigo internazionale* (Milano:
        Chiarelettere, 2011), pp. 134-135.

125   *Ibid.*, p. 144.

126   *Ibid.*, p. 145.

127   D. Biacchessi and F. Colarieti, *Punto Condor, Ustica: il processo*
        (Bologna: Pendragon, 2002), pp. 88-94.

128   G. Fasanella and R. Priore, *Intrigo internazionale*, cit., p. 146.

129   *Ibid.*, p. 147.

130   *Ibid.*, p. 145 [Sila is a mountainous plateau in the Calabria region.
        translator's note].

131   *Ibid.*, p. 151.

132   *Ibid.*, p. 149-50.

133   *Ibid.*, p. 149-51.

134   *Ibid.*, p. 151.

135   *Ibid.*, p. 152.

136   *Ibidem.* For an account of the Ustica disaster, regarding the responsibility of the French and judicial proceedings, see A. Purgatori, "Ustica e quei quattro aerei nascosti. Gli indizi portano ai francesi, 31 anni dopo", in *Il Corriere della Sera*, 26 June 2011. In any case, we have a further interpretation of the events according to which Israel would appear to have been responsible for the disaster, through an error (the intended target was a plane which had in fact already reached Iraq with its cargo of enriched uranium two days earlier). This interpretation, arrived at following lengthy research, appeared in a work that was not widely distributed despite the renown of the publishing house: C. Gatti and G. Hammler, *Il quinto scenario* (Milano: Rizzoli), 1994, p. 260-263.

137   *Ibid.*, p. 157.

138   A declassified CIA Special Memorandum dated 9 December 1981 reveals that a bellicose speech made by Gaddafi on September 1 1977 marked the turning point. The Americans now came to consider Libya an accomplice of international terrorism. Gaddafi had urged the Egyptian people to punish their president, Sadat, who had allied himself with Israel and was responsible for an attack on Libya in July 1977. The attack led to about a hundred deaths; cf. M. Cricco and F. Cresti, *Gheddafi, I volti del potere* (Roma: Carocci, 2011), p. 83.

139   "CIA Anti-Qaddafi Plan Backed. Reagan Authorizes Covert Operation to Undermine Libyan Regime", in *Washington Post*, 3 November 1985. On this question, see also B. Woodward, *Veil, The Secret Wars of the CIA, 1981-1987* (New York: Simon & Schuster), 1988.

140   J. N. Maclean, "Tactics Used Against Gadhafi Prompt Kalb to Quit US Job", in *Chicago Tribune*, 9 October 1986; D. Beckwith, "Bernard Kalb's Modest Dissent", in *Time Magazine*, 21 June 2005; G. L. Simons, *Libya: the Struggle for Survival* (New York: St. Martin's Press, 1993), p. 325.

141   For an analysis of the effects of the economic sanctions on Libya, cf. M. O'Sullivan, *Shrewd Sanctions. Statecraft and State Sponsors of Terrorism* (Washington DC: Brookings Institution Press, 2003), pp. 186-223; see also G. Barbera, *Il dittatore utopista. Storia e controstoria di Muammar Gheddafi* (Siena: Bàrbera, 2011), pp. 131-139.

142   An overview of the history of relations between the United States and Libya can be found in R. B. St. John, *Libya and the United States: Two Centuries of Strife* (Philadelphia: University of Pennsylvania

Press, 2002). As to the harm caused by the Resolutions, "in just the first nine months of sanctions, Libya's economic losses were estimated as enormous: about 2.5 billion dollars" (A. Del Boca, *Gheddafi. Una sfida dal deserto*, cit., p. 257).

143   *Ibid.* pp. 188-189; A. Aruffo also points a finger at Syria; see A. Aruffo *Gheddafi. Storia di una dittatura rivoluzionaria* (Roma: Castelvecchi, 2011), p. 85.

144   N. Chomsky, "Il gendarme globale", in *il manifesto*, 9 April 1986.

145   G. Dottori, "Guerra all'italiana, ovvero: a chi affittiamo la nostra forza?", in *Limes*, no. 2, April 2011, p. 199.

146   R. B. St. John, *Libya and the United States: Two Centuries of Strife*, cit., pp. 153-154.

147   Greenstream is the Mediterranean's longest underwater gas pipeline (520 kilometers), running from Melitah to Capo Passero, in Sicily. The maximum capacity of the pipeline is 9 billion cubic metres of methane gas per year. Greenstream was inaugurated on 7 October 2004 in the presence of Gaddafi and Italy's PM, Silvio Berlusconi (cf. E. Borriello, "Al via il gasdotto Italia-Libia", in *la Repubblica*, 8 October 2004).

148   The treaty included the provisions for payment to Libya by Italy of 5 billion dollars over a twenty-year period. A number of infrastructural works were also foreseen (a coastal motorway stretching from the Tunisian border to the Egyptian border, and construction of homes and guest houses for Libyans injured by landmines left by the Fascist Italian colonialists). Libya, for its part, undertook to strengthen its patrols to counter "slave traffickers", with joint Italian and Libyan surveillance of the Strait of Sicily. The Libyans also undertook to intensify controls of its frontiers with Chad, Niger and Sudan (including radar control).

149   "Serpents, thirst and burning sand are all welcomed by the brave; endurance delights in hardship; virtue delights in having to pay dear for its existence. Only in Libya with all her torments, can fleeing be no disgrace to the brave." (My translation; cf. *The Civil War*, Books I-X, Lucan, translation: J. D. Duff—*translator's note*).

150   The Ministry of Defence, the Ministry of the Interior, the Foreign Ministry and the Ministry of Finance, Trade and Industry in Tunisia were taken over by members of the disbanded Democratic Constitutional Assembly, and by exponents of the old regime. Cf. R. G. Khouri, "The Arab Military is Not the Solution", in *Agence Globale*. 5 February 2011; S. Ghannoushi, "Obama, hands off our Spring", in *The Guardian*, 26 May 2011.

151   N. Gaouette and V. Gienger, *Clinton will Travel to Egypt, Tunisia, Meet with Libyan Opposition Leaders*, in "*Bloomberg*", 10 March 2011. As part of a process that was to be made immediately effective at

the G8 meeting held on 26-27 May 2011 at Deauville, the powers that attacked Libya attempted to bring about 'integration' of these countries of the MENA (Middle East and North Africa). During the meeting, the attending powers agreed to create a global financial package of 40 billion dollars to back up the Arab Spring ("G8 a Libia e Siria: cessino le violenze dei regime", in *Ansa.it*, 28 May 2011).

152   D. Frattini, "La partita sauditi-iraniani in Bahrein", in *Il Corriere della Sera*, 15 March 2011.

153   Egypt, the United States and the European Union urged moderation from the demonstrators and from the Mubarak regime. They urged the various parties also to negotiate. They thus placed Egypt's people and authorities on a par (and yet the former were both unarmed and peaceful while the latter were armed and anything but peaceful!). The request should have been made only to the Mubarak regime. During the rebellions, the Bahraini and Tunisian authorities were treated with kid gloves.

154   Resolution 1973 was passed by a majority vote. Germany, India, Brazil and two Council members (Russia and China) abstained. This abstention was dubbed the BRIC+G vote.

155   The measures enshrined in paragraph 4 of Resolution 1973 were included at the insistence of France. Surprisingly, they received very little attention in Italy and abroad and were overshadowed by speculation over a no-fly zone.

156   ICISS, *The Responsibility to Protect: Report of the International Commission on Intervention and State Sovereignty*, Ottawa, December 2001 (<http://www.reponsibilitytoprotect.org/>).

157   L. Baiada, "La Responsibility to Protect, rebus geopolitico", in *Il Ponte*, no. 5, May 2011, pp. 23-29. For further discussion, cf. N. Chomsky, "UN Address: Dialogue on the Responsibility to Protect", in z communications, 5 August 2009.

158   La «responsabilità di proteggere»: la legittimazione dell'ingerenza?, interview by S, Cattori with J. Bricmont, in Voltairenet, 1 December 2008. The jurist, Bricmont, talks of "Western governments, media and NGOs, calling themselves the 'international community' [...] will judge the responsibility for a human tragedy quite differently, depending on whether it occurs in a country where the West, for whatever reason, is hostile to the government, or in a friendly state." (Statement by Professor Jean Bricmont to the United Nations General Assembly, 23 July 2009).

159   The full wording of *Resolution 1973 of the United Nations Security Council* can be found at <http://www.nato.int/nato_static/assets/pdf/pdf_2011_03/20110927_110311-UNSCR-1973.pdf>

(retrieved, September 2015).

160 P. Beaumont, "Bahrain, Terror as Protesters Shot", in *The Guardian*, 17 February 2011.

161 F. Sabahi, "La rivolta araba: banco di prova per l'Occidente", in *Italianieuropei*, no. 4, April 2011, p. 33.

162 G. Olimpo, "Bahrein, l'esercito spara sui dimostranti", in *Il Corriere della Sera*, 19 February 2011.

163 M. Dinucci, "Un partner modello per Hillary", in *il manifesto*, 15 June 2011.

164 F. Rizzi, "Mediterraneo in rivolta", *Castelvecchi*, Roma 2011, p. 103.

165 The GCC was founded in 1981 by the monarchs of Saudi Arabia, the United Arab Emirates, Qatar, Kuwait and Oman.

166 N. Gaouette, "Clinton Says Arab League Vote for No-Fly Zone Changed Minds", in *Bloomberg*, 16 March 2011.

167 C. Jean. "L'intervento in Libia: la situazione attuale e gli scenari future", in *Italianieuropei*, no. 4, April 2011, pp. 21-22.

168 The Sanusis idolized the King when the movement rose once more to power in 1951 following the declaration of independence of Libya. Muhammad Idris I reigned until 1969 (Gaddafi and his Free Officers declared the end of the monarchy on 1 September 1969).

169 R. Norton-Taylor and C. Stephen, "Libya: SAS veterans helping NATO identify Gaddafi targets in Misrata", in *The Guardian*, 31 May 2011; M. Hosenball, "US agents were in Libya before secret Obama order", in *Reuters*, 31 March 2011; C. Jean. "L'intervento in Libia: la situazione attuale e gli scenari future", cit., pp. 23-24.

170 G. Gaiani, "Soldati occidentali tra i ribelli", in *Libero*, 1 June 2011.

171 G. Gammel, N. Meo and J. Kirkup, "Libya: SAS Mission that Began and Ended in Error", in *The Daily Telegraph*, 6 March 2011.

172 A. Jamal, "US, UK, French Forces Land in Libya", in *Pakistan Observer*, 28 February 2011.

173 V. E. Parsi, "Il nuovo protagonismo internazionale nel mediterraneo", in *Italianieuropei*, no. 4, April 2011, p. 15.

174 O. Karmi, "US deploys Naval and Air Forces near Libya", in *The National*, 1 March 2011; I. Black et al., "Libya Crisis: Britain, France and US prepare for Air Strikes against Qaddafi", *The Guardian*, 17 March 2011.

175 In article appearing in *The Telegraph*, General Younis, former Minster of the Interior under Gaddafi who then became the military commander of the 'rebels', expressly asked *"that the west should be ready to launch airstrikes against Colonel Gaddafi's palace in Tripoli to prevent him attacking the Libyan people with chemical weapons or causing terrible casualties in some other way. He was also in favour*

of establishing an international no-fly zone as soon as possible. (N. Meo, "Libya's rebel army struggles to create order from chaos", in *The Telegraph*, 5 March 2011).

176   S. Gowans, "West on Guard against Outbreak of Peace in Libya", in *The Herald*, 20 April 2011.

177   Cf. "MPs rebel over Libya mission creep as Cameron, Obama and Sarkozy promise to keep bombing until Gaddafi Regime is Gone", in *The Daily Mail*, 15 April 2011.

178   U. "De Giovannangeli, Libia, l'obiettivo della NATO è assassinare Gheddafi. Intervista ad Angelo Del Boca", in *l'Unità*, 26 June 2011 [the article consists of an interview with Libya historian A. Del Boca— *translator's note*].

179   T. Cartalucci, "NATO's Terror over Tripoli", in Infowars, 20 June 2011.

180   UNCLASSIFIED U.S. Department of State Case No. F-2014-20439 Doc No. C05779612 Date: 12/31/2015 RELEASE IN PART

181   J. Kirkup, "Libya: Arab States urged to Train and Lead Rebels", in *The Daily Telegraph*, 22 April 2011.

182   P. Escobar, "What's Really at Stake in Libya", in *Asia Times*, 30 June 2011. M. D. Nazemroaya has collected evidence of the use of depleted uranium missiles in Libya: see *NATO War Crimes: Depleted Uranium found in Libya by scientists*, on "Voltairenet", 5 July 2011; C. Hallinan, *Using up USA's Depleted Uranium—for Weapons in Libya*, in "Nuclear News", 13 April 2011. See also the study conducted by Professor M. Zucchetti, of the Politecnico di Torino, "Missili Cruise all'uranio impoverito sulla Libia: studio delle conseguenze", in *Libyan Free Press*, 7 July 2011. However, F. Lamb, a first-hand witness of many of the developments of 2011 (and no friend of NATO), does not believe depleted uranium was used during the Libya campaign. "What I have observed personally," he writes, "is that nearly all the reports on events in Libya on certain internet sites are false. This was also the case during the summer months here in Libya when patently false claims about NATO using MAP 108 Spanish manufactured cluster bombs against civilian or loyalist military targets, NATO using depleted uranium, or that 150,000 Libyan civilians were killed were posted as truth 'from reliable sources inside Libya.'". Lamb warned that "grossly exaggerated and unsubstantiated claims and conspiracy theories only aid the aggressors, in this case, NATO", F. Lamb, "Rumor and Anger Mount in Libya", *Counterpunch*, 13 January 2012

183   One source, by way of illustration, is "Lockerbie and the Libyans", in

The Economist, 8 April 1999.

184   D. Vandewalle, *A History of Modern Libya*, cit., p. 169.

185   A. Cramb, "Lockerbie bomber Abdelbaset Ali Mohmed al Megrahi expected to be Freed", in *The Telegraph*, 20 August 2009.

186   "Gaddafi to give Lockerbie 'evidence'", in *BBC news*, 5 February 2011.

187   "A former Scottish police chief has given lawyers a signed statement claiming that key evidence in the Lockerbie bombing trial was fabricated", in M. Mega, "Police chief: Lockerbie evidence was faked", in *The Scotsman*, 28 August 2005.

188   *Lockerbie Settlement*, in *The New York Times*, 14 August 2003.

189   K. Hamadé, "Khdaffi gav order om Lockerbie-attentatet", in *Expressen*, 23 February 2011.

190   The Lockerbie affair has been, to say the least, controversial. The UN observer at the trial in Scotland, distinctly unsatisfied at the manner in which it had been handled, went so far as claim that Scotland did not deserve independence before addressing its failings within the judicial system (M. Macaskill, "UN observer says Scots law is flawed", *Sunday Times*, 7 October 2007); cf. O. Schmidt, *The Intelligence Files*, Clarity Press, Atlanta, 2001.

191   T. Pearce, "Ex-Minister says Gaddafi Ordered Lockerbie Bomb", in *Reuters*, 23 February 2011.

192   The entire affair has been reconstructed by R. Backer, "Libya: Connect the Dots-You Get a Giant Dollar Sign", in *Who What Why*, 6 June 2011.

193   K. Fahim, "Rebel leadership in Libya shows strain", in *The New York Times*, 3 April 2011.

194   Cf. C. Boucek, "Islamist terrorists are running loose in Libya. Why isn't the US paying attention?", in *The Christian Science Monitor*, 11 May 2011.

195   T. Meyssan, "L'OTAN face à l'ingratitude des Libyens", Voltairenet, 11 July 2011. "Nato and the ingratitude of the Libyan people", Voltairenet, 17 July 2011.

196   Self-appointed Prime Minister of the Republic of Libya, Jibril graduated at the University of Pittsburgh. France, Portugal, Italy, the United Kingdom and Qatar promptly recognized his government (an artificial construct set up by NATO after the failed coup d'état of February 2011). The Jibril government was accepted as the only legitimate representative of Libya. As on 22 August 2011, the vast majority of UN Member States were clearly not enthusiastic about this 'new boy in town'. As a representative of the NATO-supported opposition, Jibril shared his responsibilities with another militant from

the United States, Khalifa Belqasim Haftar. The latter had once been colonel in the Libyan army, and had resided in Falls Church, Virginia (located seven miles away from the CIA's Headquarters in Langley). Many knew that Khalifa Belqasim Haftar was on the payroll of the CIA (cf. P. Martin, Mounting Evidence of CIA Ties to Libyan Rebels, in Uruknet, 4 April 2011; G. Raz, "In Libya, A Civil War, not Uprising", in NPA, 2 April 2011; K. Nimmo, "CIA Operative Appointed to Run al-Qaeda Connected to Libyan Rebels", in Infowars, 29 March 2011).

197   K. Dilanian, "CIA officers in Libya are aiding rebels, US officials say", in *Chicago Tribune*, 30 March 2011. The Anglo-Americans claimed that they knew very little about the National Transitional Council. Admiral James Stavridis told the United States Armed Services Committee that, as supreme commander of the military operations of the European Command of the United States (EUCOM) and of NATO, he was deeply concerned over the behaviour of the Libyan opposition (United States Senate Armed Services Committee, U.S. European Command and U.S. Strategic Command in review of the Defense Authorization request for fiscal year 2012 and the Future Years Defense Program, 112th Congress, 2011, 1st Session, March 20 2011).

198   See the interview with Saif al-Islam Gaddafi published by the Algerian newspaper *El-Khabar*, 11 July 2011; see also "Trattative con Gheddafi, Parigi smentisce", in *La Stampa*, 12 July 2011; R. Monteforte, "Libia, il figlio del rais annunica: Contatti diretto con la Francia", in *l'Unità*, 12 July 2011.

199   B.-H. Lévy, "What Can We Do for the Young Libyan Revolution?", in *Huffpost World*, 6 March 2011.

200   B.-H. Lévy, "Scènes de la vie dans la Libye libre", in *Le Point*, 10 March 2011.

201   E. Oliari, *Libya: una guerra fatta soprattutto di disinformazione. Intervista a Fausto Biloslavo*, in Oliari.wordpress, 28 May 2011.

202   M. Correggia, "Libia: e se fosse tutto falso?", in *Famiglia Cristiana*, 14 June 2011. Confirmation of such incidents may also be found in an interview with Peter Bouckaert, a Human Rights Watch activist: *HRW: No mercenaries in eastern Libya*, in Radio Netherlands Worldwide, 2 March 2011. It was learned that *"nightly manhunts"* were organized *"for about 8,000 people named as government operatives"* (D. Zucchino, "Libyan Rebels appear to take Leaf from Kadafi's Playbook", in *Los Angeles Times*, 24 March 2011).

203   R. Nordland, "Libyan Rebels Say They're Being Sent Weapons", in *The New York Times*, 16 April 2011.

204   J. Kirkup, "Libya: Arab States urged to Train and Lead Rebels", in *The*

Daily Telegraph, 22 April 2011.

205   M. D. Nazemroaya, "Operation Libya: Recognizing the Opposition Government Constitutes a Pretext for Military Intervention", in Global Research, 13 March 2011.

206   K. DeYoung and G. Miller, "In Libya, CIA is gathering Intelligence on Rebels", *Washington Post*, 30 March 2011.

207   See G. F. Will, "Is Obama above the Law?", *Washington Post*, 28 May 2011.

208   Cit. in J. Weisenthal, "Obama Overruled by Two Top Lawyers. Who told him War must be Terminated", in *Business Insider*, 17 June 2011; "It doesn't Pass the Straight Face Test: Republican Speaker pours scorn on Obama claim of Authority for Libya Mission", in *Daily Mail*, 16 June 2011.

209   W. G. Tarpley, "The CIA's Fake "Arab Spring" Becoming a Long, Hot Summer of War", in Tarpley.net, 20 June 2011.

210   J. Gelman, "Tribulaciones Libias", in *Página* 12, 3 April 2011.

211   J. Felter and B. Fishman, *Al Qa'ida's Foreign Fighters in Iraq: A First Look at the Sinjar Records* (West Point, NY: Harmony Project, Combating Terrorism Center, Department of Social Sciences, US Military Academy, December 2007).

212   W. G. Tarpley, "The CIA's Libya Rebels: The Same Terrorists who Killed US, NATO Troops in Iraq", in Tarpley.net, 24 March 2011; Id. "Al Qaeda; Pawns of CIA Insurrection from Libya to Yemen", in Tarpley.net, 3 April 2011.

213   Cf. R. Fisk, "America's Secret Plan to Arm Libya's Rebels", in *The Independent*, 7 March 2011.

214   WikiLeaks secret cables: Chris Stevens, CDA, Embassy Tripoli, Dept. Of State, 2 June 2008, 08TRIPOLI430, CONF/NOFORM; 08TRIPOLI120 "Extremism in Eastern Libya", 15 February 2008; EO 12958: DECL: 02/15/2018; TAGS; PGOV PREL KISL PTER LY IZ (in CableSearch.org).

215   J. Felter and B. Fishman, *Al Qa'ida's Foreign Fighters in Iraq: A First Look at the Sinjar Records*, cit., pp. 8-9.

216   C. Jean, "Il secondo risveglio arabo e le lezioni della Libia", in *Quaderni speciali di Limes*, no. 2, April 2011, p. 63.

217   "Libia; il governo riconosce gli insorti. Frattini: «Armare i ribelli? Non escluso»", in *Il Corriere della Sera*, 4 April 2011.

218   "Libia: Frattini, Gheddafi controlla situazione altrimenti esplosiva", in *Adnkronos*, 8 January 2011.

219   M. Caprara, «Arginare il fondamentalismo. È questa la priorità dell'Europa» Frattini indica Gheddafi come modello per il mondo arabo", in *Il Corriere della Sera*, 17 January 2011.

220   "Libya protests: EU Condemns Violence and Fears Influx", *BBC news*, 21 February 2011. When, three days after these declarations, the Italian ambassador to Libya talked of a "calm situation", his superiors in Rome were not at all pleased. In Rome, Foreign Minister Frattini saw "dramatic" events taking place across Strait of Sicily. Media rumours circulated of some 10,000 deaths (G. Cadalanu, "La Libia in un bagno di sangue—'I morti potrebbero essere dieicmila'", in *la Repubblica*, 24 February 2011). On 31 May, Frattini wrote out a memorandum of understanding with Benghazi, thus raising the level of dealings to that of diplomatic relations (including a broadening out of the scope of relations to provide also for supplies of fuel and money). It was calculated that, in 2011, Italy was spending about 235-240 million Euros per month on the Libyan campaign.

221   See Part 1, Chap. 3, *The Sanusis.*

222   J. Felter and B. Fishman, *Al Qa'ida's Foreign Fighters in Iraq: A First Look at the Sinjar Records*, cit., p. 12.

223   *Ibid*, p. 19.

224   For an overview of this group, see G. Gambill, "The Libyan Islamic Fighting Group (LIFG)", in The Jamestown Foundation, 5 May 2005.

225   Cf. A. Baldinetti, "Le istanze amazigh in Libia: la nascita di una società civile?", in A. Baldinetti and A. Maneggia, *Processi politici nel Mediterraneo: dinamiche e prospettive*, Morlacchi, Perugia 2009, p. 231.

226   B. Selwan El Khoury, "Il nuovo fronte dei guerrieri di Dio", in *Limes*, no. 2, April 2011, p. 208.

227   B. York, "Jihadis who Killed Americans get US support in Libya", in *The Examiner*, 28 March 2011.

228   AQIM's main information agency, in Pakistan and Afghanistan.

229   W. Madsen, "NATO's 'Alternate Universe'" in Libya", in Strategic Culture Foundation, 8 June 2011.

230   "I conservatori di Benghazi faranno rimpiangere Gheddafi". Conversazione con Hanas Ahmad, direttrice del quotidiano "Oea", ed. A. Ricucci and C. Tinuzzi, in *Limes*, no. 3, July 2011, p. 206.

231   J. Felter and B. Fishman, *Al Qa'ida's Foreign Fighters in Iraq: A First Look at the Sinjar Records*, cit., p. 27.

232   *Ibid.*, p. 28 (my emphasis).

233   G. Chiesa and P. Cabras, *Barack Obush* (Milano: Ponte alle Grazie, 2011), p. 94. For confirmation of the massive presence of Al-Qa'ida militants among the 'rebels' of Cyrenaica, see R. Winnet and G. Gardham, "Libya: al-Qaeda among Libya Rebels, NATO Chief Fears", *The Telegraph*, 29 March 2011.

234   Of course, part of the official history of what happened later takes us

to the WTC and Pentagon incidents of 11 September 2001, and to that 'genius of evil', Osama Bin Laden, and his organization, Al-Qa'ida (who were immediately blamed for the attacks). There are, of course, many extensively researched works, widely read, that debunk the official accounts of the events of 9/11.

235   R. Gates, *From the Shadows. The Ultimate Insider's Story of Five Presidents and How they Won the Cold War* (New York, Simon & Schuster, 1996), p. 349; see also G. Tenet and B. Harlow, *At the Center of the Storm. My Years at the CIA* (New York, HarperCollins), 2007, pp. 121-122, 178). See *Filibuster Al Qaeda Founder Robert Gates*, in Infowars, 8 December 2008.

236   See R. Cook, "The struggle against terrorism cannot be won by military means", *The Guardian*, 8 July 2005, and P-H. Bunel, "Al Qaeda: The Database", in Wayne Madsen Report, 20 November 2005.

237   An influential Islamic preacher, for five years he was one of Bin Laden's comrades-in-arms at Khost, a training camp in eastern Afghanistan.

238   J. Rosenthal, "Al-Qaeda and the Libyan Rebellion", in *National Review*, 23 June 2011; *Libya Releases scores of prisoners*, in Al Jazeera, 9 April 2008.

239   I. Black, "Libya rebels reject Gaddafi's al-Qaida Spin", in *The Guardian*, 1 March 2011.

240   R. Bongiorni, "Noi ribelli, islamici e tolleranti", in *Sole-24 Ore*, 22 March 2011. [*Rais* is a term of Persian origin that is occasionally used in Italy to identify powerful leaders in various third world countries, including Italy's former colonies—*translator's note*].

241   P. Swami, "Libyan Rebel Commander admits his fighters have al-Qaeda links", in *The Telegraph*, 25 March 2011; C. Levinson, 'Ex-Mujahedeen Help Lead Libyan Rebels', in *The Wall Street Journal*, 2 April 2011.

242   L- Declich, "Al-Q'aida in Libia, la polpetta avvelenata di Gheddafi", in *Limes*, no. 1, March 2011, p. 72.

243   P. Dale Scott, "Who are the Libyan Freedom Fighters and Their Patrons?", in *The Asia-Pacific Journal*, no. 3, 28 March 2011.

244   "US military advisers in Cyrenaica. Qaddafi's [sic] loses his air force", in DEBKA*file*, 25 February 2011.

245   C. Levinson and M. Rosenberg, "Egypt Said to Arm Libyan Rebels", in *The Wall Street Journal*, 17 March 2011; see also G. Chetoni, "Armamenti: i nostri aiuti umanitari ai ribelli libici", in *Rinascita*, 11-12 June 2011.

246   Gaddafi's second wife, Safiya—the daughter of a leading figure of the Firkeche clan—belongs to the Bara'asa tribe.

247   There are more than 140 tribes in Libya. Thirty are of a demographically

significant size. For a detailed account of Libya's tribes, see E. Griffini, *L'arabo parlato della Libia* (Milano: Cisalpino-Goliardico, 1985).

248   On the circumstances of the assassination of Younis and his entire general staff, see M. Chossudovsky and M. D. Nazemroaya, "The War on Libya: Divisions within the Transitional Council and Rebel Forces", in Global Research, 29 July 2011. The incident is ascribed to mafia-style feuding within the Transitional Council in Benghazi.

249   M. Introvigne, "La guerra delle tribù", in Id., *Islam. Che sta succedendo?* (Milano: Sugarco, 2011), pp. 43-46.

250   V. Rainey, "Who are the Rebels we are Fighting to Protect?", in *The First Post*, 21 March 2011.

251   G. Dottori, "Disinformacija: l'uso strategico del falso nel caso libico", in *Limes*, no. 1, March 2011, p. 46.

252   Cf. D. Bandow, "L'improbabile terza guerra Americana", in Quaderni Speciali di *Limes*, no. 2, April 2011, p. 175; "Evidence: NATO-backed Libya "Rebels" are Clearly Terrorists", in *Black Star News*, 13 July 2011.

253   For an account of the tribal composition of the revolt, see A. B. Mariantoni, "Libia: evviva i 'buoni'!", in *Civium Libertas*, 21 March 2011. Key evidence confirming the scheme of developments as described here is to be found in a joint study undertaken by two French think tanks, the *Centre Internationale des Recherches et d'Études sur le Terrorisme & l'Aide aux victimes du Terrorisme* (CIRET-AVT) and the *Centre Français de Recherche sur le Renseignement* (CF2R), *Libye: un avenir incertain. Compte-rendu de mission d'évaluation auprès des belligerants libyens*, Paris 30 May 2011, pp. 23-44. The Sanusi movement was represented in the NTC by Sayyid Mohammed al-Rida bin Sayyid Masan ar-Rida al-Mahdi El Sanusi (whose great uncle was none other than the ill-famed, deposed King Idris).

254   L. Cremonesi, "'Elezioni in Libia, tanto vincerà mio padre'. Intervista a Sayf al-Islam Gheddafi", in *Corriere della Sera*, 16 June 2011.

255   The Fact Finding Commission on the Current Events in Libya collected many eye-witness reports on the atrocities committed by the 'rebels' and NATO against the civilian population. In all likelihood the material archived by the commission has been destroyed or confiscated. The findings were summarized in the editorial of 23 June 2011 of the Italian daily newspaper, *Rinascita*, "NATO Canaglia. Cronache di una tragedia". Further descriptive material, accompanied by photographs of the rebels' crimes committed against civilians, was published together with an article by Hassan Alliby, "Témoignage et photographes des crimes de l'OTAN en Libye", in *La Voix des Opprimés*, 21 June 2011; J. Blood, "Libya's Rebels Execute, Behead,

Mutilate Gaddafi Army who Surrender! Where is CNN now?", in *Deadline Live*, 20 April 2011; T. Cartaluccci, "Libya's Not-so-Noble Rebels", in *Land Destroyer Report*, 13 July 2011.

256   M. Robinson and N. Carey, "Rebels Eye Tripoli push, Gaddafi Son offers Election", in *Reuters*, 17 June 2011.

257   F. Stockman, "Libyan Reformer New Face of Rebellion", in *The Boston Globe*, 28 March 2011; P. Gelie, "La France a parachuté des armes aux rebelles libyens", in *Le Figaro*, 28 June 2011.

258   L. Cremonesi, "Se Gheddafi tiene in scacco la NATO", in *Il Corriere della Sera*, 14 June 2011.

259   C. Gazzini, "Perché in Libia la rivoluzione è andata diversamente", in *Italianieuropei*, no. 4, April 2011, pp. 29-30.

260   C. M. Blanchard and J. Zanotti, *Libya, Background and U.S. Relations*, in Congressional Research Service, 18 February 2011, p. 6. The activist, Fethi Tarbel, is generally referred to as Fathi Terbil.

261   HRW, *Libya: Security Forces Fire on 'Day of Anger' Demonstrations*, 17 February 2011.

262   Institute for National Security and Counterterrorism, *Libya in Conflict. Mapping the Libyan armed conflict*, Syracuse University College of Law, 2012

263   *Agenda item 4, Human rights situation that require the Council's attention, Report of the International Commission of Inquiry to investigate all alleged violations of international human rights law in the Libyan Arab Jamahiriya, A/HRC/17/44, Advance Unedited Version*, Human Rights Council, 1 June 2011.

264   *Agenda item 4, Human rights situation that require the Council's attention, Report of the International Commission on Libya, A/HRC/17/68, Advance Unedited Version*, Human Rights Council, 8 March 2012.

265   F. Lamb, "Amnesty International's Flawed Syrian Hospitals 'Investigation'", *Counterpunch*, 1 November 2011.

266   I. Black, "Libyan revolution casualties lower than expected, says new government", *The Guardian*, 8 January 2013

267   IPPNW, *Body Count, Casualty Figures after 10 Years of the War on Terror*, First international edition, Washington, Berlin, Ottawa, 2015, p. 33.

268   <http://twitter.com/#!/JoReport/statuses/40458755497918464>. The messages were vehicled with hashtags, tags and keywords, used on microblogging platforms to link a given message to a topic. The links providing information on the events in Libya included the following hashtags, #feb17, #gaddafi, #Libya and #Tripoli. A highly tendentious account of the role played by social networks in spreading the revolt

in Libya is to be found in G. Loccatelli, *Twitter e le rivoluzioni. La primavera araba dei social network: nulla sarà più come prima* (Roma: Editori Riuniti, 2011), pp. 127-159.

269   *Clarification on media information regarding the ICC position on the Libyan situation* (ICC-CPI-20110224-MA88), 24 February 2011.

270   I. Galushko, "Airstrikes in Libya did not take place"—Russian military, *Russia Today*, 1 March 2011.

271   For a summary of the falsehoods relayed by the media as part of their campaign in favor of intervention in Libya, see, for example, the video, <http://www.youtube.com/watch?v=hPej4Ur_tz0>.

272   G. Cadalanu, "La guerra sceneggiata per i media occidental", in *Limes*, no. 3, July 2011, p. 209.

273   A. J. Kuperman, "False pretense for war in Libya?", in *The Boston Globe*, 14 April 2011.

274   See B. Gwertzman, "Shultz Advocates US Covert Programs to Depose Qaddafi", in *The New York Times*, 28 April 1986; C. Krauss, "Failed Anti-Qaddafi Effort Leaves US Picking Up the Pieces", in *The New York Times*, 12 March 1991; J. T. Stanik, *El Dorado Canyon: Reagan's Undeclared War with Qaddafi* (Annapolis: Naval Institute Press, 2003).

275   In regard to the brutally repressive measures adopted by the Israeli army on 15 May 2011 in Palestine, leading to 15 deaths and more than 200 injured on the sixty-third day of the commemoration of the Palestinian *Naqba* (Catastrophe), journalist Angelo Pezzana—a master in the art of double standards—claimed that "The Israeli soldiers had no choice but to fire, to defend the security of a country threatened by very real invaders, as indeed any other army of any other country would have done" (A. Pezzana, "Il 1948, vera Catastrofe per i profughi. Ma i mandanti furono gli 'amici' arabi", in *Libero*, 17 May 2011, p. 23).

276   See "Zionist al-Jazeera's propaganda and the Reality in Libya", in *Qatar Wakeup Call*, 17 June 2011.

277   "Ghassan Bin Jeddo to El Shorouk newspaper: Resignation reason from al-Jazeera is its way of covering ME events", in Champress, 25 April 2011.

278   "La situazione in Siria mette in crisi i grandi network panarabi", in *Megachip*, 12 May 2011.

279   E. Oliari, *Libya: una guerra fatta soprattutto di disinformazione. Intervista a Fausto Biloslavo*, in Oliari.wordpress, 28 May 2011.

280   "Siria: conduttrice lascia *Al Arabiya* per contrasti si coperture proteste", in *Adn-kronos*, 12 May 2011.

281   G. Delorme, "Et une démission de plus (et nondes moindres) à

Al Jazeera!", in INFO Syrie, 4 December 2012; P. Jay. "Al Jazeera Journalist Explains Resignation over Syria and Bahrain Coverage", *The Real News*, 20 March 2012.

282   "Siria: dopo Al Jazeera anche la Reuters si scusa per diffusione di foto false", in IRIB World Service, 13 May 2011; see also M. Bernabei, "Disinformazione e mistificazione per impadronirsi di Damasco", in *Rinascita*, 14-15 May 2011.

283   K. Parrish, "Task Force Commander Provides Libya Update", in *American Forces Press Service*, 22 March 2011.

284   M. Kennedy, "Canada Joins UN Coalition Aerial Mission on Libya", in *Edmonton Journal*, 19 March 2011.

285   M. D. Nazemroaya, "Journalism as a Weapon of War in Libya", in *Global Research*, 29 June 2011.

286   These pre-packaged 'horror stories', *ad usum delphini*, were debunked by a journalist, Amedeo Ricucci, from the Italian national broadcasting authority, RAI. See the interview of 24 March 2011: *Guerra libica, ecco tutte le bugie che ci hanno raccontato...* (<http://www.youtube.com/watch?v=ISDFhdu3d6k>).

287   Admittedly, Bernard-Henri Lévy has mastered this game to perfection. The undeniable services rendered by this super-egocentric 'philosopher' to the cause of the war against Libya have earned him the admiration of certain circles close to France's military establishment. The philosopher was even promoted into the ranks of the French *Armée*. Serge Dassault—a powerful billionaire (the proprietor of the arms manufacturing concern of the same name), and a member of parliament for Nicolas Sarkozy's UMP (Union for a Popular Movement)—proposed that Lévy should assume the rank of French Air Force colonel. BHL duly received this rank on 7 September 2011 (he is also on the reserve officers' list). See S. Verrazzo, "Convinse Sarkò a cacciare Gheddafi. Il filosofo BHL nominato colonello", in *Libero*, 8 September 2011.

288   "L'importanza di essere democristiano. Colloquio con Ettore Bernabei di Malcom Pagani", in *L'Espresso*, 5 May 2011.

289   Human rights investigations, *The cluster bombing of Misrata: The case against the USA*, 25 May 2011 (<http://humanrightsinvestigations.org/>).

290   On the significance of this friendship treaty, see A. Del Boca, *Gheddafi. Una sfida dal deserto*, (Roma-Bari: Laterza, 2010), pp. 328-332;

291   On 20 June 2011, on the occasion of World Refugee Day, Napolitano had to face the wrath of the Northern League party, which urged the government to order Italy's forces to discontinue the airstrikes against Libya. Napolitano claimed that "Our commitment, ratified

by parliament, is to ally ourselves in Libya with the forces of other countries that have responded to the appeal of the United Nations. Italy could not look upon the events in Libya with indifference" (M. Breda, "Il Colle e la politica estera: non sia piegata a fini interni", in *Il Corriere della Sera*, 21 June 2011). While Napolitano urged a "continuation of humanitarian intervention in the name of peace", NATO managed to kill (in 'error') about thirty civilians during heavy bombing missions over Libya.

292   M. Nese, "Il generale: solita ipocrisia. Come capitò per il Kosovo", in *Il Corriere della Sera*, 29 April 2011.

293   G. Lazzaretti, *Gheddafi speranza per l'Africa*, in EFFEDIEFFE.com, 29 May 2011.

294   T. Di Francesco, "'È una guerra che abbiamo dimenticato'. Intervista ad Angelo Del Boca", in *il manifesto*, 16 June 2011.

295   The author's first-person account of his visit to Libya (15-20 April 2011)

296   M. Fetouri, *The Libyan Conflict. A Revolution or Armed Rebellion?*, p. 6 (the author cites material archived by the Fact Finding Commission). See <http://www.academia.edu/11263794/The_Libyan_Conflict_A_Revolution_or_Armed_Rebellion>.

297   [In English in the original text—*translator's note].*

298   For an analysis of the strategy adopted by Obama in Libya, see G. Chiesa and P. Cabras, *Barack Obush* (Milano: Ponte alle Grazie, 2011), pp. 85-96.

299   According to Fausto Biloslavo, one of the few journalists to interview him after Italy entered the war alongside NATO, Gaddafi's attitude was as follows, "When he talked about the British, well… His gestures were enough. He detests them. When he talked about Sarkozy, he put a finger to his head, meaning a loose cannon—in his own words, a mental case. When he spoke of the Italians and Berlusconi, he said he was shocked at the conduct of friends—and of his friend. 'You! You, with whom we'd settled all our outstanding problems, the traditional friendship between Italy and Libya': he was scandalized at this stab in the back, so to speak. A feeling, I still think, not of hatred or dislike—as with the British and French—only amazement." (E. Oliari, *Libya: una guerra fatta soprattutto di disinformazione. Intervista a Fausto Biloslavo*, in Oliari.wordpress, 28 May 2011).

300   In mid-July, after nearly four months of constant bombing, support for Gaddafi was as strong as ever. About 1,700,000 people took to the streets in demonstrations to defend the regime (see "One Third of Libya Turns Out to Support Qaddafi in World's Largest March Ever", in *Mathaba*, 7 July 2011; "Overview of Anti-NATO Rebel Alliance

& Pro Government Demonstrations in Libya", in *Waterpunt*, 16 July 2011). Furthermore, after NATO intervention, the troops loyal to Gaddafi managed to regain control of 20% more of the territory of Libya [27 July 2011] than they had been in control of on 17 February when the troubles began (see K. Sengupta, "Libyan Rebels have conceded Ground since Bombing began", in *The Independent*, 27 July 2011).

301   "Libia; Hugo Chavez propone piano di pace. Sì di Gheddafi", in *la Repubblica*, 2 March 2011.

302   During the raid of 10 May, not only were the usual targets in the Bab al 'Aziziyah complex hit but also a building that had already been struck on 30 April 2011. The building housed the High Commission for Infancy. Four children were injured there. As many as eighteen bombs struck the complex during another NATO raid two weeks later: "three people died and one hundred and fifty were injured" (M. Molteni, "Caccia a Gheddafi: strage di civili", in *Libero*, 25 May 2011).

303   L. Scaraffia, "Musulmani e cristiani in dialogo. Intervista con monsignor Martinelli, vicario apostolico di Tripoli", in *L'Osservatore Romano*, 6 June 2008.

304   See M. and Y. Brondino, *Il Nord Africa brucia all'ombra dell'Europa* (Milano: Jaca Book, 2011), p. 50.

305   K. Mezran, "Perché il colonello si sentiva sicuro", in *Limes*, no. 1, March 2011, p. 53.

306   *A Country Study: Libya* (<http://lcweb2.loc.gov/frd/cs/lytoc.html>).

307   P. Henningsen, "Globalists Target 100% State Owned Central Bank of Libya", in *The Market Oracle*, 20 March 2011.

308   E. Brown, "Libya all about oil, or central banking?", *Asia Times*, 14 April 2011.

309   See <http://hdr.undp.org/en/statistics/>.

310   World Bank data (2010).

311   Index Mundi (<http://www.indexmundi.com>).

312   *ISTAT, Rapporto annuale 2007: dati statistici.*

313   K. Mezran, *Perché il colonello si sentiva sicuro*, cit., p. 54

314   The Great Man-Made River Authority's site (http://www.gmmra. org/en/>) is no longer online. It should be remembered that NATO attacked the project, as reported by *Human rights investigations* (*NATO bombs the Great Man-Made River*, Human rights investigations, 27 July 2011).

315   A. Del Boca, *Gheddafi. Una sfida dal deserto*, cit., p. 290.

316   S. Cossu, "L'oro blu sotto la sabbia libica che fa gola alle multinazionali", in *Libyan Free Press*, 6 September 2011.

317   C. L. Cooper, "Oil Drillers Hit Water in Sahara", in *Washington Post*,

15 March 1969.

318 P. della Sala, "Libia, acqua dolce sotterranea grande come la Germania", in *Il Secolo* XIX, 25 March 2001.

319 "Libya targeted Civilian Protesters—War Crimes Court", in *BBC news*, 6 April 2011.

320 V. Walt, *Gaddafi, Lies and Video Tape: Libya's Rumor Mill*, in *Time Magazine*, 15 May 2001.

321 *ICC Prosecutor, Gaddafi used his absolute authority to commit crimes in Libya. Situation in the Libyan Arab Jamahiriya, prosecutor's Application Pursuant to Article 58 as to Muammar Abu Minyar Gaddafi, Saif Al-Islam Gaddafi and Abdullah Al-Senussi*, 16 May 2011.

322 G. Stabile, *L'Aja ha deciso: "Arrestate Gheddafi"*, in *La Stampa*, 28 June 2011.

323 K. Leigh, "Rape in Libya; the Crime that Dare not Speak its Name", in *Time Magazine*, 8 June 2011. "Gruesome Details of Gadhafi's Rape of Teenagers and Other Crimes Revealed", *Haaretz*, 26 January 2014.

324 E. Flock, "Iman Al-Obeidi: Rape as a Weapon of War", in *Washington Post*, 29 March 2011.

325 K. Leigh, "Rape in Libya; the Crime that Dare not Speak its Name", cit.

326 A. Dilks, "The 'International Criminal Court': Prosecuting Gaddafi with Questionable Evidence While Ignoring NATO-Israeli Atrocities", in *Global Research*, 17 May 2011.

327 See "Libya, Amnesty questions the Hague's findings: Are the rebels making up claims of mass rape?", in *International Business Times*, 27 June 2011; cf. D. South, "Amnesty International and Human Rights Watch expose lies on Libya", in *Mathaba*, 5 July 2011.

328 P. Cockburn, "Lies, damn lies, and reports of battlefield atrocities", in *The Independent*, 19 June 2011; see also D. Murphy, "No Evidence of Libya Viagra Rape Claims. But War Crimes? Plenty", in *The Christian Science Monitor*, 24 June 2011; G. Micalessin, "Viagra e stupri di massa? Solo balle dei ribelli", in *il Giornale*, 25 June 2011; P. Cockburn, "Don't believe everything you see and read about Gaddafi", in *The Independent*, 26 June 2011.

329 P. Dale Scott, "Rape in Libya: America's Recent Wars have all been Accompanied by Memorable Falsehoods", in *The Asia-Pacific Journal*, no. 4, 13 June 2011; "Libia, stupri di massa? I dubbi dell'ONU", in *Blitz quotidiano*, 9 June 2011.

330 R. Baker, "Did Qaddafi Really Order Mass Rapes? Or is the West Falling Victim to a Viagra Strength Scam?", in *Business Insider*, 11 June 2011.

331   C. Marsden, "Threat of War Crimes charges levelled against Gaddafi and Son", in *Axis of Logic*, 9 May 2011. According to the information provided by the spokesman for Unified Protector, Mike Bracken, a total of more than 7,000 ground airstrikes had been carried out, as reported at the end of June 2011 (see G. Chetoni, "Libia: le balle dell'informazione Atlantica", in *Rinascita*, 1 July 2011).

332   To cite just two cases that came to the attention of the press, N. Hopkins, "NATO Investigates Claims of Civilian Deaths during Libyan Raid", in *The Guardian*, 19 June 2011; "Libia, la NATO ammette due bombardamenti per 'errore'", in *Il Corriere della Sera*, 20 June 2011.

333   In regard to the 'mass rape' accusation against Gaddafi's forces, the American analyst, Sara Flounders, points to the lack of proceedings against the USA regarding many proven instances of the murder of civilians, and of torture and other crimes. Flounders also cites a parallel issue of some significance. A fairly well documented study published by the *Journal of Military Medicine* claims that 71% of the female recruits had undergone sexual violence while serving in the ranks of the US army (see S. Flounders, "Libya—Behind the Phony ICC "Rape" Charges: Are NATO Forces Preparing a Ground Attack?", in *Global Research*, 10 June 2011).

334   J. Stone, "Tony Blair duped me over Iraq and I feel ashamed, former Labour MP who voted for war says," in *The Independent*, 19 October 2015. Readers will most surely remember the events surrounding the last days of another British politician, Robin Cook.

335   Cit. in S. Lindauer, "Going Rogue: NATO War Crimes in Libya", in *Dissident Voice*, 7 June 2011.

336   M. Mariani, *L'equilibrio degli egoismi* (Milano: L'Idea, 1925), pp. 9-10.

337   M. Paolini, "Greggio e tribù", in Quaderni Speciali di *Limes*, no. 2, April 2011, p. 40.

338   G. Chazman, "For West's Oil Firms, No Love Lost in Libya", in *The Wall Street Journal*, 15 April 2011.

339   M. Dinucci, "L'attacco a Tripoli? Strategia economica", in *il manifesto*, 2 May 2011.

340   S. Agnoli, "La partita del petrolio", in *Limes*, no. 3, July 2011, p. 219.

341   "On 16 April 2008, Gaddafi finally gave Putin the green light. After a preliminary agreement was successfully reached between the two companies, Gazprom was to have 33% rights to exploit the fields. The agreement was ratified in Moscow just four days later by Alexey Miller and Paolo Scaroni." (G. Chetoni, "Geopolitica del conflitto libico", in *Rinascita*, 21-22 May 2011.

342   See M. Paris, "Guerra alla Libia. E all'ENI", in *Altrenotizie*, 19 May

2011.

343   R. Takeyh, "The Rogue Who came in from the Cold", in *Foreign Affairs*, no. 80, May-June 2001, pp. 62-67.

344   M. Caprara, "D'Alema in Libia: vengo da amico", in *Il Corriere della Sera*, 2 December 1999.

345   Relations between Libya and the United Kingdom were so fruitful that arms sales continued until the close of 2010. "According to the Department for Business Innovation & Skills (BIS), £181.7 million (Dh1.09 billion)-worth of arms export licences were granted from the UK to Libya in the third quarter of 2010—up from £22 million in second quarter.", A. Johnson, "Fox defends West's arms sales to Libya", in *Gulf News*, 3 April 2011. Police officers from Libya were receiving training at Huddersfield University (West Yorkshire, UK) when the conflict began (D. Barret and R. Lefort, "Britain trains 100 members of Gaddafi's feared Police", in *The Daily Telegraph*, 6 March 2011).

346   I. Werenfels, "How to Deal with the 'New Qaddhafi'? Risks and Opportunities of Libyan-European Rapprochement", in "SWP Comments, no. 29, October 2004, pp. 1-4.

347   The claim was made by Saif al-Islam Gaddafi in a video interview (<http://www.youtube.com/watch?v=6xQxIB_5enY>). See, A. Chrisafis, "French inquiry opens into allegations Gaddafi funded Sarkozy 2007 campaign", in, *The Guardian*, 19 April 2013.

348   "Incontro Gheddafi-Sarkozy, polemiche e contratti miliardari", in *La Stampa*, 11 December 2007.

349   F. Bechis, *Ma quale Gheddafi! Sarkò ha dichiarato guerra all'Italia*, in Bechis' Blog, 22 March 2011; Id., *Sarkò manovra la rivolta libica*, in Libero, 23 March 2011.

350   G. Beretta, *UniCredit, Finmeccanica, i capitali libici e le armi italiane a Gheddafi*, in Unimondo.org, 4 March 2011.

351   *Gheddafi in Finmeccanica. I libici al 2%, gli Usa in allarme*, in la Repubblica, 22 January 2011.

352   *La Libia ora punta al consiglio di Finmeccanica*, in Il Sole-24 ore, 23 January 2001.

353   *Gheddafi in Finmeccanica. I libici al 2%, gli Usa in allarme*, cit. These and other investments—approx. 4 billion euros—were economic in nature, but they were also of political significance (e.g. ENI 1%, Juventus Football Club 7.5%, FIAT 2%).

354   G. Dossena, *Aerei italiani per le Forze armate americane*, in *Il Corriere della Sera*, 14 June 2007.

355   *Finmeccanica si aggiudica commessa da 570 milioni di sterline*, in Investire Oggi, 17 January 2011.

356   See A. Monk, *Gaddafi Investment Authority, 2006-2011, RIP*, in Oxford SWF Project, 4 March 2011.

357   A brief, informative account of the piratical conduct of the major investment banks in their dealings with Libya may be found in M. Dinucci, "Goldman Sachs, Tripoli", in *il manifesto*, 5 July 2011.

358   See M. Dinucci, "I volenterosi puntano al fondo sovrano libico", in *il manifesto*, 22 April 2011.

359   CIRET-AVT—CF2R, *Libye: un avenir incertain. Compte rendu de mission d'évaluation auprès des belligérants libyens*, Paris 30 May 2011. China had invested considerably in Libya in the years leading up to 2011. It had dispatched to Libya more than 30,000 energy technicians for hydrocarbon extraction. About 29,000 were evacuated by sea immediately as NATO launched its offensive.

360   A. Del Boca, *Gheddafi. Una sfida dal deserto*, cit., p. 326. Senator Giulio Andreotti—one of Italy's most noted senior statesmen—had been in contact with Gaddafi over a period of many years. He wrote an introduction to the anthology of speeches made by Gaddafi during his visit to Italy in June 2009. Andreotti, too, stressed the "historic significance of this personage": *Il viaggio del Leader. Muammar Gheddafi in Italia* (Roma: Trenta Giorni Società Cooperativa, 2010), pp. 7-9.

361   For a summary account of Libya's activities under Gaddafi in Africa, see A. Aruffo, *Gheddafi. Storia di una dittatura rivoluzionaria* (Roma: Castelvecchi, 2011), pp. 69-78.

362   See R. I. Lawless, "History (Libya)", in *The Middle East and North Africa 2009* (London & New York: Routledge, 2009, pp. 765-791).

363   L. Rolandi, "Primo satellite africano in orbita", in *La Stampa*, 20 December 2007.

364   See the video dedicated to RASCOM, providing a detailed account of the RASCOM project's various stages: <http://www.youtube.com/watch?v=cSJba-_doM8&NR=1>.

365   The arrangement on this occasion was that the constructor, Thales-Alenia Space, should contribute 12% to the funding (the idea was to motivate the company to provide optimal technological services).

366   I. Lasserre, "Premières leçons de la guerre en Libye", in *Le Figaro*, 25 May 2011.

367   P. Magnaschi, "I francesi provano le bombe sulla pelle dei cittadini libici", in *Italia Oggi*, 27 May 2011.

368   M. Dinucci, "A La Bourget il Salone Libia", in *il manifesto*, 21 June 2011.

369   M. Arpino, "La trappola interventista", in *Quotidiano Nazionale*, 10 April 2011.

370   "'The United States of Africa' may become Reality", in *CBS news*, 15 March 2011.

371   "Gaddafi's Gold Reserves Among the Top 25 in the World", in *The Wall Street Journal*, 22 March 2011.

372   See G. Eugenio, "Signoraggio contro Gheddafi", in Mass Medium Blog San Pietroburgo, 11 May 2011.

373   E. Brown, "All About Oil, or All About Banking?", in *Asia Times*, 14 April 2011.

374   UNCLASSIFIED U.S. Department of State Case No. F-2014-20439 Doc No. C05779612 Date: 12/31/2015 RELEASE IN PART

375   The CFA franc is an entity consisting in two currencies: the West African CFA franc and the Central African CFA franc, pegged to the Euro and guaranteed by France's treasury.

376   For clarification in this regard, see the interview with His Majesty Jean Gervais Tchiffi Zié, Permanent Secretary General of the Forum of Kings, Sultans, Princes, Sheiks and Traditional Chiefs in Africa (video: <http://www.youtube.com/watch?v=GXnPM5MuQdE&featu re=email&email=comment_received>)

377   N. Egnatz, "Libyan War; Just another Bailout for the Banking Class", in *Intrepid Report*, 14 June 2011.

378   "Libyan Rebels Form Central Bank", in *Economic Policy Journal*, 28 March 2011. The funds have not been made available to the Libyan authorities: see L. George, "Libya's $67 billion frozen funds must remain on ice says would-be investment chief", *Reuters*, 17 July 2015. See also A. Newman, "Libyan Rebels Create Central Bank, Oil Company", *The New American*, 30 March 2011.

379   C. Marroni, "A Bengasi nasce la 'Banca Centrale' dei ribelli", in *Il Sole-24 ore*, 27 April 2011.

380   The offensive began on the evening of 20 August 2011. RAF GR4 Tornados armed with Paveway IV laser-guided bombs struck a telecommunications center and other key targets in Tripoli. The Tornados were based in Italy. According to a *France Soir* investigation, at least 500 British commandos took part in the operation, flanked by hundreds of French troops. The French forces were flown in from the amphibious assault helicopter carrier, Tonnerre. The helicopters were provided by the French Army Light Division (*Aviation légère de l'Armée de Terre* (ALAT)).

381   M. Correggia, "Sirte, Bani Walid, Sebha: non tutti gli assedi sono uguali: E anche i civili", in *il manifesto*, 7 September 2011.

382   L. Phelan, "'Free Tripoli'—just don't mention the corpses", in *Libya 360°*, 5 September 2011.

383   A 'civil death' was pronounced upon one party to the conflict. The Libyan government loyalists became *"Gaddafi hardliners"* and the army, *"Gaddafi squads"*. Opposing them were noble "insurgents" and "revolutionaries".

384   M. Dinucci, "Il futuro della Libia secondo i piani delle potenze europee", in *il manifesto*, 4 September 2011. Another Italian newspaper, *Il Corriere della Sera*, also provided information on the 'rebel' commander in Tripoli. Unsurprisingly, it managed to omit the more embarrassing highpoints of Belhadj's 'career path'.

385   Human Rights Watch came across a number of confidential documents in Tripoli. A Belhadj scandal had erupted. During a BBC interview, *Il Corriere della Sera* stated that the treatment that he and his family had received was illegal. Belhadj asked the British and American governments to formally apologize for their conduct. To end the scandal (and, more importantly, to placate the ire of his new Libyan friends), British PM Cameron announced that a commission of enquiry would look into the matter (see A. Carlini, "Gli 007 di Cameron aiutavano il raìs", in *Libero*, 6 September 2011; F. Calda, "CIA e MI6 collaboravano con Gheddafi", in *Rinascita*, 6 September 2011). In 2013 the high court dismissed Abdel-Hakin Belhadj's claim on the grounds that it related to activities in foreign states. Belhadj appealed. The UK Court of Appeals allowed the torture claim to proceed. That such a lawsuit should even have been attempted raises questions as to the parameters of the relationship between Belhadj and the UK (West). See <http://www.redress.org/case-docket/belhadj-v-jack-straw-and-others>

386   P. Escobar, "Al-Qaeda Asset is Military Commander of Tripoli", in *Russia Today*, 27 August 2011.

387   W. Tarpley, "NATO uses al-Qaeda to topple Gaddafi", in *Press TV*, 28 August 2011.

388   "US confirms al Qaeda members' role in rebel Command. Qaddafi contacts them", in DEBKA*file*, 1 September 2011.

389   *About Libya*, UNDP (<http://www.ly.undp.org/content/libya/en/home/countryinfo.html>); *Human Development Index*, United Nations, 2010.

390   F. Arbuthnot, "Looming Tragedy: Vision of the 'New Libya': Visit the 'New Iraq'. Another 'Liberation', another Unimaginable International Criminal Tragedy", in *Global Research*, 3 September 2011.

391   U. Mazzantini, "Gli "Amici della Libia" e l'accordo segreto Sarkozy-CNT: il 35% del petrolio libico ai francesi", in *Greenreport*, 1 September 2011.

392   P. Escobar, "Libya: the Real War starts now", in *Asia Times*, 7

September 2011.

393   J. Pack and K. White, "Rebuilding Libya", in *New Atlanticist*, 1 September 2011.

394   M. Delammare,"Sarkozy gaspille l'argent des français pour aider Al Qaeda à prendre le contrôle de la Libye", in *Planète non violence*, 28 August 2011.

395   K. Sengupta, "Nato strikes 'kill 354', says Gaddafi's spokesman", *The Independent*, 18 September 2011.

396   Major J. R. Greenleaf, "The Air War in Libya: Implications for the US, NATO, and the future role of airpower, Master of Military Studies Research Paper", USAF, USMC Command and Staff College, Marine Corps University, Quantico, 24 March 2012, pp. 10-19

397   "The Air War in Libya: Implications for the US, NATO, and the future role of airpower, Master of Military Studies Research Paper", cit., p. 21.

398   *Shattered lives, Civilians suffer from the use of explosive weapons in Libya*, United Nations Office for the Coordination of Humanitarian Affairs, September 2015 (second, modified version), pp. 24-25. The poor performance of such bodies as OCHA is notable. *Shattered lives*, it was claimed, "is not intended to provide a detailed or systematic analysis of explosive violence in Libya". This is quite clear even at first glance. Adorned with large photographs and generously proportioned, colourful infographics, the few dozen pages of the publication are also dedicated in large part to anecdotal or human-interest stories. For its data on the toll, in terms of the civilian casualties of the regime change operation and its predicted aftermath (2011-2015), *Shattered lives* relies—to the practical exclusion of all else—on the "Report of the International Commission on Libya, A/HRC/17/68" (a document written by UN colleagues dating back to 2012, with updates to 2015 provided only informally by the said Commission's military advisor), and on data collected by Action on Armed Violence (AOAV). AOAV is rather an interesting source. It is a British organization falsely classified by OCHA as an NGO, as explained below. It produces annual "datasets" relative to the use and effects of "explosive violence" worldwide. However, the term used by AOAV, "dataset", is equally misleading. The data presented for 2011 are heterogeneous in nature and source, and are presented 'as is' (not having been assessed with reference to any declared standards of proof). AOAV relied on press reports for its 2011 data on Libya. It did not carry out on-site investigations. Here as elsewhere, we are dealing with an informational 'closed circuit'. The organization's objectivity is open to challenge also because of conflict of interest issues.

The AOAV report concerning Libya for 2011 (H. Dodd and R. Perkins, "Monitoring Explosive Violence – The EVMP dataset 2011", AOAV, London, March 2012.) —mentioned among the sources for *Shattered lives*—was funded by the Norwegian government. Norway was a (particularly aggressive) member of the alliance set up to take out Gaddafi. Incidentally, it is also a rival hydrocarbon energy player. It is perfectly feasible that Norway financed its military intervention entirely through the windfall generated by global oil price fluctuations at that time.

399   C. Chivers and E. Schmitt, "In Strikes on Libya by NATO, an Unspoken Civilian Toll", *New York Times*, 17 November 2011.

400   F. Lamb, "Anatomy of a NATO War Crime", *Counterpunch*, 16 December 2016.

401   See <https://www.foia.state.gov/searchapp/DOCUMENTS/HRCEmail_DecWebClearedMeta/31-C1/DOC_0C05782401/C05782401.pdf> (retrieved on 7 January 2015).

402   "NATO strike in Sirte area, 20 October 2011. NATO and Libya, Operational Media Update, For 20 OCTOBER", Allied Joint Force Command, 21 October 2011.

403   A. E. Mayer, "Building the New Libya: Lessons to Learn and Unlearn", *University of Pennsylvania Journal of International Law*, Winter 2013. Mayer also describes how "Omran Shaban, one of the rebels who had apprehended him, was captured in July 2012 by men from Bani Walid, a stronghold of Qaddafi supporters. The latter sought revenge by beating Shaban and repeatedly slashing his chest with razors, inflicting grievous injuries that led to his death. Shaban's murder then provoked a military attack on Bani Walid from his hometown, Misrata, which, in turn caused denunciations and protests. Allowing such spirals of lethal vengeance to continue could only lead to unremitting violence. There was no army capable of curtailing the violence, because Libya's military had been deliberately enfeebled by Qaddafi due to his fear of potential coups. He had relied on his security forces to maintain his stranglehold on power. Once he was overthrown, his security apparatus disintegrated, leaving no force that could exert control over the disparate rebel militias that had sprung up to fight Qaddafi, militias whose members seemed eager to utilize their weaponry and who were not above indulging in wanton violence and criminality". The bottom line (portrayal of Gaddafi as a callous, irrational despot) never changes. Fearing a *coup*, Mayer assures us, Gaddafi had acted in a manner that had placed his country

and his own life at risk, and ultimately exposed innocents to the violent acts of those who opposed him.

404   M. Chulov, "Gaddafi's last moments: 'I saw the hand holding the gun and I saw it fire'", *The Guardian*, 20 October 2012.

405   See Conor Friedersdorf, "Hillary Defends Her Failed War in Libya", *The Atlantic*, 14 October 2015.

406   I. Black, "Libyan revolution casualties lower than expected, says new government", *The Guardian*, 8 January 2013

407   Anon., "At least 30,000 Killed, 50,000 Wounded in Libyan Conflict", *The Tripoli Post*, 8 September 2011

408   G. Shupak, "The Disaster in Libya, Western-led military interventions aren't motivated by humanitarian concerns", *Jacobin*, 9 February 2015. Gazzini is anything but an anti-institutional figure. Her organization, International Crisis Group (ICG) is not, in truth, a non-governmental organization, since it openly receives funds from a number of governments. Indeed, ICG is a truly élite 'revolving-door' type of organization, chaired and presided over by a dazzling group of one-percenter celebrities, top businesspeople, former UN functionaries, former diplomats, former ministers, and opinion leaders (see "Crisis Group's Board of Trustees", <http://www.crisisgroup.org/en/about/board.aspx>, retrieved in 23 December 2015). Billionaire philanthropist George Soros is a trustee of ICG. As revealed by T. Cartalucci, Amnesty International, too, receives public moneys (perhaps less openly) through its 'charity' wing (see "Amnesty International is US State Department Propaganda", *Global Research*, 22 August 2012). AI appears not to be the NGO many believe it be. George Soros is a private donor to ICG and AI, as well as to many other purported human rights and social project organizations, as noted above.

409   B. Obama, "Remarks by the President in Address to the Nation on Libya", White House, Office of the Press Secretary, 28 March 2011.

410   "Libya's indiscriminate attacks on civilians in Misrata may be international crimes – Pillay", United Nations, Human Rights, Office of the High Commissioner, 20 April 2011.

411   HRW's stance at the time differed sharply from Mahmoud Jibril's, who claimed genocide was about to occur: "'At that point, we did not see the imminence of massacres that would rise to genocidelike levels,' said Sarah Leah Whitson, executive director of the Middle East and North Africa division for Human Rights Watch. 'Gadhafi's forces killed hundreds of overwhelmingly unarmed protesters. There were threats of Libyan forces approaching Benghazi, but we didn't feel that rose to the level of imminent genocidelike atrocities.' J. S. Schapiro, K.

Riddel. "Exclusive: Secret tapes undermine Hillary Clinton on Libyan war", *Washington Times*, 28.1.2015. According to Schapiro and Riddel, HRW's view largely coincides with that of the Defense Intelligence Agency ("Hillary Clinton's 'WMD' moment: U.S. intelligence saw false narrative in Libya", *Washington Times*, 29.1.2015). We may contrast HRW's and DIA's assessment of the Gaddafi forces' conduct at the time with the wanton disregard for the lives of civilians displayed later by the warring factions in 2014 (the NATO-backed factions that brought Gaddafi down three years earlier)—as documented, at least in part, in *Shattered lives, Civilians suffer from the use of explosive weapons in Libya*, cit.

412   See *World Report 2015: Libya*, Human Rights Watch, 7 January 2015

413   UNCLASSIFIED U.S. Department of State Case No. F-2014-20439 Doc No. C05782401 Date: 12/31/2015 RELEASE IN PART. Unsurprisingly, the mainstream media have paid little attention to these documents. For a brief roundup of some of the more shocking remarks and their implications, see R. Parry, "What Hillary Knew about Libya", *Consortium News*, 12 January 2016.

414   *Ibid.*

415   From the very start, these militias had been backed by French and British special ground forces, and would have soon been defeated without this covert aid.

416   C. Hughes, "Britain's Secret War in Libya: British Special Forces uncovered on the ground", *Daily Mirror*, 27 January 2012. A Rand Corporation report of 2014, glossing over the legality of the deployment of special forces on the ground in Libya, skilfully spins this illegality as an instance of the alliance's generous actions, empowering the people of Libya: "NATO adopted an airpower-heavy strategy, ground forces were limited to small numbers of special forces from Europe and the Gulf States. Precision airpower allowed NATO to avoid large numbers of civilian deaths, keep costs down, and ensure it was the rebels themselves who took the capital. The limited number of ground forces, however, also greatly reduced the extent of control and influence that NATO and its partners could exert after Qaddafi was gone". C. S. Chivvis, J. Martini, *Libya After Qaddafi, Lessons and Implications for the Future*, Rand Corporation, 2014, p. 4.

417   Bouchard was the commander of the NATO intervention forces, appointed on 25 March 2011.

418   C. Chengu, "Libya: From Africa's Richest State Under Gaddafi, to Failed State After NATO Intervention", *Global Research*, 22 February 2015.

419   J. Steele, "Motivated To Believe The Worst", *The Guardian*, 18 August

2000 (the article could not be retrieved from the web archive of the "*The Guardian*" at the time of writing: see <http://www.commondreams.org/headlines/081800-01.htm>).

420   *How America Switched Sides in the War on Terror. An Interim Report by the Citizens' Commission On Benghazi, The Citizens' Commission on Benghazi (CCB), 22* April 2014. The CCB is a *"self-selected group of former top military officers, CIA insiders and think-tankers"* *(hence, a pressure group presumably of some standing)*. We note that the CCB report garnered little media attention. This lack of attention may indicate that no independent evidence has actually emerged since 2012 to confirm the validity of the CCB's findings and/or that the report includes many inconvenient truths. Interestingly, the testimony provided in person by Rear Admiral Charles Kubic is altogether rather too brief, decidedly imprecise in its wording, and perhaps even contradictory. Kubic nevertheless provides a fascinating account of the objects of the negotiations, as he understood them, between AFRICOM and the Libyan authorities, including the terms of Gaddafi's supposed offer to abandon Libya (cf. D. Martosko, "Benghazi attack could have been prevented if US hadn't 'switched sides in the War on Terror' and allowed $500 MILLION of weapons to reach al-Qaeda militants, reveals damning report", *Daily Mail*, 28 April 2014). The account provided by Kubic (who acted it would appear, directly on behalf of the Joint Chiefs of Staff) was reiterated in 2016, at least in part, by veteran reporter Gareth Porter via other separate sources. However, Porter indicates that Gaddafi was prepared only to resign (presumably from all public offices). Porter rules out Gaddafi's exile as a condition acceptable to the Libyans (G. Porter, "US military leadership resisted Obama's bid for regime change in Syria, Libya", *Middle East Eye*, 4 January 2016).

421   The Barqa council called for a boycott of the upcoming parliamentary elections. The Council's platform was not secession but federalism, with its own parliament, police and justice system based in in Benghazi. However, its approximately sixty militias did set up roadblocks, hampering trade and traffic across the country.

422   C. S. Chivvis, J. Martini, *Libya After Qaddafi, Lessons and Implications for the Future*, cit., p. 8. On 15 February 2014, a report was circulated to Security Council members (S/2014/106), which analyses the proliferation of weapons to and from Libya, considered a major challenge for the stability of the country and the region. According to this report, "most weapons are still under the control of non-state armed actors and border control systems remain ineffective". The task of destroying the mustard gas stockpile, initiated while Gaddafi was

still in power, was completed in early 2014.

423   "Held on July 7, 2012, in the face of considerable skepticism about their feasibility, the elections became the bright spot in the international postwar effort. UNSMIL [the UN mission to Libya] and nongovernmental organizations like the International Foundation for Electoral Systems (IFES) worked with the Libyan electoral commission to register voters, design and implement an electoral formula, and stage the polls. There were some issues with administration and small irregularities, but the international community judged the elections free and fair". However, on a slightly less upbeat note, Chivvis and Martini also observe that "Although there were some positive developments, including successful elections in July 2012, these were overshadowed by mounting violence that stunted efforts to establish functioning political institutions through which the Libyan people could realize their aspirations for self-rule. Jihadist groups—some linked to al Qaeda in the Islamic Maghreb (AQIM), an al Qaeda affiliate—meanwhile made use of the security vacuum to establish a foothold nationwide. Libya today is thus in a very precarious situation, as are conditions in the broader Sahel and Maghreb regions. Jihadist activities in Mali, Tunisia, Algeria, and Egypt do not favor a rapid improvement in the outlook". C. S. Chivvis, J. Martini, *Libya After Qaddafi, Lessons and Implications for the Future*, cit., p. 2, p. 41, 51.

424   Interview with C. Gazzini on the occasion of the conference, "The Libyan crisis: military intervention or political solution?", organised by IAI (Istituto Affari Internazionali). Claudia Gazzini explains the political situation in Libya and the possible alternatives to military intervention (https://www.youtube.com/watch?v=e8L0zmwyiFM, retrieved on 23 December 2015).

425   D. Hearst, "The West wants unity in Libya so it can bomb it", cit.

426   J. Hersh, "CIA Role In Benghazi Attack Comes Into Focus", *Huffington Post*, 11 February 2012.

427   Cf. D. L. Barlett and J. B. Steele, "The Oily Americans", in *Time Magazine*, 13 May 2003; T. Henriksen, "The 'Blowback' Myth", *The Weekly Standard*, no. 5, 15 October 2001; Anon., "Imperial Hubris", *Washington Post*, 11 July 2004; R. Baer, *See No Evil: The True Story of a Ground Soldier in the CIA's War Against Terrorism* (New York: Crown Publishers, 2002; F Heisbourg, *Après Al Qaeda: la nouvelle génération du terrorisme* (Paris: Stock, 2009); Cf. J-C. Brisard and G. Dasquié, *Bin Laden: La verité interdite* (Paris: Denoël, 2001); E. Alterman, "Blowback the Prequel", *The Nation*, 25 October 2001. In fall 2001, during the BBC transmission, *Newsnight*, Springmann (former head of the US visas office in Jeddah from 1987 to 1989) declared that,

while he was in Saudi Arabia, high-ranking State Department officials repeatedly ordered him to issue visas to unqualified applicants. These applicants had no ties with Saudi Arabia or their own country of origin. Springmann's complaints to Washington fell on deaf ears. He admitted that he had issued visas for terrorists recruited by the CIA and by Osama bin Laden. The terrorists travelled to the United States to be trained for operations in Afghanistan against the Soviets (cit. in "Has Someone Been Sitting on the FBI?", *BBC News* 6 November 2001; R. MacInnes-Rae, "Interview with Michael Springmann", *CBC Radio One*, 3 July 2002; see also W. G. Tarpley, *9/11 Synthetic Terror: Made in USA* (Joshua Tree, Progressive Press, 2006); S. Zunes, *Tinderbox: US Middle East Policy and the roots of terrorism* (Monroe, Common Courage Press, 2003).

428   Arshad Mohammed e Samuel P. Jacobs, "Intrepid U.S. Envoy Stevens Nurtured Libyan Democracy", *Reuters*, 12 September 2012.

429   B. Klapper, "Chris Stevens: US Envoy to the Arab World", *Associated Press*, 13 September 2011.

430   "Hillary Clinton: What to know about her recent controversies, scandals", *Russia Today*, 10 April 2015. It has been reported that "Hillary Clinton's top State Department aides turned to Clinton Foundation employees for political help in the immediate aftermath of the Benghazi terrorist attack, and that Clinton withheld the emails from the House Benghazi Committee investigating her conduct. Clinton currently faces federal investigation for allegedly allowing people without a security clearance to access classified information, in violation of the Espionage Act. Newly-discovered emails, considered classified by the State Department, were going to Clinton Foundation staffers who did not have a security clearance to view classified information." P. Howley, "Exclusive: Hillary Aides talked Benghazi with Clinton Foundation Staff, withheld Emails", *Breitbart*, 23 September 2013.

431   D. Martosko, "Benghazi attack could have been prevented if US hadn't 'switched sides in the War on Terror' and allowed $500 MILLION of weapons to reach al-Qaeda militants, reveals damning report", cit.

432   "US envoy dies in Benghazi consulate attack", *Al Jazeera*, 12 September 2012; cf. "Libya official says Gaddafi loyalists killed US Diplomats", *Reuters*, 12 September 2012.

433   *The authors of the aforementioned CCB report*—"How America Switched Sides in the War on Terror"—failed to note, or *chose not to comment on* the declarations made by high-ranking Libyan officials immediately after the attack. According to these officials, the perpetrators were pro-Gaddafi resistance militants. Interestingly,

the CCB report nevertheless slammed the White House for its "false claim" that the attack was in some way spontaneous, or that it was perpetrated by protesters or fundamentalists offended by the American video production.

434   J. Dettmer, "Despite Arrests in Consulate Attack, Chaos Persists in Libya", *The Daily Beast*, 15 September 2012.

435   As for a number of US-appointed top Libyan officials, Abushagur returned to Benghazi in May 2011, well after the start of rebellion.

436   "Clinton praises Libya for its move to rein in militias", *CNN*, 25 September 2012; D. D. Kirkpatrick, "A Deadly Mix in Benghazi", *The New York Times*, 28 December 2013. Rand Corporation analysts Chivvis and Martini do note that "Libyan officials claimed that Qaddafi supporters were behind these attacks, but most evidence pointed to the jihadists". This "most evidence", based on mere hearsay, is laughably facile ("The social and historical conditions in the east are particularly conducive to militancy, and the east had been a center of jihadist activities for decades"). Given the Rand Corporation's resources and outreach, this is decidedly fuzzy, and the entire affair smacks of a cover-up concerted at the highest levels. See C. S. Chivvis, J. Martini, "Libya After Qaddafi, Lessons and Implications for the Future", cit., p. 25.

437   "Libya demands return of Benghazi suspect, slams US raid as attack on sovereignty", *Russia Today*, 18 June 2014.

438   J. Robes, "Green Libyan Flags are waving once again—Interview", *Voice of Russia*, 22 January 2014.

439   S. Morgan, "Saddened, Heart-sick, Disgusted, Enraged...", *Susannah Morgan's Blog*, 3 November 2012.

440   For a rapid overview of the controversy over these events, see J. S. Robins, "Is a General losing his job over Benghazi?", *Washington Times*, 28 October 2012, and J. S. Robins, "General at center of Benghazi-gate controversy retiring", *Washington Times*, 29 October 2012.

441   "Everything You Want to Know About Migration Across the Mediterranean", *The Economist*, 4 May 2015; an estimated 500,000 immigrants reached Italy by sea in 2015: cf. "Record 432,761 Refugees, Migrants have Crossed Med this Year", *The Daily Mal*, 25 September 2015.

442   "I morti nel Mediterraneo nel 2014 sono 3.419", *Internazionale*, 10 December 2014; A. N. Mauro, A. Cimarelli and J. Ottaviani, "Migranti, la guerra del Mediterraneo", *l'Espresso*, 31 March 2014.

443   "Il vertice Ue triplica i fondi per l'operazione Triton", *La Stampa*, 23 April 2015.

444   "Letter dated 13 August 2015 from the Permanent Representative of Libya to the United Nations addressed to the President of the Security Council", UN document.

445   "Libya's Government Seeks Support It May Not Get", *Stratfor Global Intelligence*, 21 August 2015; S. Avni, "In Libya, a Rift Widens Over How to Defeat ISIS", *Newsweek*, 14 March 2015; T. Dahl, "Exclusive: Libya peace talks negotiator: UN arms embargo 'deeply hampering' fight against ISIS", *Breitbart*, 17 August 2015. Cf. United Nations Security Council, "7485th Meeting Transcript", UN Document S/PV/7485, New York, 15 July 2015

446   "Libya's Government Seeks Support It May Not Get", *Stratfor Global Intelligence*, cit.; cf. P. Sensini, "Isis, terroristi? Ecco le colpe dell'Occidente", *Affaritaliani.it*, 22 November 2015.

447   "US Embassy Cables: Hillary Clinton Says Saudi Arabia 'A Critical Source of Terrorist Funding'", in *The Guardian*, 30 December 2009; "WikiLeaks Cables Portray Saudi Arabia as a Cash Machine for Terrorists", in *The Guardian*, 5 December 2010.

448   "Held on July 7, 2012, in the face of considerable skepticism about their feasibility, the elections became the bright spot in the international postwar effort. UNSMIL [the UN mission to Libya] and nongovernmental organizations like the International Foundation for Electoral Systems (IFES) worked with the Libyan electoral commission to register voters, design and implement an electoral formula, and stage the polls. There were some issues with administration and small irregularities, but the international community judged the elections free and fair". On a slightly less upbeat note, Chivvis and Martini also observe that "Although there were some positive developments, including successful elections in July 2012, these were overshadowed by mounting violence that stunted efforts to establish functioning political institutions through which the Libyan people could realize their aspirations for self-rule. Jihadist groups—some linked to al Qaeda in the Islamic Maghreb (AQIM), an al Qaeda affiliate—meanwhile made use of the security vacuum to establish a foothold nationwide. Libya today is thus in a very precarious situation, as are conditions in the broader Sahel and Maghreb regions. Jihadist activities in Mali, Tunisia, Algeria, and Egypt do not favor a rapid improvement in the outlook". C. S. Chivvis, J. Martini, "Libya After Qaddafi, Lessons and Implications for the Future", cit., p. 2, p. 41, 51.

449   M. Rout, Australian lawyer Melinda Taylor, freed after being held in Libya, is reunited with her family, *The Australian*, 3 Juky 2007.

450   Mohammed El-Magariaf resigned as President of the General National Congress, since this law was to apply also to him. Other leading

politicians and officials resigned for the same reason. Mohammed El-Magariaf resigned as President of the General National Congress, since this law was to apply also to him. Other leading politicians and officials resigned for the same reason.

451   Abdul Haq al-Ani & Tarik al-Ani, *Genocide in Iraq,Volume II: Obliteration of a Modern State*, Clarity Press, Inc., 2015, p. 104ff.

451   *Ibid.*

452   C. S. Chivvis, J. Martini, "Libya After Qaddafi, Lessons and Implications for the Future", cit., p. xi; the authorities increased subsidies for food, fuel, and electricity first to 11 percent of GDP and then to 14 percent. Government wages were increased as a means of "temporarily reducing the chances of conflict while insecurity prevails, but they do so at a risk to Libya's long-term economic health", p. 62 (N.B. In Washington, of course, wage hikes are always bad news!).

453   United Nations Security Council, "Report of the Secretary-General on the United Nations Support Mission in Libya", UN Document, New York, 5 September 2013 < http://www.un.org/en/ga/search/view_doc. asp?symbol=S/2013/516>.

453   United Nations Security Council, "7075th Meeting Transcript", UN Document S/PV/7075, New York, 9 December 2013.

454   *Ibid.*

456   Cato Institute, "Did the Military Intervention in Libya Succeed?", cit. 457 UNSC, "Report of the Secretary-General on the United Nations Support Mission in Libya", 26 February 2014.

458   "Islamist groups have enjoyed more financial support as the Muslim Brotherhood-controlled Congress gave them around $700 million of funding", S. Warnes, "Libya's civil war: why is the government paying both sides?", Mirror (<http://ampp3d. mirror.co.uk/author/sophie-warnes/>, retrieved December 2015); cf. "Lawless Libya: Can peace be achieved?", BBC, 17 December 2015; K. Mezran and F. Lamen, "Security Challenges to Libya's Quest for Democracy", Atlantic Council Issue Brief, September 2012; International Crisis Group, "Holding Libya Together: Security Challenges After Qadhafi", Crisis Group Middle East/North Africa Report No. 115, 14 December 2011; B. McQuinn, "After the Fall: Libya's Evolving Armed Groups", Small Arms Survey, Geneva, October 2012; C. S. Chivvis, J. Martini, "Libya After Qaddafi, Lessons and Implications for the Future", cit.

459   D. Hearst, "The West wants unity in Libya so it can bomb it", Middle East Eye, 16 December 2015. In its "Events of 2014" report, HRW states that "Political infighting and clashes between rival militias escalated, triggering armed conflicts in Benghazi and other parts of the east in May, and in Tripoli and its environs in July. The fighting

caused widespread destruction of property, and civilian injuries and deaths. Around 400,000 were internally displaced in Libya, including about 100,000 residents of Tripoli. Another 150,000 people, including foreigners, fled Libya" ("World Report 2015: Libya", Human Rights Watch, 7 January 2015). These HRW figures for 2014 are compatible with Hearst's, figures for Libyan refugees or displaced persons as a whole since 2011. As noted above, before 2011, very few Libyans emigrated. They did so mainly as professionals and business people.

460 As noted above, between one and two million Libyans may have fled the country since 2011, lowering the population numbers considerably.

461 G. Micalessin, "Viaggio in una Libia che non esiste più", in "Immigrazione S.p.A.", *Il Giornale*, Milano 2015, p. 63.

462 *Ibid.* p. 64.

463 Michael Moss, "Rising Leader for Next Phase of Al Qaeda's War", *The New York Times*, 4 April 2008.

464 K. Mezran, "Overcoming Political Polarization in Libya", Atlantic Council, 5 March 2013.

465 See "The former 'Gate of Africa': Libya's deserted frontier", Middle East Eye, 15 December 2015.

466 G. Micalessin, "Viaggio in una Libia che non esiste più", cit., p. 69.

467 J. Carney, "Libyan Rebels Form Their Own Central Bank", CNBC, 28 March 2011. As the coup got underway in February-March 2011, the 'rebels', buoyed up by their rapid advances, moved immediately toward bolstering the financial infrastructures required for democratic state-building. According to CNBC, "The rebel group known as the Transitional National Council released a statement [19 March 2011] announcing that they have designated the Central Bank of Benghazi as a monetary authority competent in monetary policies in Libya, and that they have appointed a governor to the Central Bank of Libya, with a temporary headquarters in Benghazi (...) Is this the first time a revolutionary group has created a central bank while it is still in the midst of fighting the entrenched political power? (...) This suggests we have a bit more than a ragtag bunch of rebels running around and that there are some pretty sophisticated influences. 'I have never before heard of a central bank being created in just a matter of weeks out of a popular uprising,' Wenzel writes".

468 Federico Fubini, "All'ombra del conflitto la battaglia sotterranea per il tesoro di Gheddafi", *la Repubblica*, 4 March 2015.

469 See A. Monk, "Gaddafi Investment Authority, 2006-2011, RIP", in "Oxford SWF Project", 4 March 2011. M. Dinucci, "I volenterosi puntano al fondo sovrano libico", *il manifesto*, 22 April 2011.

470 A brief but informative account of the piratical conduct of the major

investment banks in their dealings with Libya may be found in M. Dinucci, "Goldman Sachs, Tripoli", *il manifesto*, 5 July 2011.

471   E. Brown, "Libya all about oil, or central banking?", *Asia Times*, 14 April 2011.

472   "UN Proposes Unity Government to End Libya Conflict", *Al Jazeera*, 9 October 2015.

473   D. Hearst, "The West wants unity in Libya so it can bomb it", cit.

474   R. Ramesh, "UN Libya envoy accepts £1,000-a-day job from backer of one side in civil war", *The Guardian*, 4 November 2015.

475   RUSI is a key élite British military and strategic think tank with 2,000 members (military officers, diplomats, politicians etc.). Given its Westminster address and membership roll, we may class the organisation, founded by the Duke of Wellington, as Britain's shadow foreign ministry.

476   "More war drums: 1,000 crack British Special Forces deployed to Libyan oil fields to 'halt the advance of ISIS'", *Russia Today*, 4 January 2016.

477   D. Hearst, "The West wants unity in Libya so it can bomb it", cit.

478   P. Sensini, "Usa & Co. non cambiano rotta. 'Regime Change' in Siria e Libia", *Affaritaliani*, 20 December 2015. Numerous attempts were made on Faiez's life by suicide bombers and gunmen in Misrata and Zliten on 9 January 2016. He fled to Tunisia. It was to be the day of his first public appearance as PM.See G. Micalessin, "Libia, la sfida del 'premier' accolto da una bomba", Il Giornale, 10 January 2016. Some two weeks later, Faiez's 'government' project looked as divisive as ever (see R. Musa, M. Michael, "Libya's Rivals Declare Unity Cabinet Under UN Plan". ABC, 23 January 2016), and has since been rejected by the vast majority of the members of the parliament in Tobruk, Indeed, of the 104 members of this internationally recognised assemby, 15 voted in favour and 89 against (A.Spinelli Barrile, "Libia, ultime notizie: il governo non ottiene la fiducia", Blogo, informazione libera e indipendente, 25 January 2016.

479   R. Crilly, "Islamic State is building a 'retreat zone' in Libya with 3000 fighters, say UN experts", The Telegraph, 2 December 2015.

480   See M. O'Hanlon, Deconstructing Syria, Towards a regionalized strategy for a confederal country, Center for 21st Century Security and Intelligence, The Brookings Institution, Washington D.C., June 2015; see also Oded Yinon, "The Zionist Plan for the Middle East", Kivunim. *A Journal for Judaism and Zionism,* republished by the Association of Arab-American University Graduates, Inc., Belmont, Massachusetts, 1982.

481   "At least 65 killed in bomb attack on Libya police training center", Russia Today, 7 January 2016.

NAMES INDEX